Women in the Islamic World

Women in the Islamic World

FROM EARLIEST TIMES TO THE ARAB SPRING

Irene Schneider

Translated from the German
by Steven Rendall

Markus Wiener Publishers
Princeton

The translation of this work was funded by Geisteswissenschaften International—Translation Funding for Humanities and Social Sciences from Germany, a joint initiative of the Fritz Thyssen Foundation, the German Federal Foreign Office, the collecting society VG WORT, and the Börsenverein des Deutschen Buchhandels (German Publishers & Booksellers Association).

For information, write to: Markus Wiener Publishers
231 Nassau Street, Princeton, NJ 08542
www.markuswiener.com

Library of Congress Cataloging-in-Publication Data

Schneider, Irene.
   [Islam und die Frauen. English]
   Women in the Islamic world : from earliest times to the Arab Spring / Irene Schneider ; translated from the German by Steven Rendall.
   pages cm
   Includes bibliographical references and index.
   ISBN 978-1-55876-573-3 (hardcover : alk. paper)
   ISBN 978-1-55876-574-0 (pbk. : alk. paper)
   1. Women in Islam. 2. Islamic law. 3. Islamic modernism. 4. Feminism—Islamic countries. I. Rendall, Steven, translator. II. Title.
   BP173.4.S3713 2014
   297.082—dc23
                                        2013027946

Markus Wiener Publishers books are printed in the United States of America on acid-free paper and meet the guidelines for permanence and durability of the Committee on Production Guidelines for Book Longevity of the Council on Library Resources.

CONTENTS

PREFACE

Is there any movement that could be identified as Islamic feminism? What legal rights do women have in contemporary Muslim states, and what human rights are withheld from them? How do women go about trying to gain a firmer legal standing in Islamic societies? What is the role of the Quran and its interpretations in controversies concerning women's rights? These were the fundamental guiding questions I confronted in writing this book on women in the Islamic world. A positive answer to the first question posed above will immediately encounter strong objections: how is it possible to speak of feminism in nation-states where women are massively oppressed and exploited? Isn't it obvious that the Quran contains clear statements about men's and women's positions in society and religion? Shouldn't sharia and human rights be regarded as contradictions? However, the answers to these questions are complex. Given the vast diversity of Islam, today and in history, no single answer can be given to these questions. They are taken up repeatedly in different chapters relating to different societies, denominations, traditions, periods, and regions. In particular, it is necessary to differentiate among the various Muslim states, regions, and communities, and to consider historical periods as well as the present day.

It is not possible to understand modern societies in Muslim countries without knowing the historical background that has contributed to the development of Islam and its diversity. The current debate about gender roles is characterized by a clear orientation toward the past, as is shown by the appeal in many

Muslim states today to the relevant passages in the Quran and to the sayings of the Prophet. Moreover, Islamism, which in the 1970s made its entrance onto the stage of world politics as a political power to be reckoned with, takes the first Islamic community under Muhammad in Medina (622-632) as the ideal model for the modern state in the twenty-first century. Islamism, which is also sometimes called "fundamentalism," is at the same time—and this is often misunderstood —a modern, twentieth-century ideological movement whose central characteristics are the politicization of the Islamic religion, a retrospective idealization of the early period of Islam, and a demand for the reintroduction of sharia. The representatives of these movements see this goal as something that has not yet been achieved and criticize modern Muslim nation-states, even though modern family law is based on sharia, albeit with alterations and developments that will be explained in this book.

Many women are active in Islamist, Muslim, and liberal or secular political movements: at the beginning of the twentieth century, during the colonial period, movements and organizations that fought for women's education and women's rights were already being formed. They took an interest in education and especially in the "heart" of the discourse on gender, family law. Starting from a broad definition of feminism as active engagement on behalf of greater rights for women, this book will describe the multiplicity of such movements and actors.

*   *   *

With this book, I aim to achieve two goals: first, to de-essentialize the idea, widespread in the West, of *the* Muslim woman by drawing attention to the variety of life plans, approaches, and activities of women (and men) in Muslim states, because Muslim women define and understand themselves in many different ways. We will look into different life stories and introduce some women's organizations in their social and political contexts; follow different theological, legal, and literary discourses; and examine different approaches to understanding gender and sexuality, taking into consideration the most recent research. Here law plays a central role, because it sets the norms according to which the state, the society, and the family are organized. In present-day Muslim countries, Islamic family law is shaped by pre-modern sharia, but it is no longer identical with it.

My second goal is to emphasize, through the presentation of examples and quotations, the active role played in Muslim countries by women in politics and society, and to correct the still widely prevalent image of the passive, apolitical Muslim woman who is under patriarchal domination and avoids the public sphere. Here I will present Islamist activists—men and women—as well as secular advocates for the implementation of human rights conventions and the separation of state and religion.

The gender hierarchy connected with a still patriarchal social order and existing political repression of women in many Muslim states is evident. What is not sufficiently seen is that precisely in the context of political systems that are still (or again) repressive, women are active and help shape their societies, often encountering strong resistance and threats to their bodies, their freedom, and their lives. In the demonstrations that took place in Tunisia, Egypt, Libya, Bahrain, and Yemen during the spring of 2011, women were marching alongside men to protest against repressive regimes. The developments since 2012, however, show that a patriarchal society and a not yet democratic regime still strongly oppose women's participation in the public sphere.

In view of the broad regional diversity of Muslim states—there are also Muslim minorities today in many states around the globe—and the cultural, spiritual, social, and political diversity of ways of life from the seventh to the twenty-first centuries, the task this book undertakes is not an easy one. It goes without saying that it was necessary to be selective regarding topic and emphasis. In this book the Muslim world will be identified with the Islamic heartland—that is, with the countries of the Near East and North Africa, as well as Turkey, Iran, and Afghanistan. Because of space limitations, large parts of Islamically influenced regions such as South Asia and Southeast Asia, Sub-Saharan Africa, and the Soviet Union's successor states in Central Asia could not be taken into account. In the section on women's movements, I have discussed the example of Egypt and compared it with Iran and Morocco; in particular, legal developments are described through a comparison of classical law and the Moroccan personal law promulgated in 2004. My scholarly focus on law guided my choice but did not confine it. Furthermore, I see no great advantage in singling out, eclectically and without attention to their specific historical, political, and social contexts, specific points in the development of the women's movement and of law in many different countries. On the contrary, describing the background of the developments specific to each country seems to me the best way to proceed.

The concepts "woman" and "man" always have to be used carefully; women and men are not considered as "natural" categories but as social constructs connected with special concepts of "femininity" and "masculinity." These gender concepts, gender roles, and hierarchies have changed over time and are spelled out differently in different regional and local contexts in history and today. Furthermore, gender roles can be determined only by examining the interaction of the sexes, whether in normative texts or on the actual social and political level. One important focus is on the hierarchical relationships of gender—especially in the legal context—and the associated power play. Beyond the dominant conception of the two genders, transsexuality and same-sex relations play an important role in the law, literature, and society of Muslim countries, even if they are almost always tabooed by the dominant discourse. They will also be discussed here. "Islamic" may designate the societies and cultures of people who consider themselves Muslims, but it would be a grave mistake to infer that these societies and cultures are exclusively shaped by religion.

For a long time Wiebke Walther's book *Women in Islam* (first published in German in 1980) was the standard reference on the topic. Leila Ahmed, calling Walther's book "more anecdotal than analytical," made a convincing new contribution to the topic with her book *Women and Gender in Islam* (1992), which adopted a feminist approach and concentrated on different discourses. Like Ahmed, I concentrate on certain discourses, especially those that refer mainly but not exclusively to legal history and legal developments in modern times, both of which have been among my main fields of research; however, I also take into consideration discourses on sexuality, theology, and literature. Unlike Ahmed, I do not approach the topic chronologically, but rather, thematically. In my view, research in many areas of gender studies, especially regarding the premodern era, is still in its infancy, and it is difficult because of the scarcity of source material. For this reason, many results remain tentative; sometimes no more than hypothesis can be offered, whereas in later times with more sources it is possible to identify and compare different discourses and thus construct a more complete picture.

One further important scholarly approach to gender in Islam should be mentioned, the *Encyclopedia of Women & Islamic Cultures* (2003), which provides information on many different topics concerning Muslim societies.

*   *   *

To reproduce the Arabic alphabet I use a simplified transcription that indicates only macrons. The letters 'Ain (ʿ) and Hamza (ʾ) are indicated only by '. However, in the Glossary, the proper scholarly transcription of each word is given. Names and concepts that are used in English, such as the names of authors who have published in European languages or persons whose names appear on the Internet and in the press in Romanized form, are given accordingly.

*   *   *

I would like to thank all those who have contributed to the publication of this book. First of all, I wish to acknowledge my friend and colleague Angela Schwarz, with whom I was able to have many stimulating discussions. She read the German manuscript critically and offered me many valuable suggestions that improved the text. My assistants in the department of Arabic and Islamic Studies at the University of Göttingen, Hanane El Boussadani and Kathrin Zeiß, Naseef Naeem and Mohsen Zakeri, and also Nadjla Al-Amin, Mehdi Vazirian, and Rebecca Stengel, have made contributions to certain parts of the book, for which I am very grateful. Fritz Schulze and Thomas Weische undertook the difficult task of proofreading the whole of the German text.
I am indebted to Steven Rendall for an accurate translation into English, and I thank Simon Fuchs for checking the quo-

tations in English text editions. Furthermore, I am thankful to Shanti Hossain for her conscientious proofreading of the final manuscript, and especially to Markus Wiener, for his many efforts to get the book translated and for publishing it in this English version.

Docendo discimus. I thank the participants in my seminar on the "Women's Movement and Colonialism in Egypt" in the summer semester of 2010 and on "Key Texts of Modernity" in the winter semester of 2010-2011 for their fruitful discussions and contributions.

My husband and my two sons always kept me (the only woman in the family) and my mind agile in our discussions of gender relations, and for that I thank them most heartily.

Göttingen, May 2013

The Beginnings

Pre-Islamic Arabia

Terra Incognita?

In his biography of the Prophet Muhammad, the historian Ibn Ishāq (d. 767)[1] tells how 'Abdallāh, the future father of the Prophet, was traveling with his father to visit Āmina's family in order to be introduced and married to her. On the way there, he passed another woman. She saw a light emanating from him and offered to give him a gift if he immediately had sexual intercourse with her. Looking at his father, whom he was accompanying, 'Abdallāh declined. When, on the following day—after having married Āmina and begotten the prophet—he returned to the woman in order to take her up on her offer, she no longer seemed interested in him. When

1

he asked why, she said "The light that accompanied you yesterday has left you. So I no longer need you." Ibn Ishāq further reports that this woman was the sister of a Christian named Waraqa and had learned from him about the expected arrival of a new prophet.

If we set aside the question of the historicity of this tradition, the story depicts an offer of sexual intercourse that is made by a woman to a man and is not found objectionable on the narrative level; at the same time, it attests to the idea of a metaphor of light—that is, of a light that is conceived as an expression of divine election, which is associated with Muhammad's family line, and is apparently inherent in 'Abdallāh's sperm. After the Prophet was conceived, Āmina now carried the light within herself.

Can we conclude from this story that, in the pre-Islamic society of Mecca into which Muhammad was born around 570, a sexual initiative on the part of a woman was considered acceptable? Or was the woman interested only in receiving the semen in which the "light of Muhammad" slumbered, thus acquiring for herself the prestige of being the Prophet's mother? What was women's social status at the time, and what rights did they have? Two opposite positions are usually taken on this question. On the one hand, it is argued that the status of women was better in pre-Islamic times, because women had more freedom of movement and action; on the other hand, it is claimed that Islam introduced many improvements and gave women rights they did not have in pre-Islamic times. The truth is that the difficult and very meager sources allow us to make reasonably certain statements about only a few points.

It is clear that the prophet Muhammad was born around 570 in the city of Mecca, on the Arabian peninsula. His father was, at that point, already dead, and his mother died a few years after he was born. Muhammad was raised as an orphan by his uncle, Abū Tālib, who belonged to the clan of the Hāshim and the tribe of the Quraysh. Abū Tālib fed the orphaned child and gave him shelter, without which he could not have survived in the contemporary tribal society. Life on the Arabian peninsula was marked by frequent feuds between the partly nomadic tribes that lived there. Family, clan, and tribe determined the individual's place in society and provided legal security. At the same time, there were urban centers of supra-regional commercial, religious, and political importance: examples include, Mecca, Muhammad's birthplace, but also Yathrib, which later became Medina, the city to which Muhammad emigrated in 622. Blood feuds between tribes were suspended at certain times and in certain places— Mecca, for example—in order to allow people to assemble in a conflict-free atmosphere on cultural and religious occasions. Because of its position on the trade route from southern Arabia to the Levant, Mecca was not only an important commercial and business center, but also a religious center, because the Ka'ba shrine was located there. This site, which was later to become the focal point of the Islamic pilgrimage, was considered a holy place even in pre-Islamic times.

It is true that in Mecca and the surrounding settlements several gods and goddesses were worshiped, but we can already discern at this time tendencies toward monotheism— toward the veneration of a single God known simply by the name al-ilāh, "the God," which became in the Quran the name of the Islamic God (Arabic *Allāh*). At that time, the Arabian peninsula lay between the great powers of the Byzantine Empire in Asia Minor and the Sassanid Empire in the area of modern-day Iran, and the existence of Christian and Jewish communities there has been proven. Thus, for example, the relative of the woman who offered herself to 'Abdallāh is thought to have been a Christian, and Jewish groups had settled in Medina.

The historical sources date from the centuries that followed. Ibn Ishāq's biography comes down to us through Ibn Hishām (d. 830), who lived two hundred years after the Prophet. In these Islamic traditions, the time before Muhammad is seen as the "Age of Ignorance" (Arabic *jāhiliyya*), meaning, from a religious perspective, the time before divine revelation; the designation nonetheless implies a rupture in the continuity of history, so that pre-Islamic customs and practices are judged from the point of view of the newborn religion. Many of the documents relating to the pre-Islamic period are therefore unreliable, incomplete, and contradictory, and in many cases historians are unable to advance beyond hypotheses. Since the 1970s, the view that Islam's early period in the seventh century should be regarded as the political model for modern-day Muslims as well has established itself in the Islamic world. As a result, a backward-looking idealization has set in, a transformation from the point of view of the twentieth or twenty-first century of a past that is, in any case, difficult to reconstruct historically.

The fundamental source for this period is and remains the Quran, which Muslims believe contains God's revelation to Muhammad and to humanity as a whole. According to the broad consensus among Muslim and Western scholars, it was written down a few decades after the Prophet's death. It is the principal source not only of Islamic spirituality, ethics, and religiousness, but also of Islamic legal and social norms, especially regarding gender status and a few areas of criminal law. In addition, the *sunna* ("way"), in the sense of the "Prophet's way" (Arabic *sunnat al-nabī*), is the second-largest source for theology and law. The latter includes the statements and acts, raised to the status of legally binding precedents, handed down in traditions (Arabic *hadīth*, pl. *ahādith*). These traditions were first collected in canonical works in the ninth century; the two most important of these, from the Sunni-Muslim point of view, are that of al-Bukhārī (d. 870) and Muslim (d. 875). The Shiites, the second largest religious group in Islam, recognized other works as central, for example that of Ibn Bābūya (d. 991). Muslim traditional scholars consider these works to be authentic and actually going back to the Prophet, whereas modern scholarship is more circumspect on this point and on the basis of a historical and critical analysis of these sources does not unreservedly recognize them as an expression of the historical reality of the seventh century. Nonetheless, they contain numerous statements about the social, economic, and political role of women in pre-Islamic times.

Gender Roles in "The Age of Ignorance"

Khadīja, a widow belonging to the Quraysh tribe to which Muhammad also belonged, ran a flourishing trading operation in Mecca in the late sixth century. The sources tell us that her employees accompanied caravans as far as modern-day Syria. She hired the young, penniless Muhammad to manage her merchandise and sent him, presumably in 595, to the city of Basra in Syria. After he had completed his task satisfactorily, she offered to marry him. Muhammad is supposed to have been twenty-five years old at this time, and Khadīja forty, though other sources say she was twenty-eight. Thus for a second time a woman's initiative with regard to a man in pre-Islamic times is reported.

During her lifetime, Khadīja was the only woman to whom Muhammad was married. The marriage brought him financial and emotional security, and the couple had at least five children, four girls and one or two boys. Only one of the daughters, Fātima, (d. 632) became an important figure in Islamic history, as the mother of Muhammad's two surviving grandsons, Hasan (b. 624) and Husayn (b. 625). Fātima was married to 'Alī b. Abī Tālib, the Prophet's cousin and the son of Abū Tālib, who had raised the orphaned Muhammad. Ruqayya (d. 624), another daughter, married 'Uthmān, who later became the third caliph (reigned 644-656). Her eldest sister Zaynab died in 629, while Muhammad was still alive.

The marriage with Khadīja should be seen as a turning point in Muhammad's life not only because it afforded him a secure social position and a regular family life, but also because Khadīja supported her husband, increased his self-confidence, and believed in him when, in the month of Ramadan, 610, he received his first revelation from the archangel Gabriel. As Ibn Ishāq reported, Muhammad, still completely shaken by the impact of the revelation, went first to Khadīja and told her what had happened to him. She is said to have replied: "Rejoice, son of my uncle, and be steadfast! By him in whose hand my soul lies, truly, I hope you will be this people's prophet."[2] Khadīja was apparently wealthy as well as financially and socially independent, and was therefore in a position that enabled her to choose her husband by herself. Her economic and social position also allowed her to support her husband when he broke with all the religious ideas of the powerful elites of Mecca and proclaimed a new religion.

The pre-Islamic religion of Arabia was characterized by a richly varied spectrum of gods and goddesses, along with the cult rituals that accompanied them. The Quran itself refers by name to the female deities al-Lāt, al-'Uzza, and Manāt (53:19-20),[3] whose cults have also been proved by archaeological research and who played prominent roles in the religious life of Mecca associated with the Ka'ba. In a revelation described as proceeding from Satan, Muhammad is said to have named the three goddesses as mediators between humans and God. The revelation in these verses was retracted; they were removed from the Quran and declared to be in error, although several historiographical sources testify to them. These are the so-called "Satanic verses" that the Anglo-Indian author Salman Rushdie took up in his eponymous novel (1988) and reworked in a literary way. For the Meccan elite, the inclusion of these three highly-respected goddesses would have meant an integration of their traditional cult into the new religion, which might have been of interest to them on purely economic grounds, since the flow of pilgrims brought money to Mecca and increased the prosperity not only of the merchants but of the whole city. If they turned away from the traditional cults, this source of income would be in danger of drying up. Muhammad realized, however, that there could be no place for these goddesses in his strictly monotheistic world-view.

Similarly, in the theological domain there were different forms of marriage on the social level. "Temporary marriage" (Arabic *mut'a*), which was tolerated by the Shiites but not by the Sunnis, was traced back to Quran verse 4:28. This verse was interpreted by the Shiites as referring to a temporally limited marriage contract between a man and an unmarried woman, the validity of which can range from a few hours to several decades. This form of marriage is still permitted by the family law of Shiite-influenced Iran.

In Bukhārī's traditional work we find a statement about marriage in the pre-Islamic period made by the Prophet's wife 'Ā'isha after the death of Khadīja:

4834: It is related from 'Urwa ibn az-Zubayr that 'Ā'isha, the wife of the Prophet, may Allah bless him and grant him peace, informed him that there were four types of marriage in the Jahiliyya. There was the marriage which is that still practiced by people today in which a man asked another man for his ward or daughter, paid her dower and then married her. Another type was that a man would say to his wife after she was pure from menstruation, "Send for so-and-so and have intercourse with him." Her husband would stay away from her and not have sex with her until she became pregnant by that man with whom she was sleeping. When it was clear that she was pregnant, then her husband would sleep with her if he wished. He did that out of the desire for a child of noble descent. This marriage was called al-Istibda'. Another type of marriage was that a group of less than ten men would go to the same woman and all have intercourse with her. If she became pregnant and gave birth, some days after the birth she would send for them, and none of them could refuse to come. When they were gathered together before her, she would say to them, "You know what you did. I have given birth. It is your son, so-and-so!" She would name whichever of them she wanted to name, and her child would be attributed to him and the man could not deny that. The fourth type of marriage was that many men would go to a woman who would not refuse whoever came to her. They were prostitutes and they used to set up flags at the doors as signs. Whoever wanted could go to them. If one of them became pregnant, when she gave birth, they would

be brought together and they would call the phys-
iognomists who would then attach the child to the
one they thought was the father. He would be ascribed to him and called his son. None of them
could reject that. When Muhammad, may Allah
bless him and grant him peace, was sent with the
truth, he abolished all of the marriages of the
Jahiliyya except the marriage practiced by people
today.[4]

It is questionable whether 'Ā'isha described the forms of
marriage in pre-Islamic times exhaustively and accurately,
but it is confirmed by other sources that different forms of
marriage existed. The focus in this tradition is on the question
of paternity. In the second category the woman is lent out to
another man so that a child of good descent can be procre-
ated. This form of marriage is also known to have existed in
pre-Islamic Iran. In the third category, a woman who has had
sexual relations with several men has the right to name the
father of her child and thus to determine the genealogical relationship and descent. In 'Ā'isha's report, this form of marriage is clearly distinguished from prostitution, in which
paternity is determined by independent scholars. 'Ā'isha remains silent regarding the role of the genders in marriage, the
division of labor, finances, inheritance, and the two partners'
social and family duties. But with the third category she
refers to a form of marriage in which women clearly had the
right to make their own decisions regarding their bodies, their
sexuality, and the descent of their child. This seems diamet-
rically opposed to the second category, in which the women
are "lent out."

However, the existence of different forms of marriage
should not be equated with a dominant political or social role

for women, or even with matriarchy. We may take as an il-
lustration of this, even if it is of uncertain historicity, a statement attributed to the second caliph, 'Umar (reigned
634-644), according to which Quraysh men in Mecca had
always been in charge of their women, whereas among the
people of Medina, who were later called "helpers" (Arabic
ansār), women were dominant. 'Umar complains that
Quraysh women then imitated this custom.[5] Both the aforementioned self-confident offer a woman made to Muhammad's father and the financially and socially independent
position enjoyed by Muhammad's first wife Khadīja, who
came from Mecca, seem to contradict this statement. On the
other hand, hints in the Quran suggest that customs discriminating against women existed in pre-Islamic times, and that
these customs were restricted or prohibited by Islam. For instance, it was forbidden to kill a new-born girl (81:9) or to
marry a widow to her deceased husband's brother against her
will (4:23), while the number of times a man could repudiate
a wife was limited (2:229). The contradictory nature of the
source statements is evident, and the problems faced by the
historian seeking to reconstruct early Islamic history in general and ideas of gender in particular, become clear. The same
holds for the question of the character and role of Islamic
figures such as the Prophet's male and female companions
and his wives.

Muhammad and Women

The Prophet's Female Companions

The Prophet's followers who were in direct contact with him, both male and female, are known as his "companions." Because of this proximity and the knowledge of the Prophet's thoughts and acts connected with it, they had great practical and symbolic significance in Islamic history and became, through the Prophet's statements handed down by them, part of the line of transmission-chain (Arabic *isnād*) that is supposed to ensure the credibility of these reports. Their names, dates of birth and death, and information regarding the circumstances in which they lived were collected in biographical lexicons so that their reliability with regard to the traditional statements was considered proven. Through their proximity to the Prophet they enjoyed considerable prestige, which has endured down to the modern age, and they have frequently become figures with whom modern Muslims identify, serving as models for Islamic conduct that was religiously and ethically righteous and virtuous. The statements made by the Prophet's female companions were considered to be just as reliable as those made by his male companions.

Ibn Sa'd (d. 845), the author of a biographical lexicon, listed 117 women who followed Muhammad, including Umm Ayman (in Arabic names, *Umm* stands for "mother," *Abū* for "father"), his former nursemaid, whom he regarded as part of his family. Moreover, Ibn Sa'd mentioned 359 additional women as converts in Medina. He begins his life histories of these women with a discussion of the so-called "women's oath," which Ibn Ishāq interprets as a declaration of support for Muhammad on the basis of religious and social ideas: the latter included, for example, not associating God with a partner, that is, affirming an absolute monotheism, and declaring that one would not engage in fornication, kill newborn girls, or lie. Thus the oath contained fundamental religious-spiritual and legal-social rules like those found in the Quran. However, in contrast to the men's oath, the "women's oath" excluded supporting the Prophet in battle. Such a loyalty oath for women is mentioned in the Quran (60:12), in a verse in which God addresses Muhammad as follows:

> O Prophet, when believing women come to thee, swearing fealty to thee upon the terms that they will not associate with God anything, and will not steal, neither commit adultery, nor slay their children, nor bring a calumny they forge between their hands and their feet, nor disobey thee in aught honorable, ask God's forgiveness for them; God is All-forgiving, All-compassionate.

Muhammad had already gathered a few followers around him when, in 619, Khadīja and Abū Tālib died and he lost the most important members of his family, those who had supported and protected him. Since his situation in Mecca therefore became precarious and he found himself facing increasing hostility from the residents of that city, in 622 he decided to accept an offer and move to Medina. The Islamic calendar begins with this emigration (Arabic *hijra*), so that for the supporters of the new religion a new epoch began. In Medina Muhammad's role changed fundamentally; there, he was recognized by the residents and became not only the spiritual but also the political leader of a young community consisting of a few adherents who had followed him from Mecca and the "helpers" in Medina. The cornerstone for a religiously-shaped political community was laid, and we can discern new processes of negotiation regarding political and social themes as well as gender roles. The character of the divine proclamations changed. During the period spent in Mecca, religious and eschatological themes referencing both God's mercy and the threat of the Last Judgment were dominant; in Medina, however, numerous specific rules regulating peoples' everyday lives developed.

The philosopher and human rights activist Abdullahi al-Na'im (b. 1946), who lives and teaches in the United States, sees here the dividing line for the understanding of the revelation. Whereas the "spirit" of the Quran—that is, its religiousness and spirituality—is to be found in the early verses, the suras and verses from Medina reflect above all the social, political, and economic reality of the Arabic peninsula in the early seventh century. In his view, the Medina verses, which often also concern gender relationships, should be interpreted in this context, and can no longer serve as norms for the communal life of the faithful in the twenty-first century.[6]

Umm Kulthūm, a woman from Mecca, was the first woman to migrate to Medina, and asked the Prophet for help when her brother tried to take her back to Mecca. In addition, a considerable number of women were supposedly present at the numerous battles that were fought between Medina and Mecca after Muhammad's emigration. They served as nurses, but according to some reports, they also took part in the fighting. Thus a woman from Medina, Umm Umāra, is supposed to have been present at various warlike conflicts and to have fought and even been wounded at the battle of Uhud in 625, when the Muslims suffered a bitter defeat.[7] In Medina, a young woman, Umayya bt. Qays,[8] is supposed to have asked the Prophet's permission to care for the wounded in the battle of Khaybar in 628. According to Ibn Sa'd, for doing so she received as war booty a necklace that the Prophet himself put around her neck, while Ku'ayba bt. Sa'd sheltered the Prophet and cared for the wounded from a campaign in a tent in the Medina mosque.[9] The Prophet's wives also seem to have accompanied him on military campaigns. On the other hand, there are reports according to which he forbade a woman to participate in a battle on the ground that he did not want it said that he had fought with a woman at his side.[10]

The Prophet's female—as well as the male—companions enjoy great prestige. They are thought to be the first who saw Muhammad as the Prophet and adhered to Islam, the first who heard his statements and also questioned him in certain situations. The traditions that go back to them explain many details of religious law, rites, and practices of worship, along with interaction between the genders and social and legal guidelines. The same goes for Muhammad's wives, who have an even more prominent rank.

Wives and Daughters

Khadīja, Muhammad's first wife, and 'Ā'isha, his favorite wife, as well as Fātima, his daughter, later became figures to be identified with and role models that premodern and modern Muslim women were expected to follow. Denis Spellberg analyzes the medieval Muslim scholar's view on the women of the Prophet. According to her research, Khadīja is depicted in the earliest biographical dictionaries not just as the Prophet's first wife, but also as the first convert to Islam. She is described as a woman of wealth and honor within Meccan society. She, like the other wives, was counted among the *ummahāt al-mu'minīn*, the "Mothers of the Believers." Thus the most famous of honorary titles bestowed upon the most elite women of the first Muslim community is an allusion to a basic female biological role. Spellberg reports an anecdote according to which 'Ā'isha, being addressed as "mother," replied, "I am not your mother, I am the mother of your men," a grammatically savvy statement as well, since the masculine—not the feminine—plural is employed for the Arabic word "believers."[11]

Traditionally, the Prophet's wives often appear as models for righteous conduct, as 'Ā'isha's following statement about Khadīja shows:

> 4931. It is related that 'Ā'isha said, "I was not jealous about any of the wives of the Prophet, may Allah bless him and grant him peace, as I was jealous about Khadīja because of the frequency with which the Messenger of Allah, may Allah bless him and grant him peace, mentioned her and praised her, and it was revealed to the Messenger of Allah, may Allah bless him and grant him peace, to give her the good news of a house of pearls in the Garden.[12]

Khadīja's legacy in the Muslim community is based on her being presented as a steadfast supporter of her husband's mission; her virtues were, according to the sources, often mentioned by the prophet.

Information about Fāṭima is sparse in the earliest sources compared with the tremendous elaboration of detail about her life in later sources, particularly among Shiite authors.[13] Fāṭima is often referred to by the byname *al-Zahrā'*, "the radiant." She had the closest relationship to her father of all his children, and the family tree of the Prophet's descendants *(*Arabic *shurafā'*, sing. *sharīf)* developed through her sons

Hasan and Husayn, whom the Shiites call imāms (Arabic *imām*, pl. *a'imma*). According to Shiite doctrine, they were supposed to be the community's only legitimate leaders after 'Alī . This claim made by the Shiites was not recognized, however, since first Abū Bakr and then 'Umar held the caliphate, until 'Alī was finally recognized in 656 as the leader of the Muslim community.

The sources report that Fātima and 'Alī initially lived in very poor conditions. Fātima is said to have had no helper in the household and to have ground her own wheat, because Muhammad was not prepared to give her a slave to do this work for her. Such poverty affected many households among the early Muslims, but abated later on. In addition to their sons Hasan and Husayn, the couple also had two daughters, Umm Kulthūm and Zaynab. It is said that Fātima frequently complained to her father about the harsh treatment she received from her husband, and Muhammad is supposed to have supported her efforts to prevent 'Alī from taking a second wife. Regarding this domestic dispute between his daughter and 'Alī, Muhammad is supposed to have remarked that Fātima was a part of him and that anyone who injured her injured him. She is described as a reserved woman who never meddled in political matters while the Prophet was alive.

After Muhammad's death, which upset her greatly, Fātima supposedly spoke out against the choice of 'Umar as his successor. She died not very long after her father. There is a saying that on Judgment Day she will be the first to enter Paradise after the resurrection. Everyone will have to cast down their eyes when, preceded by seven virgins of Paradise, she passes over the bridge that leads from Hell to Paradise.[14]

The key to the special veneration of Fātima among Shiites lies in her genealogical function. Verena Klemm has studied the way in which fragmentary historical and biographical information was used to create a coherent and meaningful story of a heroine named Fātima. Whereas in the *hadīth* she appeared as a shadowy figure chiefly in relation to her father and husband, later Shiite narratives transformed these references into a religious *vita* that emphasizes her passivity and compliance. In her family roles she combines love, motherliness, loyalty, and obedience. In the Islamic conception, she is chaste, pious, and absolutely consistent. Her position in the Shiite tradition is comparable to that of Mary in Christianity, especially with regard to sexuality and motherhood.[15]

After Khadīja's death in 619, and while he was still in Mecca, Muhammad married again; in fact, he married two women at once: Sawda and 'Ā'isha, tradition emphasizing that 'Ā'isha was the only virgin he married. In Medina he married other women, so that Islamic tradition assumes that he had thirteen or perhaps fourteen wives in all. The precise number cannot be determined because Muhammad also had relationships with concubines. Thus, for example, it is not clear whether the Jewess Rayhāna was married to Muhammad or was only his concubine. She and Safiyya bt. Huyayy, whom he married, converted to Islam. The Copt Maria, who was only his concubine, bore him a son named Ibrāhīm, who died, however, around the age of two. He gave Safiya al-'Anbariyya, a prisoner of war, a free choice between marrying him and returning to her own tribe. She decided to go back to her tribe. Various sources report that women proposed marriage to the Prophet, among them, according to some sources, Umm Salama Hind bt. Abī Umayya,[16] who had been, with her earlier husband, among the Prophet's first followers. She brought four children to the marriage, handed down numerous statements by the Prophet, and was considered by many sources to be the legal specialist among the Prophet's female companions and wives. She was the last of the Prophet's wives to die, in 679 or 680.

A few of these marriages might have been politically motivated, because Muhammad married, for example, not only 'Ā'isha—the daughter of Abū Bakr, his closest advisor, companion in arms, and supporter—but also 'Umar's daughter Hafsa. Both men succeeded the prophet, in the capacity of political and military leaders of the young Islamic state, as caliphs. Abū Bakr ruled from 632 to 634 and 'Umar from 634 to 644.

Since according to a Quranic revelation Muslim believers are allowed to marry no more than four women, the higher number of Muhammad's wives is justified by a special law (33:50). As stated above, in sura 33, his wives are given the byname "Mothers of the Believers" (33:6). However, this rank was associated with special conditions connected with their status. In sura 33:32-34 we read:

> Wives of the Prophet, you are not as other women. If you are god-fearing, be not abject in your speech, so that he in whose heart is sickness may be lustful; but speak honorable words. Remain in your houses; and display not your finery, as did the pagans of old. And perform the prayer, and pay the alms, and obey God and His Messenger. People of the House, God only desires to put away from you abomination and to cleanse you. And remember that which is recited in your houses of the signs of God and the Wisdom; God is All-subtle, All-aware.

A topic closely related to the Prophet's wives is, as this verse shows, the practice of seclusion and veiling. Thus we read in sura 33:59:

O Prophet, say to thy wives and daughters and the believing women, that they draw their veils close to them; so it is likelier they will be known, and not hurt. God is All-forgiving, All-compassionate.

In sura 33:53 we read:

And when you ask his wives for any object, ask them from behind a curtain.

The Arabic word for "curtain," *hijāb*, was later equated with clothing, so that a "veil," whether it now covers the face or only the hair and neck, is generally called a *hijāb*.

'Ā'isha was incontestably the Prophet's favorite wife. According to a few sources, she was married to the Prophet when she was only six years old, and the marriage was consummated after the emigration to Medina, when she was about nine. Early marriages were apparently usual in the pre-Islamic and early Islamic context and were not considered objectionable. Islamic premodern law later viewed these early marriages as exemplary, and established nine as the minimum age for marriage. Even in discussions about modern personal law in the twentieth century, the example of 'Ā'isha was adduced. Nonetheless, many modern family law codes indicate a far higher minimum age for marriage. For instance, in Morocco it has been set at eighteen for both sexes since 2004.

In 627, 'Ā'isha's marriage was put under serious strain when she accompanied her husband on a military expedition and was caught up in the affair known as "the slander" (Arabic *hadīth al-ifk*). The traditions vary in many details, but we can nonetheless make out a few points of agreement in this tale. When the caravans set out, 'Ā'isha was left behind in the camp, but she was found by a young man, who put her on his camel and returned her to the group. In view of the strict segregation of the prophet's wives and the latent hostilities toward Muhammad, suspicions concerning 'Ā'isha immediately arose. In this case, honor and dishonor were not seen as private matters but instead as having public relevance, because they affected Muhammad's position in the community. In a community that was still strongly marked by public monitoring, such behavior could not be swept out of the way simply by the Prophet forgiving his wife. In this connection, a divine revelation (24:11) was issued that exonerated 'Ā'isha of any charge with regard to the suspected adultery. In addition, it was established that adultery or extra-marital sexual intercourse must always be established by four male witnesses, whereby the strict punishment prescribed in the Quran for this sexual crime was connected with rigorous proof. If the act cannot be proven, the accuser is to be punished by being given eighty lashes.

According to the Sunni tradition, the story did not result in a decrease of the Prophet's love for his favorite wife; Muhammad is reported to have died in 'Ā'isha's arms. With his death in 632, 'Ā'isha became a childless widow at the age of eighteen and, like all of the Prophet's wives, was not allowed to marry again. When in 656 the third caliph, 'Uthmān (reigned 644-656), was murdered, she publicly criticized the assassination and moved with a thousand Quraysh against 'Alī, the fourth caliph (reigned 656-661), who had become the target of her criticism because he had not sufficiently distanced himself from the killing. In the Battle of the Camel (656)—so called because the heaviest fighting took place around the camel that was carrying 'Ā'isha's sedan chair— 'Alī was victorious, and 'Ā'isha's reputation was damaged. She returned to Medina and afterward refrained from all political activities until she died at the age of sixty-six.

Because of this political incident, Shiite sources are critical about 'Ā'isha. As Denise Spellberg has outlined, her participation in the battle was later also criticized because she did not, as laid down in Quran (33:33), stay in the house. Sunni and Shiite Muslims disagreed about 'Ā'isha's responsibility and culpability in the first civil war, but they agreed fundamentally about her potential as a negative political example for all women. The emphasis on 'Ā'isha's transgression of the Quran 33:33 is the basis for reports—from both Sunni and Shiite sources—that share the assumption that if 'Ā'isha had not left her house—if she had followed the revealed word of the Quran—the Battle of the Camel would not have occurred. Her involvement in the politics also made her a central figure to the debate, in Islamic medieval sources, over the relationship of all women to the Islamic government. It is here that 'Ā'isha is connected to the so called *fitna* ("civil war" or "chaos"),[17] a term which both denotes the Battle of the Camel as the first civil war in the Muslim community, but which also connotes male assumptions about the dangerous chaos inherent in female sexuality. Though never defined directly as a female linked to *fitna*, 'Ā'isha played a role in the connotations the term would have when applied to women later.[18]

Exercising all the necessary caution, we can deduce from the sources certain differences between 'Ā'isha and Fātima. For example, Fātima was politically rather passive, whereas 'Ā'isha's participation in the Battle of the Camel, and in certain political activities, has been proven. Both women were very close to the Prophet and today both enjoy great respect in the Islamic world. The conduct ascribed to them is considered exemplary. 'Ā'isha's portrayal in the earliest written Arabic material developed, according to Spellberg, into an implicit and explicit comparison with Khadīja and Fātima.[19]

At the same time, interpretations of the character and actions of those women could turn out to be very different. For example, the Moroccan sociologist Fatima Mernissi[20] describes Muhammad's wives as dynamic, influential, and active members of the community who initiated a genuine protest movement. She creates the impression that they were prototypes of actors in the women's movement in the late nineteenth and early twentieth centuries. However, given the sketchy state of the sources to which we have already alluded, this and other far-reaching interpretations must be considered more as projections of present-day ideas onto the past than as historically proven facts.

Theology and Law

The Quran and the Hadīth

Quranic Regulations Concerning the Gender Relationship

In its present form, the Quran consists of 114 suras. Suras are large sections of text provided with names, and are further subdivided into individual verses (Arabic *āya*, pl. *āyāt*). Of the 6,238 verses, about a hundred concern legal regulations, the juristic interpretation of many of which was and is controversial. The Quran's revelations are sometimes directly addressed to "believing men and women," but grammatically and thematically they are usually addressed exclusively to men.

In general, these regulations concern questions of detail such as the position of the Prophet's wives and their conduct with regard to other men. A pre-Islamic background can often be discerned behind the concrete examples, but they also show a new kind of legal thought and new ethics. The regulations concern the group's communal life and thus also questions of gender roles and family law, particular points in criminal law, and to a small extent, procedural or business law. Other domains of law, such as the question as to what an Islamic state should be like, remain largely untouched. Similarly, the interpretation of the Quran and the *hadīth* is difficult. Many statements in these two fundamental sources of Islamic law cannot be read directly but require interpretation, and they have been debated ever since the beginning of the commentary literature on them. The disciplines of Quran interpretation (Arabic *tafsīr*) and jurisprudence (Arabic *fiqh*) developed in this context.

Commentators on the Quran have developed an extensive toolkit for exegesis. This toolkit includes, in addition to the "occasions of revelation" (Arabic *asbāb an-nuzūl*), whose importance is shown by the example of 'Ā'isha's story, the classification of verses as generally valid or only valid for a particular group of people. Moreover, it includes the question whether certain verses have been superseded by other, later verses and have lost their validity. This path of supersession or restriction is mentioned in the Quran itself (2:106). Thus for example the possibility of testamentary inheritance (2:176) is limited by the establishment of fixed shares (4:12).

In modern times, verses concerning gender relationships have been the subject of intense controversies. Feminist interpreters of the Quran have criticized the fact that for centuries, men representing a patriarchically-structured society have interpreted verses in a way advantageous for them. Whereas on the one hand modern legislators, such as those in Tunisia, Morocco, and Egypt, have begun to redefine gender relationships through new interpretations, on the other hand traditional interpretations based on the assumption of a hierarchy of genders persist.

In the Quran, gender relationships are based on marriage as the most important institution. The *mahr*, a specified amount of money or possessions to be paid by the groom, was a fundamental part of the marriage contract, and it was paid to the bride herself, not to her father (4:4). In later Islamic law as well, the bride had the right to dispose of these assets, and they could not be taken from her by her husband. If the husband repudiated the wife before the marriage was consummated, half of these assets went to the bride (2:237). This gave the wife a certain financial independence. Levirate marriage, a custom that was obviously pre-Islamic, and in which a man's widow was married to his surviving brother, was forbidden (4:23).

In addition, exchanging women—for example, sisters—in order to avoid paying the *mahr* (as was apparently previously done), was prohibited not by the Quran but by tradition.[1] Today, the *mahr* is still an indispensable part of an Islamic marriage contract.

As to the question of interfaith marriages, Muslim men were permitted to marry non-Muslim women belonging to the category of "the people of the book"—that is, Christians and Jews, and also, according to later law, Zoroastrians, whereas Muslim women were not permitted to marry non-Muslims (2:220). According to the Quran, adoption is not allowed (33:4-5).

Men were not allowed to marry their own mothers, wives from their father's earlier marriages, and close female relatives, or their nursemaids or children who had been nursed by her, so that blood relationships were in this respect equated with relationships arising from being nursed by the same woman. The simultaneous marriage of two sisters to the same man was also forbidden (4:27 ff.). All these regulations es-

tablished the boundaries, defined by the degrees of relationship between two persons, that "forbade" (arabic *mahram*)
them to marry or "allowed" (arabic *halāl*) them to marry.
They became the foundation for interactions between the
genders and defined the rules for the separation of the sexes.
The killing of a new-born girl was forbidden (81:9) and the
rejection of a new-born girl (16:60) was declared to be
immoral.

In addition to the payment of the *mahr* (4:4, 33:46), it became common in law that the husband was held responsible
for the maintenance (Arabic *nafaqa*) of his wife (65:7, 2:233).
Regarding the relationship between parents and children, in
sura 2:233, it is said that the mother should nurse her children
for two full years, and that even in the event of a divorce, the
father must provide for their support during this period.

According to the traditional view of the commentators, a
legal hierarchy of the genders is implied by verse 2:228—
"but their men have a degree above them"—and by verse
4:38:

> Men are the managers of the affairs of women for
> that God has preferred in bounty one of them over
> another, and for that they have expended of their
> property. Righteous women are therefore obedient,
> guarding the secret for God's guarding. And those
> you fear may be rebellious admonish; banish them
> to their couches, and beat them. If they then obey
> you, look not for any way against them; God is All-
> high, All-great.

In the history of Quran interpretation, the husband's financial
responsibility for his wife has been inferred from these and
other verses. Moreover, depending on how sura 4:38 is un-

derstood, a general physical and psychological hierarchy may be inferred as well.

The verse regarding polygyny (4:3) sets the maximum number of wives at four:

> If you fear that you will not act justly towards the orphans, marry such women as seem good to you, two, three, four; but if you fear you will not be equitable, then only one, or what your right hands own; so it is likelier you will not be partial.

Traditionally, this passage was interpreted as asserting the right of the man to marry a maximum of four women and also to take slaves as concubines, the statement "if you fear that you will not act justly" being taken as a moral recommendation but not a legal obligation to treat wives equally. This was understood to imply above all financial fairness and thus equal amounts paid for living expenses and *mahr*.

Asked how to interpret this verse, 'Ā'isha explained that it was sent from on high on a specific "occasion of revelation":

> 4777. It is related by 'Urwa that he asked 'Ā'isha about the words of the Almighty, "If you are afraid of not behaving justly towards orphans, then marry other permissible women, two, three or four. But if you are afraid of not treating them equally, then only one, or those you own as slaves. That makes it more likely that you will not be unfair."(4:3) 'Ā'isha said, "Nephew, an orphan girl may be in the care of her guardian who is attracted by her wealth and beauty and then he wants to marry her for a bride-price less than what is customary for someone like her. They were forbidden to marry them unless

they are fair to them and give them their full bride-price. They were commanded to marry other women instead."[2]

In pre-Islamic times, repudiation (Arabic *talāq*) as a form of divorce evidently proceeded from the man and he could use it as often as he wished. He had to utter the formula and during the waiting period (Arabic *'idda*) he could make it retroactive, which seems to have led to abuses: the husband repudiated the wife, decided to take her back before the end of the waiting period and then immediately repudiated her again, thus keeping her in a constant situation of waiting—being neither married nor divorced. This was intended to put pressure on her so that in the end she would forego payment of her *mahr* just to be free of marital bondage. Sura 2:229 limits repeated repudiation:

> Divorce is twice; then honorable retention or setting free kindly. It is not lawful for you to take of what you have given them unless the couple fear they may not maintain God's bounds; if you fear they may not maintain God's bounds, it is no fault in them for her to redeem herself.

This last sentence is used to justify the so-called "redemption" of the wife (Arabic *khul'*), and in the latest family law—for example, the Egyptian law passed in 2000—wives are given the right to divorce even against the husband's will, although at a financial loss. Recent Shiite law refers to sura 65:2, in which it is said that two witnesses must be present at the divorce.

After a divorce, a woman had to observe a waiting period corresponding to three periods of menstruation, in order to ensure that she was not pregnant (2:228). If she was pregnant, she was not allowed to remarry until forty days after she delivered. Sura 2:234 required widows to observe a mourning period of four months and ten days before remarrying.

In the Quran, slaves are often mentioned as concubines (4:3, 23:6; 33:50, 70:30), but in the time of the Prophet slavery was common and was restricted by Islamic laws only insofar as a Muslim could not be enslaved. A child engendered by a free Muslim and a female slave was considered legally free, the mother, the so-called "mother of the child" (Arabic *umm al-walad*) won her freedom after the death of her owner. Prisoners of war were also slaves. The conversion of Christian or Jewish slaves did not automatically grant them emancipation, however. But in Islamic society slave owners were expected to treat their slaves well (4:40), and emancipating them was considered religiously desirable (90:12-13). Today, slavery has been legally abolished in all Muslim states, and the corresponding international accords have been adopted. This is remarkable given that in the domain of family law and also in inheritance law—particularly, insofar as polygyny, inheritance and repudiation are concerned—improvements have been made in many places but gender equality—except in Turkey—has not been achieved. A possible explanation for this is that the gender relationship and its regulation are seen as inherent and central components of the Muslim cultural identity. Giving them up is considered tantamount to abandoning this identity.

In the domain of criminal law, the blood revenge of pre-Islamic times was not generally abolished, but rather restricted. Only exact retaliation (Arabic *qisās*) was still allowed, though it was connected with gender and status:

O believers, prescribed for you is retaliation, touching the slain; freeman for freeman, slave for slave, female for female (2:174).

In the Quran, the punishments for certain sexual acts and other crimes are called "boundaries" (Arabic *hudūd*, sing. *hadd*), because the corresponding crimes are considered transgressions of the boundaries set by God. For example, both men and women who engaged in illicit sexual intercourse (Arabic *zinā'*) (24:2) were punished with eighty lashes (24:4). Stoning as punishment for illicit sexual intercourse is found not in the Quran but in the tradition. Classical Sunni law punishes by stoning violators who have been married, regardless of whether they are still married or divorced or widowed at the time of their offense, whereas Shiite law punishes only adultery. The corresponding Quranic revelation was issued, as we noted above, in connection with the slander of 'Ā'isha.

Inheritance law attributes fixed shares to be accorded to wives. However, even today these almost always amount to only half the man's share (4:15-16). In procedural law according to the Quran, testimony given by female witnesses has only half the weight of testimony given by male witnesses (2:282), a rule that is still contained in many modern family law codes:

And call two witnesses from among your men; and if two men be not available, then a man and two women, of such as you like as witnesses, so that if either of two women should err in memory, then one [who does not err] may remind the other [who errs, of the true facts].

A large number of Quran verses concern veiling and the segregation of the sexes, for example sura 24:30-31:

> Say to the believers, that they cast down their eyes and guard their private parts; that is purer for them. God is aware of the things they work. And say to the believing women, that they cast down their eyes and guard their private parts, and reveal not their adornment save such as is outward; and let them cast their veils over their bosoms, and not reveal their adornment save to their husbands, or their fathers, or their husbands' fathers, or their sons, or their husbands' sons, or their sisters' sons, or their women, or what their right hands own, or such men as attend them, not having sexual desire, or children who have not yet attained knowledge of women's private parts; nor let them stamp their feet, so that their hidden ornament may be known.

In this verse men and women are addressed, but the latter are urged at greater length to adopt restrained behavior. The second part of the verse seems to assume that certain parts of the body were in any case visible.

Changes

It is frequently argued that Islam brought with it a significant improvement over the "Age of Ignorance." In this comparison, reference is often made to the verses in the Quran that prohibited the killing of new-born girls, took women into account in the apportioning of inheritances, and put restrictions on the repudiation of a wife. On the other hand, Leila Ahmed[3]

31

points to the greater freedoms enjoyed by pre-Islamic women and the more restrictive sexual rules in the Islamic age. She describes Khadīja and 'Ā'isha as the protagonists of two periods in which women had different legal and social positions.[4] Whereas Khadīja, as a prosperous businesswoman, chose her husband by herself, proposed marriage to him, and supported him financially, spiritually, and psychologically after what was for him the shocking experience of divine revelation, 'Ā'isha was given to the Prophet at an age when, according to the sources, she was still playing with dolls. In Ahmed's view, after Khadīja there was no longer any monogamy and autonomy for Muhammad's women. But to oppose the two women almost as personifications of the pre-Islamic and Islamic periods would seem simplistic, given the aforementioned problem of contradictory and non-contemporaneous sources.

An example from the topic of freedom and slavery, or of sexuality and gender relationships, may be used to clarify this and illustrate the difficulty of interpreting the sources, on the one hand, and the complexity of the pre-Islamic period on the other. In classical Islamic law the sale of a free Muslim man or woman into slavery was just as forbidden as enslaving a foundling. From a modern point of view, this may look like progress. Various ways of selling children were recognized by certain late antique legal systems that were then in force in Islamized areas and shaped legal practice there.[5] Great social pressure forced the Byzantine emperor Justinian (reigned 527-565) to temporarily legalize this custom, which was rooted in the far-reaching paternal power of Roman law (Lat. *patria potestas*). The sale of children was presumably practiced because of poverty and especially in times of natural catastrophes such as droughts.

How did the first Muslim legal scholars react to this preexisting practice? The answer can be found in a statement by Zuhrī, a jurist from Medina:

> Zuhrī (d. 742). A man sold his daughter to a buyer who had intercourse with her. Her father [justifying his criminal act] said: "Misery forced me to sell her!" He [Zuhrī, IS] decided: "The father and the daughter should both be punished with a hundred strokes of the whip, if the girl was of age. Then the buyer should have the money paid returned to him but he would be required to pay [the father] the *mahr* because of what he had inflicted upon her. However, the father should pay this back [the *mahr* to the buyer] as a fine. If the buyer had known that she was a free person then he would have to pay the *mahr* and the father would not have to pay it back to him as a fine and [the buyer] would also be whipped a hundred times. If the girl was a minor, then [only] the father would be punished as an example."[6]

Thus a daughter is sold and the buyer has sexual intercourse with her. Zuhrī plays out several scenarios: whether or not the girl was of age determines whether or not she is punished and whether or not the buyer knew her status as a free person will determine whether or not he is punished. The sale is retroactively legitimated as a marriage by the payment of the *mahr*. The punishment meted out to the father, the girl who is of age, and the buyer who is aware of her status is a hundred lashes, and thus refers to the punishment stipulated in the Quran for illegitimate sexual intercourse, though Zuhrī does not make this explicit. Thus the sexual offense, that is, the buyer's sexual intercourse with the girl, is apparently punished. The father cannot be punished for illegitimate sexual intercourse, since in the Quran this punishment is to be inflicted only on the two persons taking part in the sexual intercourse. He apparently receives the hundred lashes for the sale of his daughter, but here, too, Zuhrī gives no reason for the severity of the punishment. In addition, the father has to give back the *mahr* to the buyer, as the equivalent of a monetary fine, even though according to the Quran the *mahr* must be paid to his daughter. The daughter not only loses her *mahr*, but is also punished for sexual intercourse along with the buyer who knew about her status.

From the point of view of a modern understanding of law, it might be objected that although the sale of a human being is recognized as a criminal act, the daughter is punished for a sexual relationship for which she is not responsible, since she was sold. Neither does Zuhrī mention the power of disposal over the child granted the father by Roman law; he takes it into account no more than he does their poverty. The punishment is cancelled only if the daughter was not of age, which corresponds to later law in the case of *hadd* punishments that were not inflicted on those deemed incapable of crime. As already in the Quran, severe punishments for illegitimate sexual intercourse are foregrounded, and show the need for a legal regulation of sexual relations. That is the case here, since although the girl is a victim of poverty and paternal control, she is nonetheless punished because she has engaged in illegitimate sexual intercourse. On the other hand, the re-shaping of a specifically Islamic family structure does not go so far as to adopt the Roman law construction of far-reaching paternal power or especially the legal practice implying the right to kill or to sell.

Regarding the question of whether Islam was an improvement over life in the "Age of Ignorance," nothing is to be gained from this debate; value judgments such as have been made since the beginning of the twenty-first century from the point of view of gender equality cannot be projected back on the past.

With the caution required by the difficult state of the source materials, the following can be said regarding gender relationships in pre-Islamic and early Islamic times:

- The kinds of marriage contracts current in pre-Islamic times were replaced by a form of the patriarchal family under the leadership of a man with prerogatives, though the new Islamic marriage did not include the father's power of disposal over his children found in Roman law.
- A few pre-Islamic forms of marriage apparently gave women greater freedom of action and the possibility, as in the case of Khadīja, of choosing a husband by themselves, and of indulging in sexual relationships with several men, even simultaneously. At the same time, the Quran's prohibition of levirate marriage, in which the brother of a deceased man inherited the latter's wife, and the "loaning of women" 'Ā'isha described both point to the fact that these existed alongside patriarchically oriented forms of marriage, in which the woman is seen as an object. They were also subjected to restrictions.
- Thus a legal protection emerged that was unknown in pre-Islamic Arabia.
- Strict punishments for illegitimate sexual intercourse as well as a waiting period for women after a divorce or the death of her husband were clearly intended to safeguard patrilineal descent of the children in the father's household.
- Regulations reflecting gender equality and gender hierarchy are found in equal measure in the Quran. While

the severe punishments for illegitimate sexual intercourse were meted out in the same way for both men
and women, marriages with several partners and concu-
binage, as well as the possibility of repudiation and
receiving full shares of an inheritance, were reserved
for men.

Over the centuries following Muhammad's death, Islamic
law developed. This was a complex process that has still not
been completely studied, and because of the state of the
sources it will probably never be possible to reconstruct it in
all its details. Theology (Arabic *kalām*) emerged, and has become important for the question of gender roles, but it never
achieved the same rank as Islamic legal scholarship (Arabic
fiqh), which derived specific rules for human beings from the
holy scriptures.

Religious Equality?

Is the legal inequality delineated on the basis of the Quran
verses on polygyny and the repudiation of wives transferable
to the religious domain? Or, on the contrary, can we speak of
an equality of the genders in this domain? The idea that in
religion men and women have equal rights is frequently expressed, but must be qualified. The religious dimension consists of theological concepts and beliefs on the one hand, and
ritual practice on the other. As in the domains of law, statements in the Quran are frequently interpreted differently, and
the Prophet's statements also offer a partly contradictory picture that can be interpreted only with difficulty by historians.

The idea of God in the Quran is male. The divinity is characterized, as in the Judeo-Christian tradition, by masculine

attributes; the word for "God" (Arabic *al-Lāh*) is masculine; *al-Lāt*, its feminine form, which referred to one of the three goddesses venerated in the "Age of Ignorance," was repressed. The history of humanity's salvation and damnation as propagated by Muhammad represented a chain of repeated divine revelations to men, his messengers and prophets, such as Adam, Noah, Abraham, Moses, and Jacob.

On the other hand, sura 4, verse 1 says that all humans, both men and women, were created out of one soul. A general equality of the genders is also implied in sura 49:13:

> O mankind, We have created you male and female.

In verses 2:187, 30:20, and 42:9, men and women are described as couples and as meant for one another. In other passages women are created for men (26:165). Verse 4:36 refers to the economic equality of the genders:

> Do not covet that whereby God in bounty has preferred one of you above another. To the men a share from what they have earned, and to the women a share from what they have earned.

An equality of religious rights and duties exists, along with the possibility for both sexes to attain Paradise. The duty to believe, to pray, to obey God, and not to kill new-borns, is incumbent upon both men and women. Both sexes are expected to have the Muslim virtues of humility, uprightness, patience, modesty, and continence. The punishment for trespasses, and especially for disobeying the commands of continence, are meted out to both sexes, just as are God's reward and punishment (9:71-72, 33:35-36, 58, 73, etc.).

Women's modesty, in the sense of a safeguard against illegitimate sexuality, is discussed more often and in greater detail than that of men (e.g., 24:30). Either female sexuality was found more threatening or it was believed that women needed more guidance in order to protect their sexual purity. In any case, in matters relating to sacredness and sexuality, women are in a difficult position, because they cannot exercise their ritual duties at certain times, since praying and fasting during menstruation and childbed are not allowed.

In the prophetic tradition we find the following report:

> 298: It is related that Abu Sa'id al-Khudri said, "The Messenger of Allah, may Allah bless him and grant him peace, set out to the place of prayer on the Day of Adha or Fitr and passed by the women. He said, 'O congregation of women! Give alms for I have seen that you will make up the majority of the inhabitants of the Fire!' They said, 'Why, Messenger of Allah?' He said, 'You call down too many curses and show ingratitude to your husbands. I have not seen anyone more deficient in intellect or deen [i.e., deficient in religion; here in religiousness, IS]. Yet the mind of even a resolute man might be swept away by one of you.' They said, 'In what way is our deen and intellect deficient, Messenger of Allah?' He said, 'Is not the testimony of a woman worth only half that of a man?' They said, 'Yes.' He said, 'That is how your intellect is deficient. Is it not so that when a woman is menstruating, she neither prays nor fasts?' They said, 'Yes.' He said, 'That is how her deen is deficient.'"[7]

Here Muhammad not only urges women to give alms, but also and equally expresses a general suspicion with regard to their gender as a whole, which he has seen simmering in Hell. In addition to specific social and domestic transgressions such as swearing and ingratitude, he reproaches them for having inadequate understanding and insufficient religiousness. In their questions, the women then concentrate on these last two points, and the answer is somewhat sobering for them. The insufficient religiousness is to be attributed to the temporally determined bodily impurity during menstruation or puerperium, against which they are powerless. Muhammad gives no reason for the intellectual inadequacy of women but he refers to the Quran verse 2:282, according to which the testimony of a woman has only half the value of that of a man.

The question of purity is central, and both men and women must purify themselves before praying. A major purification is necessary after sexual intercourse. Sexuality and sacredness are closely interwoven: sexuality pollutes, and purification then prepares Muslim men and women for the sacred again. According to this view, washing has not only a physical but also and primarily a metaphysical implication. Purity (Arabic *tahāra*) can be lost and restored. The techniques of purification are exactly prescribed, and all bodily excretions are considered impure. These include not only urine and feces, but also menstrual blood, bleeding in childbirth, and sperm. According to a few scholars, pollution can take place merely by touching the other sex. The general distinction between the sexes consists in the fact that men can immediately rid themselves of this pollution by means of the corresponding ablutions prescribed before prayer, whereas women can do this only to a limited extent. During menstruation and puerperium they must wait until these pollutions inherent in their bodies have ceased, and then they can undertake the ablutions.

Another tradition says:

> If a woman says her prayers five times a day, fasts
> for a month, safeguards her honor . . . and obeys
> her husband, it will be said to her: Enter the Garden
> through whichever gate you choose.[8]

These words sound more conciliatory; they concern not a lesser female religiousness and ritual impurity, but rather chastity and sexual restraint as the factor that is under women's control. However, the blissful vision of Paradise is connected with the woman's good behavior with regard to her husband, as we have seen in the saying of the Prophet cited above and handed down by Sa'īd al-Khudrī.[9]

Sexuality and ideas of purity also play a major role in connection with ideas of the Last Days, or, more precisely, the visions of Paradise. Thus women are punished for their sins, but according to the commentators, they can nonetheless gain admission to the Beyond on their own merits. According to sura 66:10, Noah's and Lot's wives, who had behaved unjustly toward their husbands, were cast into the fire. On the other hand, in sura 4:123 we read:

> And whosoever does deeds of righteousness, be it
> male or female, believing—they shall enter Paradise, and not be wronged a single date-spot.

According to another statement of the Prophet's, Paradise lies at the feet of the mothers, which would mean that women are admitted to Paradise because of their biological function as child-bearers, not because of their good deeds.[10] In connection with the description of the apocalypse, which is seen as a complete overturning of nature, it is said that then a man will be forced to obey his wife, an idea that was apparently found unnatural.

Like men, right-believing women will also go to heaven. In the Quran, their fate in the beyond is connected with that of their husbands. Thus in sura 36:55-56 we read:

> See, the inhabitants of Paradise today are busy in their rejoicing, they and their spouses, reclining upon couches in the shade.

Believers sit on silk couches, wear elegant clothing, eat fruit, and drink the wine that is forbidden them in this world. But what about the gender relationship? Might what is "forbidden" in this domain also be allowed in Paradise? Asked which man a woman would belong to in Paradise if on Earth she had been married to several, one after the other, Muhammad is supposed to have said that she could choose the one whose nature was most congenial to her. Nonetheless, she remained imprisoned in a conventional sexual relationship.

Things are otherwise with male sexuality: it can fully develop in Paradise, at least if the "man" was pious on Earth and obeyed the commandments. Every man who has done so will be married to virgins of Paradise (Arabic pl. *hūr*) (44:54; 52:20; 55:72; 56:22), and according to the theologian Suyūtī (d. 1505), each will even receive seventy of them. Despite their sexual activities, these women remain virgins, they do not menstruate, and they thus excrete no impure bodily fluids. They are described as having "large eyes," which is supposed to emphasize their erotic charisma, and are completely devoted to the pleasure of the male inhabitants of Paradise, or, as the Tunisian sociologist Bouhdiba has put it, "unlimited orgasm."[11] To be sure, this is a very male-oriented idea of Paradise, and this statement is understood as metaphorical by modern Quran interpreters like Amina Wadud.

Thus we can speak only to a limited extent of gender

equality in the sense of common duties, commandments, and personal responsibility independent of gender. Especially in domains that have to do with ritual purity, women are, because of their physical attributes, not granted equal status. Whereas the Quran assures believing women that they will go to heaven, they have no idea what their place in Paradise will be.[12]

Role Models and Interpretive Models

Early Images of Women

Persons named in the Quran, including females, have always played an important role in theological discourses. As role models, female figures in the Quran have achieved just as much importance as the Prophet's female companions and his wives. In addition to the mention of numerous male predecessors of the Prophet and figures of Islamic religious life, there are also stories[13] about Eve and Mary, about Pharaoh's wife—that is, Moses's step-mother—and about the Queen of Sheba. These stories reflect various roles and images.

In the Quran, Eve, unlike Adam, is not designated by name. The creation of the first woman occurs at the same time and in the same way as that of the first man (4:1), and the idea of her creation from Adam's rib is thus not found in the Quran. Furthermore, the Christian story according to which Eve was responsible for Adam's seduction by giving him the forbidden fruit to eat is not found in the Quran; instead, the text is open to interpretations. Verse 2:33-34 reads:

And We said, "Adam, dwell thou, and thy wife, in
the Garden, and eat thereof easefully where you desire; but draw not nigh this tree, lest you be evil-
doers." Then Satan caused them to slip there from
and brought them out of that they were in . . .

Thus it is Satan, not Eve as in Christianity, who is responsible
for original sin. However, later interpretations drew on Christian and Jewish traditions and represented Eve as Adam's se-
ducer. In these later interpretations she is supposed to have
been punished for her offense by birth pains, menstruation,
and female duties such as weaving, spinning, and baking
bread. However, the seduction of the man by the woman is
narrated in the Quran by means of another figure who also
remains unnamed. This is Zulaykha, the wife of the Egyptian
Potiphar, who bought Joseph after he had been abandoned by
his brothers and fallen into slavery. Zulaykha tried to seduce
the adolescent Joseph, but he refused her, divine intervention
having given him the strength to resist her (12:24). As the
two ran to the door, Zulaykha tore his shirt from behind,
whereby Potiphar recognized his wife's ill intent (12:28):

So when he saw his shirt torn from behind, he said,
'Surely, this is a device of you women. Your device
is indeed mighty.'

There is a sequel to this story in the tradition. Zulaykha in-
vites the women of the city to visit her and gives them knives
with which to cut fruit. Then she has Joseph come in. Blinded
by his beauty, all the women cut their hands. The story appears in detail in the commentaries as well as in collections
of sayings and popular tales about the Prophet, and in them
women's "device" (Arabic *kaid*) is central and is proverbially

connected with the female sex and with female sexuality. Zulaykha would like to seduce Joseph; she plays the role of an active sex partner who imposes her wishes even by force. In some versions this story has a sequel according to which after her punishment Zulaykha became Joseph's wife and the mother of his children. Thus the dangerously seductive woman was bound in the corset of marriage and motherhood and reinterpreted as an ideal companion.

In the Sufi tradition—for example, in the tale of the mystic Jāmī (1414-1492)—Zulaykha becomes the true heroine of the story. Whereas Joseph, with his manly beauty, represents God, she stands for the mystic's soul, which longs for union with God.[14] Carnal love between Joseph and Zulaykha, which is realized at the end of the story, is conceived as a metaphor of love for God.

In contrast to the seductress Zulaykha, the virgin mother of Jesus, Mary (Arabic *Maryam*) is for Muslims (43:57) exemplary because of her belief and purity. She was seen as the ideal and was "chosen among women" (3:39). Although she had given birth to a child outside wedlock (66:12), she was regarded as immaculate. Mary is the sole female figure in the Quran who is designated by name. She has the privilege of being addressed in person by God, through an angel (19:16-33). Since according to the Islamic conception Jesus was a human being and was not crucified, she did not have to see her son suffer. In Islam, the prototype of the suffering woman is instead Fātima, who greatly mourned her father and died shortly after him. She plays an active role at the end of time, when she will be allowed, along with her father and the imams—that is, the direct successors of Muhammad through Fātima—to intercede with God on behalf of true believers.[15] A few Quran commentators and theologians want to see Mary and Sarah, the mother of Isaac, as well Moses's mother and

Pharaoh's wife Āsiya, as prophets, because they had received God's word from angels or through inspiration. Āsiya, whose name is also to be found only in the commentaries, persuaded her husband not to kill the child Moses. She is described as a righteous woman who served God (28:8; 66:11).

The Queen of Sheba appears in the Quran as a sovereign ruler who received from Solomon a message demanding her submission (27:22-24). After she had spoken with her counselors, she tried to mollify Solomon with gifts, which he did not, however, accept. Instead, he commanded a spirit to bring her throne to him, and the Queen came to him. After he showed her the throne and after a confrontation with him, she finally joined Solomon in submitting to God. According to the story in the Quran, the victor was ultimately not the Queen of Sheba but Solomon, who was famed for his wisdom and righteousness.

In early Islamic theology, in which there were lively controversies—for example, concerning humans' ability to act and the image of God—women apparently did not play a major role. Only in the domain of early Islamic mysticism (Sufism), which beyond or alongside formal practices of worship seeks direct access to God in an inner spirituality, did a woman by the name of Rābi'a al-'Adawiyya (d. 801) achieve fame. In many reports and narratives she was described as intellectually and spiritually superior to her male contemporaries. To express her mystical experience she used—and here she differed from her contemporaries—verses. A story reports that al-Hasan al-Basrī (d. 728), a famous theologian from Basra, Iraq, approached Rābi'a while she was deep in contemplation. With masculine ostentation, al-Hasan threw his rug on the water, sat down on it, and invited Rābi'a to come over to him and discuss with him. Thereupon she threw her prayer rug in the air and invited Hasan to come up to her.

When the latter did not speak, since he could not fly, Rābi'a said to him: "Al-Hasan, what you have done, fish can do, and what I have done a fly can do. The real act (of a holy person) lies hidden behind both these acts." She thereby referred her colleague to the true inner value of mystical piety, beyond any cocky and pretentious feats. The story can be read as an example of female superiority, but also as an example of Rābi'a's deep spirituality.[16]

The images of the women in the Quran oscillate between the seductive and sexually active but unsuccessful Zulaykha and the holy and pure Mary; they show the breadth of the different representations of women and of the role of sexuality, while not burdening them with original sin. Thus there is no explicit depreciation of women to be found in the Quran, though this is less true of later theology. Instead, the image appears to be ambivalent and allows various interpretations that were taken up in the modern period in support of a greater equality of the sexes.

Quran Exegesis by Women

The question of which image of the genders and which gender roles are rooted in the Quran, and are thus religiously justified, is central not only for Islamic theology but also, as will be shown in the following section, for Islamic law, when it is a matter of the status of the genders. In the twentieth and twenty-first centuries, interpreters—men, and increasingly women as well—have argued that precisely the central verses touching on the status of the genders were for a long time interpreted against this background by scholars who, as a result of their patriarchal education, had read a corresponding preconception into the texts. For the former, it is high time to correct this reading. In the following, we will present the debate over the interpretation of the text by focusing on the example of the Quran verse 4:38, to provide insight into the form and content of the debates that are currently taking place in the Islamic world.

The verse in question was already cited above; it reads, in Arberry's translation:[17]

> Men are the managers of the affairs of women for that God has preferred in bounty one of them over another, and for that they have expended of their property. Righteous women are therefore obedient, guarding the secret for God's guarding. And those you fear may be rebellious admonish; banish them to their couches, and beat them. If they then obey you, look not for any way against them; God is All-high, All-great.

Paret, a German scholar, translates (in his edition it is 4:34):

> Men stand over women because God has distinguished them (by nature), and because of the expenditures of their assets they have made (as a wedding gift to their wives?). And virtuous women are humbly devoted (to God), and take care of what is hidden (from outsiders) (i.e., because God is concerned that it not become public). And if you fear that (any) women might rebel, then admonish them, avoid them in the marriage bed, and beat them! If they (thereupon) obey you (again), then undertake nothing (further) against them! God is sublime and great.

Tendencies associated with different understandings of the text can be discerned in these two translations; translation is always already interpretation. *A fortiori*, the exegeses offered by Arab and Muslim commentators differ in various domains. Arberry's translation refers to men as "managers of the affairs" whereas Paret's reads "stand over . . . (by nature)." It is not clear to whom women are supposed to be humbly devoted, since in Paret's version the object of this devotion—God—is put between parentheses, while in Arberry's it is left open. Thus in the latter's version the passage could be taken to refer to a humble devotion to the husband, or it could remain ambiguous. The translation of the phrase "avoid them in the marriage bed" or "banish them to their couches" also differs. On the other hand, there is little room for varying interpretations of "beat them," since the word used in the Arabic text, *daraba*, in general means "corporal punishment" or "strike."

Thus in classical and modern exegeses the following central passages are interpreted differently:

1. "Stand over/being managers of" (Arabic *qawwamūna 'alā*): How is it intended? Physically, spiritually, or regarding status? As financial responsibility?
2. "Distinguish" (Arabic *faddala*): Who is distinguished from whom by what?
3. "Obedient" (Arabic *qānitāt*): To whom? The husband? God?
4. "Recalcitrance" (Arabic *nushūz*): What precisely does this mean?
5. "Banish/avoid them" (Arabic *wa-hjurūhunna*): Where, precisely? In bed?
6. "Beat them" (Arabic *wa-dribūhunna*): Really beat? How can/may a wife be beaten?

Whereas in his thirty-volume commentary al-Tabarī (d. 926) obviously understood the first point as referring primarily to men's financial responsibility, Jalāladdīn al-Mahallī (d. 1459) and his pupil Jalāladdīn al-Suyūti (d. 1505) interpreted the phrase "stand over" as supremacy on grounds of knowledge, understanding, and political authority or guardianship.[18]

Even modern commentators on the Quran like Muhammad 'Abdūh (d. 1905) and Rashīd Ridā (d. 1935), who are often mentioned as early advocates of greater gender equality, still supported such a meaning in their Quran commentary al-Manār (published from 1900 to 1935):

> The reason for this (for unequal assignments, especially the supervision of women), is that in creation God himself gave priority to men over women and gave (men) more power and strength than (women). Thus the differences in burdens and assignments were an effect of the difference in fundamental properties (Arabic fitra) and predispositions.[19]

The first woman who attempted to interpret the Quran in modern times was 'Ā'isha 'Abdarrahmān (1913-1969), known as Bint al-Shāti'. She studied with her husband, Amīn al-Khūlī, who was considered one of the outstanding experts in the area of Quran interpretation. Her exegesis cannot, however, be called feminist.

In contrast, Amina Wadud (b. 1952), Professor of Islamic Studies at Virginia Commonwealth University in Richmond, Virginia, seeks to arrive at a reading of the Quran based on women's experiences and without the stereotypes that have shaped the interpretive framework of many male exegetes.[20] Amina Wadud is not only a scholar, but also an activist for a more prominent position for women in the Islamic-American context. In 2005 she led a Friday prayer in New York before a community that included both men and women. This was seen as something new, and met with criticism from the Islamic world.

Wadud wants to develop an exegesis of the Quran that is meaningful for women in the modern world, drawing on the work of the Pakistani scholar Fazlur Rahmān (1919-1988). For her, the language of the Quran bears a gender connotation, since Arabic distinguishes between feminine and masculine verb-forms. She asks why in some passages the Quran distinguishes between masculine and feminine forms and in others does not. In her view, the masculine plural applies to both men and women, unless the text explicitly indicates that the passage is to be read as applying exclusively to men.

Certain discussions that have thus far been seen as gender-specific, Wadud reads as gender-neutral, whereas others that have previously been understood as universal she would like to read as reflecting the circumstances in seventh-century Arabia.[21] The point is to work out the implications of the expressions in the Quran in the time of its origin, in order to understand its actual meaning.

She calls her approach "holistic." This involves the analysis of the Quran from modern social, moral, economic, and political points of view—including those that affect women. She is aware that no method of interpretation can be completely objective. The goal of interpreting "the Quran by the Quran" is guided by traditional exegesis. However, unlike traditional Quran exegetes, she does not proceed verse by verse, but rather thematically. In doing so she lays particular store by the comparison with similar themes in the Quran, the grammatical composition, how the text says something, and the "Weltanschauung"—she uses this German concept—

that is inherent in the Quran. In this connection, Amina Wadud speaks of the "spirit" of the Quran.

According to Wadud's interpretation, the Quran recognizes the biological difference between men and women and also grants that each gender functions in accord with culturally established rules.[22] In relation to the Creation, her interpretation concedes no differences between the genders. She interprets the Creation on the basis of verse 42:9:

> He has appointed for you, of yourselves, pairs, and
> pairs also of the cattle, therein multiplying you.

She investigates the word for "pair" (Arabic *zawj*) in different passages of the Quran, for example in sura 4:1:

> Mankind, fear your Lord, who created you of a
> single soul, and from it created its mate (Arabic
> *zawjahā*).

The Arabic text reads "of a single soul" (Arabic *nafs*). For that reason, Wadud can argue that neither from this nor from other passages in the Quran does it emerge that the man was created first, but instead that in the Creation both partners are essentially equal.[23] Men and women were created from the same "soul"; she translates *zawj* as "partner" and derives from this, precisely with respect to theology, the equality of the genders. To do so she refers to Quran verse 53:46, among others:

> And that He Himself created the two kinds, male
> and female . . .

In the story of Creation, the expulsion from Paradise, and the question of humans' temptation (which in the Quran is not attributed to Eve), she finds the general concepts of guidance for human conduct, of temptation and betrayal, divine forgiveness, and finally individual responsibility. For her, proper conduct, equality, individual responsibility, and unity (Arabic *tawhīd*) are the fundamental themes of the Quran's Weltanschauung.

So far as ideas of life after death and Hell are concerned, according to Wadud's exegesis no gender-specific differences can be discerned. However, she assesses the descriptions of Paradise with its virgins against the background of Arabs' time-bound pre-Islamic ideas, and concludes that these descriptions are not to be taken literally. For her, the great value of Paradise lies instead in the nearness to God, which humans could attain independently of their gender.[24]

Regarding the position of women in this world, Wadud argues that one cannot assume that a system of gender hierarchy is given in advance, because the Quran does not prescribe men's and women's roles in detail. However, piety is obligatory for both sexes.

She interprets "distinguishing" (see point 2 above) in verse 4:38 as referring to giving priority to "some before others" and explains that this does not imply a general preference for men over women. Instead, some men are superior to some women in certain ways. On the other hand, some women are superior to some men in other cases. But above all, men are distinguished by the fact that they pay money for women. So she translates the verse in the following manner:

> Men are "qawwamun" over women in matters in which God has given some of the men more than some women, and in what men spend their money on.[25]

52

Then she turns to the interpretation of "stand over" (see point 1 above). Here she discusses women's role as child-bearers and considers men's responsibility with regard to women and a "balanced" society. She views this responsibility as less biological or inherent than "valuable." So far as "recalcitrance" (see point 4 above) and the "beating" that may follow it are concerned, she argues that in other passages of the Quran the noun *nushūz* ("recalcitrance") is also used with regard to men, and therefore cannot be translated as "disobedient to the husband;" instead, it refers to a disharmony, a disunity between husband and wife equally. As Wadud sees it, the Quran provides an incremental solution for this problem: verbal admonishment, spatial separation, and finally beating. She goes on to say that the Arabic word for "beat" (Arabic *daraba*) can also be used with other meanings, for instance in the idiomatic phrase *daraba mathalan*, which means something like to "set an example." In addition, she writes, the verb is not used here in its intensive form, which is why, considering other regulations in the Quran, for example the prohibition on killing new-born girls, a limitation of the use of force on women must be intended. Against this background she proposes to interpret *daraba* (in opposition to the traditional exegesis, which saw in this an escalation following admonishment and avoiding the marriage bed), as a warning not to beat too hard.

It seems questionable whether a general prohibition on violence can be inferred from the prohibition on killing a new-born girl. Many classical commentaries also mention that beatings should not be too severe, but rather done with a "toothbrush," that is, with a small piece of wood used to clean the teeth.

The women at the Center for Islamic Research on Women's Issues and Encouragement of Muslim Women

(ZIF) in Cologne (Germany) argue along similar lines. So far as "beating" is concerned, the authors assume that physical violence cannot be a solution for marital problems. Moreover, they argue, humiliating the woman in order to save a marriage—which in any case could not be achieved by beating—contradicts the Quran's conception of marriage. Both tradition and the Quran demanded a marriage marked by a lack of violence and by mutual support and respect, they argue.[26] These authors see the solution in Quranic marriage mediation. In a way, such an argument proceeds in accord with the principle that what should not be cannot be: physical violence cannot be a solution for marital problems; therefore it cannot be intended in this passage. A "Quranic concept of marriage" is assumed a priori and not substantiated by reference to the corresponding passages. It would be difficult to speak of such a "concept of marriage" if in sura 4:38 it is at least possible to interpret the verb *daraba* in the physical sense; "beating" is, after all, the usual understanding of the word. In any case, this passage has always been a challenge for Quran exegetes who are interested in gender equality.

In her book *Sexual Ethics and Islam*, Kecia Ali discusses several interpretations of sura 4:38 that arrives at results similar to Amina Wadud's. Summing up modern feminist Quran hermeneutics, she sees the concentration on financial support as being of central importance: if men stand over women only when they pay for them or for their living expenses and bride-money, then this becomes irrelevant when women become financially independent by working or by possessions, as is increasingly the case *de facto* in many parts of the Islamic world. On the other hand, Kecia Ali concedes that the Arabic word for "beating," *daraba*, normally implies physical violence. She concludes that although many passages in the Quran emphasize individual responsibility, men have more room for maneuver with respect to action and moral responsibility, especially in matters concerning marriage and sexuality.[27]

The authors of new interpretations mentioned up to this point publish in the non-Islamic world: Amina Wadud and Kecia Ali live in the United States, while the women of ZIF live in Germany. In Muslim countries male and female authors who seek to provide a more modern interpretation of the Holy Scriptures oriented toward greater gender equality are opposed by the patriarchal and very conservative scholarly establishment. The room for maneuver accorded intellectuals in Western countries therefore leads to further developments in the central theological discourses that cannot take place in many Arab and Muslim countries. This should be kept in mind when in Western countries Islamic discourses are regarded with fear and pursued with reservations.

The most well-known victim of the still very traditional exegetical discourses was surely the Egyptian scholar Nasr Ḥāmid Abū Zayd (1943-2010). When he tried to use modern literary theory to read the Quran against the background of its time, he was accused of apostasy—that is, of renouncing Islam—and was declared to be divorced from his wife. The divorce was later reversed, but after his promotion to full professor was blocked, he left his homeland and afterward taught Islamic Studies at the universities of Leyden and Utrecht in the Netherlands.

Thus scholars who work in their respective Muslim countries deserve all the more respect. One of them is Sedigheh Vasmaghi (b. 1962), a professor of theology and law at the University of Tehran, who published her book *Woman, Jurisprudence, Islam* (Persian *Zan, Fiqh, Islam*) in December 2008,[28] when protests against the draft of a new family law code had already reached their highpoint. A chapter was distributed as an advance copy and was immediately seized upon by the country's women's organizations for their argument. This is symptomatic of the debate in Iran, which can be conducted only "Islamically," because reference to human rights and human rights conventions is not possible. In this case, the basic question was whether in article 23 of the draft of the new 2008 law a man required a court's permission to marry a second wife, but no longer needed the first wife's consent, which had been required in the 1975 law. On the basis of the Quranic verses and the Prophet's statements, Vasmaghi demonstrated that it was absolutely possible for the state to make the first wife's consent obligatory and thus to prevent the man from marrying a second wife. In the family law of 1957, the Tunisian legislature categorized the addendum to sura 4:3, "But if you fear you will not be equitable, then only one" as legally binding. Using the argument that equal treatment of multiple wives is not possible in a modern society, monogamy was legally established in Tunisia, and polygamous husbands are prosecuted as criminals.

In contrast, Raga' El-Nimr, a female Egyptian university professor trained in Islamic Studies at the University of London and at the King-Fahd Academy in London, takes the standpoint that in Islam both men and women have specific rights, but that there are fundamental differences between the sexes that cannot be ignored. In her view, failure to recognize these facts has led Western feminists to make the false assumption that men and women have the same responsibilities. For her, Islam significantly improved women's status in comparison to the pre-Islamic period; women are equal recipients of the divine message. However, the fact that the genders are equal in value does not imply that they are the same; instead, there are gender-specific responsibilities. In her reading, verse 4:38 is to be understood as meaning that men have responsibility for women, since as mothers the latter play an eminently important role in the family. Nothing in Islam forbids women to seek work, but only such work as suits their nature and abilities. El-Nimr endorses the inequality in the value of testimony that is still found in many legal systems, according to which the testimony of two men is equivalent to that of one man and two women, and a woman's testimony thus has only half the value of a man's. She bases this on women's extremely emotional nature, appealing to a general topos in gender relations which characterizes women as not rational but emotional.[29] This was expressed in the previously cited hadīth,[30] in which the Prophet warned women about hellfire on the ground of their deficient understanding. El-Nimr believes that women should obey their husbands, but that obedience to God's commands must be central to their conduct, so that disobedience to the husband can be legitimate if he demands disobedience to God.

Finally, it is the exegesis primarily of the Quran, and to a lesser extent of the tradition of the Prophet, that is central in present-day Islamic societies when it is a question of the status of women in society and gender relationships. The growing number of women trained precisely in the "heart" of the discourse on gender, in family law, necessarily poses a challenge to the classical scholarly establishment. Unlike in the case of human rights conventions, however, this establishment has to acknowledge female scholars' interpretations when they are based on the recognized foundations of Islamic law, and this is increasingly the case.

The Legal Situation in the
Twentieth and Twenty-First Centuries

The Road to Modernity

In modern Islamic states, family and inheritance law, in contrast to criminal, business, and labor law, is based on classical Islamic law in a modernized form. Only Turkey fully abandoned the codification of Islamic law, when it adopted Swiss civil law in 1926.

Since family and inheritance regulations are mentioned in the Quran alongside criminal law prescriptions, in this domain the interpretation of the Holy Scriptures to adapt them to the changing relationships between state and society met with a special challenge.

In all Muslim countries other than Saudi Arabia family law is codified, the most recent codifications having occurred in Bahrain in 2009. Premodern sharia regulations were reformulated in the form of laws. Such an establishment of specific legal regulations on the basis of the many different schools of jurisprudence or new interpretations confronted jurisprudence in Muslim countries with great challenges: which legal opinion should be codified? From which school of jurisprudence? From the dominant opinion in each school of jurisprudence in each region? Or should minority opinions be taken into account? Is it possible to rely on the legal opinion of jurists from the period preceding the founding of schools of law in the eighth and ninth centuries? Or should the Quran and the tradition be re-interpreted by means of "independent interpretations of the text" (Arabic *ijtihād*)? The latter has been increasingly demanded by both Islamists and Muslim modernists since the 1970s.

Two questions above all are central here: What should be the criteria for choosing legal opinions? And what authority should make the decision regarding the valid interpretation? The first question is the hardest to answer, but in Muslim countries it has led to long-standing battles over the interpretation of the text. The debate regarding the "correct" interpretation runs through the whole history and present situation of Muslim countries. The second question, regarding which authority should be consulted in the interpretation, has varying answers. In the premodern period, the monopoly on text interpretation lay not with the ruler, but rather with the scholars, who had been trained in great academic centers such as Azhar University in Cairo, Qarawiyin University in Fez, Ez-Zitouna University in Tunis, and the Shiite universities in Najaf in Iraq. However, in the Ottoman Empire (15th-20th centuries) the Sultan, and therefore the central political authority, had already carried out this important task. After the collapse of the Ottoman Empire and the emergence of modern national states in the Islamic area, this function was taken over by various organs and legislative authorities such as Parliaments or institutions succeeding the sultanate, for instance, kings. The traditional scholarly establishment's monopoly was threatened and its prestige diminished, but it many countries it remained influential.[31] Regarding the introduction of the new family law code in Morocco, we will show later that the scholars vehemently defended their alleged sovereign control over interpretation against challenges proceeding from various quarters and against the claims of untrained persons belonging to civic organizations.

In addition, in the twentieth century these scholars had to deal with competing Islamic interpretations that criticized their traditional understanding of the laws and demanded a new reading of the Holy Scriptures. In the second half of the twentieth century many women took up the task of producing a new textual interpretation in theology and law, and in traditional universities such as Azhar University in Cairo, a few branches for women were established; In the Iranian city of Qom, there has been for several years a university solely for women.

Today, legislation and political discourse in Muslim countries—this became evident in the "Arab Spring" of 2011— are no longer opportunities that the most authoritarian states can impose. Instead, alongside the traditional scholarly establishment civic organizations, including women's and human rights groups as well as Islamist movements, have become major players in the process of political and legal negotiation. The question is not whether Islamic law should be followed; on that point all Muslim countries with the exception of Turkey have been in agreement since the beginning of the twentieth century. The question is which "Islamic" law is to be cast in the form of legislation. In this process, the aforementioned social actors are involved and increasingly demand their right to judge. A not insignificant influence is exercised here by international agreements that the countries have signed, which oblige them to implement in their national legislation the norms established by these agreements.

How such complex discussions and procedures can be concretely implemented, which arguments are adduced, and which institutions are involved can be shown by examining a judgment handed down by the Egyptian constitutional court. In 1994, the Egyptian Ministry of Education issued a decree[32] in which school uniforms were regulated and the facial veil (Arabic *niqāb*) was prohibited. Since the 1970s there has been a "new veil" in Egypt that identifies the wearers as belonging to the Islamist movement and is intended to express opposition to the state. The presumption that the prohibition on the veil is politically motivated thus cannot be rejected out of hand.

The Egyptian constitutional court was presented with the following case: the plaintiff, whose two daughters had been expelled from school because they wore facial veils, filed a complaint against the school's decision and described the decree as unconstitutional. First of all, the complaint said, it was contradicted by Article 2 of the constitution, according to which Islam is the state religion and the principles of sharia are the main source of legislation. Second, it was said to violate Article 46, which guarantees freedom of religion. Legislation, according to a judgment of the constitutional court, is possible only where no established, inalterable rule is present in sharia, that is, only in a case in which "independent interpretation of the text" (Arabic *ijtihād*) is applicable. However, *ijtihād* must be conducted in the framework of the sources of Islamic law, that is, on the basis of the Quran and tradition. In the matter of the facial veil, the constitutional court made the following decision: in Islam, women have to dress in a certain way; they are not fully free to choose their clothing, but must observe the rules of decency. Nonetheless among Islamic scholars there are some differences of opinion regarding how extensive the veiling must be. From this it can be concluded that there is no established regulation, and hence the decree issued by the Education Ministry is in conformity with the constitution. Thus the constitutional court itself resorted to *ijtihād*, a method that was previously reserved for classically-trained legal scholars.[33] This example shows the restriction of Islamic norms and arguments by modern institutions and mechanisms of legitimation. Sharia is not to be replaced but instead cautiously modernized, and in fact modernized in the context of new institutions.

The modernization or methodical adaptation of premodern

Islamic substantive law to present-day contexts and its translation into codifications such as now exist in many countries were carried out with the help of *ijtihād* and "choice" (Arabic *takhayyur*) among the various regulations of (Sunni) legal schools. Those involved did not feel bound to respect the dominant majority opinion; minority opinions could also make their way into the codification of the law. An example from the area of divorce: in Hanafite law a woman can ask for a divorce only if the man is incapable of consummating the marriage, or if he was absent and had also reached the age of ninety. This made a divorce agreement possible only at a very late date, if at all. On the other hand, the Malikis also allowed a judge to decree a divorce at the request of the wife (Arabic *tafrīq*) in the event that her husband treated her cruelly, refused or was unable to pay for her maintenance, was absent for one or two years, or had an illness that made the continuation of the marriage unbearable for the wife. The regulation of the Maliki school has been widely adopted in modern personal law. Today, it is possible to get a divorce in this way practically everywhere from Morocco to Afghanistan.

Furthermore, through legal prescription, optional regulations in Islamic law can become compulsory components of a legal transaction. For example, in divorce law certain possible agreements may be considered obligatory conditions of the marriage contract, the goal being to improve the status of women. They include, for instance, the woman's right to get a divorce in the event that the man marries again or is absent beyond a certain period of time.

Another area in which reforms were possible is derived from the classical right of the ruler to guide the community in the interest of the welfare of society (Arabic *siyāsa*, in the modern translation, "politics"). The doctrine of this "guidance of the community" grants the state the right to undertake administrative measures that are in the public interest if this does not involve violating the substantial rules and norms of sharia. This principle develops its effect above all in procedural regulations such as the jurisdiction of courts, the registration of births, marriages, deaths, and such like. Moreover, the introduction of a new court system has been justified on this ground. In most Muslim countries, marriages are now registered, and divorces must be decreed by the court. This creates legal certainty. Thus a valid marriage in a mosque, or a divorce in private or by text message, is not longer possible in these countries, but it is in those states where there are no regulations for a judicial divorce.

Islamic law, which has often been called "sacred" and "inalterable," can be adapted to modern conditions—and necessities—on the basis of systematic regulations. And it has in fact been so adapted. However, Turkey and Tunisia are the only Muslim states that have outlawed polygyny. In Tunisia, it was abolished on the basis of the Quran's requirement that a husband treats his wives equally, which was deemed no longer possible in a modern state. Furthermore, in Tunisia these reforms took place in the 1950s under the then President Habib Bourguiba (governed 1957-1987). Elsewhere the institution of polygyny persists, even if it is often restricted, held to legal guidelines, or connected with the woman's right to divorce.

Polygyny, Marriage, and Divorce Law

The reform of personal law[34] is of central importance for the status of the genders and, as we will see later, for the demands made by the women's movement. The following table compares the premodern provisions of Moroccan law with its current provisions. Since 2004 Morocco has had a legal code based on the classic Maliki code produced by Sahnūn (d. 854) and titled *Mudawwana*.[35] The table makes it possible to see which regulations remained the same and which were changed. In addition, the adaptability of the legislation to new situations is shown.

1. Betrothal (Arabic *khitba*)

According to classic sharia law betrothal is a non-binding promise to marry.	Article 5: Betrothal is simply a promise to marry, which can follow customary legal procedure, for example the uttering of the first sura of the Quran. The return of gifts may be demanded in the event the betrothal is cancelled.

2. Marriage (Arabic *inkāh*, *tazwīj*)

Marriageable age

The marriageable age is connected with puberty, which schools of jurisprudence set for girls at the age of nine at the earliest, for boys at the age of 12 at the earliest.	According to Article 19, marriageable age is now eighteen for both sexes.
A valid marriage is already possible between two children under the Islamic age of marriage, that is, who are not yet sexually mature, even if they are little children. In this case marriage	Article 20-21: In the matter of the minimum age, a dispensation is possible. It is issued by the court, which obtains an advisory opinion or undertakes a social investigation.

and the consummation of marriage do not coincide. Thus according to classic Islamic norms, child marriage is possible.	

Contract

The marriage contract is classically made in the mosque, in the presence of two witnesses (2:282). Conditions can be written into the marriage contract.	The marriage contract plays a central role. It includes agreements regarding the bride-money, the wife's professional activity, or the man's duty to observe monogamy. Modern marriage contracts are commonly guided by French models.

Impediments

1. Permanent impediments to marriage: kinship, kinship by nursing.	1. Article 36-38: Impediments to marriage include blood kinship, relationship by marriage, and kinship by nursing.
2. Temporary impediments: an existing marriage, an irrevocable third divorce.	2. Article 39: ditto
3. A difference in religion (2:220; 5:5): a Muslim woman cannot marry a non-Muslim man.	3. Article 39: Differences in religion are also seen as impediments to marriage.

Guardianship (Arabic *wilāya*) with reference
to marriage and child marriages

A woman needs a guardian, in general her father, in order to complete a marriage contract. Only according to Hanafite law can an adult woman herself agree to the marriage, as soon as she is of marriageable age.	Articles 24 and 25 follow the Hanafite doctrine. Article 24 reads: "Marital guardianship (Arabic *wilāya*) is the woman's right. It is exercised in relation to an adult woman according to her choice and in her interest." A forced marriage is therefore excluded. However, a supervisory guardianship of women is still very common.

3. Consequences of marriage

Bride-money (Arabic *mahr*) and maintenance (Arabic *nafaqa*)

The bride-money is paid to the bride (4:4). It is legally obligatory. If the amount is not fixed, it is determined by taking into account various criteria (the family's social position, qualifications, etc.). Payment of part of the amount is commonly delayed until a divorce or the death of the husband ensues.	Article 29: The bride-money is the wife's property, it is at her free disposal, and the husband can ask for nothing in return, such as a contribution to setting up the household. Article 30: It is also permissible to agree to defer payment of part of the bride-money. This is supposed to provide a degree of security for the wife in the event that the marriage is dissolved.
Maintenance is the woman's legal right in a valid marriage. Classically it includes food, clothing, lodging, medical expenses, and possibly servants (if the wife was accustomed to having them in her parents' house).	Article 194: According to the family code, the husband is obliged to provide maintenance for his wife.

Further follow-ups

1. A claim to guidance and protection is usually inferred from sura 4:38.	1. Article 4: The marriage is a contract between a man and a woman that is based on a mutual agreement and a legal and permanent union. Its objective is a life in fidelity and purity as well as the foundation of a stable family under the guidance of the two spouses, in accord with the provisions of this code.
2. The duty to obey is also inferred from sura 4:38; a disobedient wife can be deprived of her maintenance.	2. Article 195: A wife who refuses to obey a court order to move back into the marital home loses her right to maintenance.

Childcare (Arabic *hadāna*) and guardianship (Arabic *wilāya*)

1. Childcare is the duty of the mother until an age that varies depending on the school of jurisprudence. It refers to the direct care of the child.	1. Article 164: Childcare is incumbent upon both parents, so long as the marriage exists. If the marriage breaks down, the mother is usually accorded the prerogative of caring for her child (Article 171); —Article 166: Children have a right to childcare until they reach maturity.
2. The mother can continue to provide childcare after a divorce, unless and until she marries again.	2. Article 171: In the event of the dissolution of a marriage, custody is given to the mother, then to the father, and then to the mother's mother, unless the

	court decides otherwise in the interest of the child. In addition, when the child turns sixteen, he/she can decide whether he/she wants to live with the mother or the father (Article 166). —Articles 174 and 175: If a woman holding custody of a child marries another man who is not related to the child in a way that excludes marriage, she can lose custody. —Articles 178-179: If a divorced woman having custody of a child changes her place of residence within Morocco, this no longer has a prejudicial effect on her right to provide childcare. The guardian can however refuse to allow travel abroad; in the event of conflict, the judge decides.
3. The father is the legal guardian (Arabic *walī*).	3. Articles 230, 236, 238, 239: The legal guardian is the father, and only if he is deceased, absent, or incapable of acting as guardian can the mother take over this task.

Polygyny (Arabic *ta'addud az-zawjāt*)

Polygyny is based on suras 4:3 and 4:129, and is seen as permissible for the man. The number of wives allowed is limited to four. In general, equal treat-	Articles 40-46: Polygyny is limited and connected with a series of pre-conditions related to equal treatment of the wives and children, permission of the

ment is seen as a recommendation and not an obligation.	court, social situation, the first wife's option to request a divorce, and an "objective justification." The first wife will be summoned to provide information. Thus there is a duty to gather information regarding both wives, and the first wife has the option of divorcing, though she must petition the court; but the husband is not prevented from taking another wife.

4. Divorce

According to sharia, a marriage can be dissolved in the following ways: 1. by repudiation (Arabic *talāq*), 2. by mutual agreement (Arabic *khul', mubāra'a*) 3. by court decree (Arabic *tafrīq*) In all cases the consent of the husband is necessary.	All three variants are found in the present law.
1) Repudiation Premodern law: the classical form of the dissolution of a marriage is the repudiation of the wife by the husband. The wife's agreement is not required, and the husband needs not state his grounds for repudiating her. This is based on suras 2:228-238; 65:1-6, and many traditions.	1) Repudiation Article 89: Fundamentally, it is up to the husband to justify the repudiation. The husband can grant his wife the right to repudiate him. The judge must first attempt to effect a reconciliation in order to save the marriage (Articles 81-83). Only if this attempt fails can the divorce of the couple be made final.

2) Divorce by mutual agreement
This is based on suras 2:229 and 4:128, as well as on the Prophet's tradition and also includes the wife's self-redemption by paying compensation. In practice, after the promise of compensation the husband formally repudiates the wife.

3) Judicial divorce
Judicial divorce (Arabic *talāq amām al-qadā', tafrīq qadā'ī tatlīq bi-hukm al-qadā'*) can be requested by the wife on certain grounds that differ according to the school of jurisprudence. It must always take place before a court.

Grounds:

A) Injury or disadvantage done to the wife (Arabic *darar*) that has physical or psychological consequences that make life in common impossible;

B) The absence of the husband (Arabic *ghaiba*);

C) A prison term of several years (Arabic *habs*) imposed on the husband;

D) Non-payment of maintenance (Arabic *'adam al-infāq*) by the husband.
  Points A) to D) are originally

2)
Article 114: The dissolution of a marriage through "redemption" (Arabic *khul'*) is possible; both marriage partners or either of them can file the petition. The court decides.

3) Judicial divorce
Article 94: Divorce on the ground of marital discord and also on petition by the wife is possible. Both marriage partners or one of them can petition the court for this kind of divorce.

Further grounds are:

A) Articles 98-101.

B) Articles 98, 104: Absence of more than a year.

C) Articles 98, 106: Prison term of more than three years.

D) Articles 98, 102.

based only on Maliki, not Hana-fite law;	
E) A defect (Arabic *'aib*) such as a severe illness or the man's impotence (Arabic *'unna*), which prevents normal marital relations, which was not known to the wife at the time of the marriage, or is not accepted by the wife after the marriage.	E) Articles 98, 107.

From this comparison we can see that many Islamic regulations have persisted down to the present day, and that in some respects important further developments have also taken place. For example, the payment of bride-money and living expenses are obligatory for the man, a point that is often emphasized as a right of women and thus as a positive side of classical Islamic law. In fact, the separation of property is significant if women have sole control over their money. This is established in most personal law codes. However, the payment of bride-money and living expenses is classically seen as the husband's obligation, from which then emerged, on the wife's side, the obligation to "obey." Financial responsibility thus determines a specific behavior on the part of the wife. In Egypt, for example, before 1967 obedience was enforced by the so-called "house of obedience" (Arabic *bayt at-tā'a*). This meant that a "disobedient" (Arabic *nāshiza*) wife who had left her home lost her claim to maintenance, but not her bride-money, and was brought back into the marital home by the police. A wife can now justify her disobedience before a court, but she is still threatened with the loss of her maintenance. This is also the case in Morocco, as we have shown above, when there is a court judgment against the wife. In 1997 the Egyptian constitutional court decided that a wife does not lose her claim to marital maintenance if, contrary to her husband's wishes, she continues to hold a job and if a prohibition could be a hardship. In 2000, the same court decided that Egyptian women could be granted a passport against their husbands' will. However, the husband can obtain a court order forbidding the wife to travel abroad.

A further point of gender inequality that has been criticized by women's movements for more than a century and is still repeatedly discussed is polygyny, which is restricted in Egypt by the husband's obligation to register his marriages. It has been abolished only in Turkey, where Islamic law as a whole was replaced by Swiss law, and in Tunisia, where polygyny was criminalized in the 1950s. In Morocco it remains possible after the legal reform of 2004, but it must be legally registered and cannot be undertaken when it is feared that the husband will not treat his wives equally. Evidently, polygyny is still relatively widely permitted by the courts. In Iran (where despite its official abolition after the Revolution the 1975 law regarding the protection of the family continued to be observed *de facto* and was revised only in 2008), according to article 16f., not only the permission of the court but also the first wife's agreement must be obtained. The new Family law of 2013 does contain the necessary court's decision but not the first wife's permission for the second marriage of the husband. Thus in the case of polygyny a broad range of legal rulings exists: the classical law of complete non-restriction (Saudi-Arabia), the obligation to register (e.g., Egypt), the requirement to obtain the permission of the court (Morocco), the additional obligation to obtain the first wife's permission (Iran), and prohibition (Tunisia, Turkey).

Gender equality with regard to guardianship for children has not been achieved either, and here we must carefully distinguish between guardianship (*wilāya*) and childcare (*hadāna*). Until they reach maturity, or, for girls, until they marry, children have a right to care. In classical Islam this was always women's right, but it did not include official legal representation and disposal over the child's assets and it was restricted to the early age of children. The regulation according to which the husband alone represents the children, while only childcare in the sense of feeding and caring for children falls to the wife, persisted for a long time and is only slightly qualified in the different family codes. In Morocco both partners to a marriage have since 2004 the duty to provide childcare. In the event of a dissolution of the marriage, childcare falls to the mother, then to the father, and then to the mother's mother, unless the court decides otherwise in the interest of the child. This reservation allows the court to take specific measures in individual cases to assure the child's welfare. In addition, at the age of sixteen the child can decide whether he/she wants to live with his/her father or mother, and this too is to be considered in relation to the child's interest. However, according to premodern law the mother's right to provide childcare is lost when she marries another man who is not related to the child in a way that excludes marriage to the child. Only fathers have control over the child's assets and thus full legal guardianship, also in Morocco. Only if he is dead, absent, or incapable of acting as guardian can the mother take over this task. In contrast, the new Turkish Civil Code of 2001 gives men and women equal rights with regard to guardianship (Turkish Civil Code, Article 182).

The unified and gender-neutral establishment of marriageable age at eighteen in Morocco and some other states can be considered an improvement with regard to gender-equality, as can the responsibility of both partners for the marriage, which puts an end to the position of the husband as the head of the family. The Turkish family law code, which has long since ceased to be determined by Islamic law, only abolished this position of the husband in 2001 (Article 186) giving the marriage partners equal rights to the residence (Article 194) and to possessions acquired during the marriage.

A decisive step taken in Egypt in 2000 toward more gender equality is granting women the power to get a divorce on their own initiative, even against the husband's will, by means of "redemption" (Arabic *khul'*), which the new Moroccan law has adopted as well. In classical law, redemption was possible only with the husband's consent, but this is no longer necessary. However, it still entails financial losses. A further improvement in the 2004 Moroccan Family Codes was the implementation of the requirement for divorce proceedings to take place in court. Since the husband is forced to file for divorce before a court, he can no longer simply pronounce the divorce at discretion and without any duty to inform the wife, as in premodern law. Still divorce (*talāq*) by SMS can take place in many other Muslim states.

The legislation in Egypt, Morocco, and Iran shows that premodern Islamic regulations have certainly been restricted, though the restrictions were implemented gradually and always in response to pressure from women's organizations, and in some countries—such as Egypt under Sadat's wife Jehan and in Morocco under King Muhammad VI—they were also connected with the government's initiative.

Why have these advances towards gender equality been achieved only in small steps? One reason is that society is still patriarchically structured; another is that the the traditional scholarly establishment remains influential claiming the sole right to interpret the Holy Scriptures, expressing reservations, and critically opposing innovations in the domain of gender.

If we examine the regulations from the standpoint of the

gender equality demanded by international treaties, we find different standards in individual countries, and except in the case of Turkey and in certain legal areas in Tunisia, no equality. In general, polygyny, divorce, and childcare, as well as inheritance law, which is often not codified and thus conforms to premodern law, remain hotly debated questions. They belong to the "core" of the discourse on gender-equality.

Whipping, Stoning, and Blood Money

In the vast majority of Muslim countries—for example, Morocco, Tunisia, Algeria, Egypt, Lebanon, Syria, Iraq, and Jordan—Islamic criminal law is no longer applied. It is still valid in Iran, Pakistan, and Saudi Arabia, as well as in northern Nigeria.[36]

The following examples compare selected premodern Islamic criminal law regulations relating to gender status with Iranian codified criminal law of 1991, in order to show how classical criminal law was codified on points relevant to gender.[37]

1. Illegitimate sexual intercourse (Arabic *zinā'*) is to be punished, according to sura 24:2-5, by one hundred lashes, and according to classical law, in certain cases by stoning.	1. Article 64: Illicit sexual intercourse entails a *hadd* punishment if the male or female perpetrator is of age, of sound mind, is free to choose, and knows the regulation and the facts.
2. False accusations (Arabic *qadhf*) of illegitimate sexual intercourse are to be punished by eighty lashes.	2. Article 78: If the witnesses make statements regarding details about the object of their testimony, the statements may not deviate from each other with re-

	spect to place and time and comparable circumstances. If there are deviations in the testimony, illicit sexual intercourse is not only not proven, but the witnesses are to be condemned to a *hadd* punishment for slander.
3. Homosexuality is to be punished like *zinā'*.	3. Article 109: A *hadd* punishment is to be meted out to both the active and the passive participants in homosexual intercourse. —Article 129: The *hadd* punishment for lesbian sexual contacts consists of one hundred lashes for each participant.
4. Rape is to be punished, but the woman may be required to produce proofs.	4. Article 73: If a woman who has no husband becomes pregnant, the fact of the pregnancy alone does not justify a *hadd* punishment, except when illicit sexual intercourse is proven with one of the means of proof specified in this law.
Bodily injuries and crimes of killing are to be paid in blood money, the amount for men, women, and slaves to be determined separately in each case (2:174).	Article 300: For premeditated and also unpremeditated killing of a Muslim woman, the blood money amounts to half the blood money for a man.

In the Iranian criminal code illegitimate sexual intercourse is avenged with Quranic punishments imposed on both sexes. However, the stoning for which the code also provides is to be found only in tradition, not in the Quran. The standard of proof is higher. If the witnesses' statements differ, they are themselves punished and the accusation is invalid; that is also classical Islamic law. Thus if four witnesses have observed the sexual intercourse, but one of them is not recognized by the court, all four are considered slanderers. An existing marriage increases the punishment, and stoning is imposed as a punishment. In this case countries that have abolished Islamic criminal law have other regulations. According to the Egyptian penal code, Articles 273-277, only adultery is punishable, with a maximum of two years in prison.

In Iran, a distinction is drawn between active and passive partners in the case of male homosexuality, but not in the case of female homosexuality. The distinction between active and passive partners in male homosexuality is relevant when sexual acts (not necessarily sexual intercourse) take place and the active partner is non-Muslim but the passive partner is Muslim. Then the active partner is punished by death. In contrast, religious adherence is of no consequence in the case of women because the distinction between active and passive partners is not made (Article 130). Homosexual acts are punished by one hundred lashes.

Also among the basic principles of criminal law is the equal status of perpetrator and victim. This becomes important because men and women are not considered to have equal status. On the basis of the idea of blood revenge, a Muslim man who kills another Muslim man is to be hanged (Article 207). However, hanging can be waived at the request of the victim's family and converted into the payment of blood money. Again, a woman's blood money is half a man's. The family member taking blood revenge for the killing of a Muslim woman has the option of demanding half the blood money from the killer. However, if he demands blood revenge on the killer—that is, if he wants him to be executed—before the latter is executed the avenger must pay him half the amount of the blood money to cover the difference (Article 209). The execution of the murderer of a woman will thus not take place until the family of the murdered woman pays a substantial sum to the killers family, namely half the blood money of the man executed. Blood money was the subject of many public debates in Iran but none of these led to abolition; in 2008 the blood money for men and women was set at the same level only in the case of traffic accidents.

To sum up: In contrast to family law, the codification of criminal law in Iran did not lead to more gender equality, but instead cemented gender inequality. The cruel corporal punishments are in any case to be regarded as violations of human rights.

The example of honor. "Honor" is a complex social concept.[38] So-called "sexual honor" is part of it. In many societies around the Mediterranean, including Christian ones, family honor is connected with the sexually unobjectionable conduct of women. If this honor is injured by sexual relations on the part of a female family member—sometimes mere suspicion suffices—the "code of honor" requires the husband, father, or brother to act. In the most extreme case, the honor of the family can be restored only by killing the woman, the lover, or both. On this view, honor is not a gender-neutral concept, but highly gendered.

Such a distinction is also found in the old European Penal codes—for example, in the Prussian criminal law code of 1843, according to which a womans adultery was to be more severely punished than a man's; according to the idea during that time, the man's status was thereby injured, but not that of the woman. At the beginning of the twentieth century, duels lost their significance in Europe. On the other hand, the "crime of passion" persisted in some criminal law codes.

Until 1975, the French criminal law code contained an article (Article 324) that provided for more lenient punishment of a husband who found his wife *in flagrante delicto* with another man and killed him. Since many Muslim countries adopted French criminal law after abolishing Islamic criminal law, this article found its way into the criminal law codes of those states which abolished Islamic criminal law, such as Egypt (Article 237). According to Egyptian law the husband need not catch his wife engaging in sexual intercourse with another man; it is enough to surprise her in a situation that leaves no doubt that she has already committed adultery or is about to do so. In addition, he must kill the unfaithful wife or her lover, or both of them, on the spot. Whether adultery has taken place and what period of time is covered by the expression "on the spot" depends on the particular situation. Here the judge has room for interpretation, a fact which is strongly criticized by women's organizations and human rights groups precisely because, in their view, it usually benefits the perpetrator. When, in the opinion of the court, all the pre-conditions are met, a killing is reclassified from a crime to a misdemeanor, so that the punishment still takes place, but is lessened. The possible sentences then range from twenty-four hours to three years in prison (Article 18 of the Egyptian Criminal Law Code). Attempted murder continues—as do all misdemeanors for which punishment is not expressly envisaged—to go unpunished. From an Islamic point of view, it is frequently objected that the punishment for illicit sexual intercourse established in the Quran applies to both partners. In legal reality, however, it is almost exclusively women who are put to death in the name of honor.[39]

The Iranian criminal law code of 1926 was—as in Egypt—Europeanized and contained a corresponding article (Article 176) with regard to the case that a "man sees his wife in bed or in a similar situation with a strange man."[40] This changed after the Islamic Revolution in 1979 and in the code of 1997, (Article 630), the term "sexual intercourse" is not used, but instead *zinā'*, the Islamic term for illicit sexual intercourse. Thus the husband was granted the right to kill his wife. A few Iranian jurists and other legal scholars criticized the fact that this article abrogated the actually valid rule based on the Quran, which required four witnesses who had definitely seen the sexual act.

Illegitimate children.[41] The custom of burying new-born girls alive that was obviously practiced in pre-Islamic Arabia—a cruel custom that was attributed to poverty, but also to contempt for female progeny—was forbidden in the Quran (sura 81:1-14; 16:59-60; 6:151). In premodern law, the descent of a child from its father was based on the birth in a valid marriage. The legal connection between parents and child represented the foundation for the mutual rights to inheritance, guardianship, and maintenance. Marital fatherhood in accord with sharia was considered legitimate fatherhood by all schools of jurisprudence. The child of a repudiated or widowed woman was also considered legitimate if it was born within a certain period after the divorce from the husband or after the latter's death. Furthermore, a concept of premodern Islamic law is the so called "sleeping" child (Arabic *rāqid*), the idea that the child falls into a kind of developmental stasis his mother's uterus—a situation which was considered to possibly last for several years. According to this idea, such a child could be born as long as several years after the usual due date. Such ideas seem to have been used by the women to escape the legal and social consequences of an illegitimate pregnancy. A second effect was of course the legitimacy of the child born at such a late date. On the other hand, a child born from an illegitimate sexual relationship can in no case be recognized and according to classical Islamic law has no legal status.[42]

In modern legislation in most Muslim countries, illegitimate descent is neither taken into account nor accompanied by any kind of legal consequences. On the contrary, the subject is still widely taboo. However, here the new Moroccan law has pointed the way: in the interest of the child's legal status, children conceived outside a registered marriage can henceforth be officially recognized as legitimate in certain cases. According to Article 156 of the new family law, couples who were engaged but not married when conceiving a child "in good faith" are treated as *de facto* married couples with respect to family descent. Thus legal connections between the child and his father are produced that are significant, especially for giving the child the right to inheritance and to maintenance. In consequence, illegitimate sexual relationships, which in Morocco are punished according to Article 490 by a prison term ranging from one month to a year, are at least partially legitimized. The latest provisions of the family law code bring the families of the mother and the father into the process of "legitimation," thereby increasing the acceptance of a family descent established in this way. In its new family law of 2001, Turkey has completely dissociated itself from the concept of "illegitimate" children. According to Article 282, maternal descent is established through birth, and the term "illegitimate children" is no longer used.

Customary Law

In a few geographical regions and areas of law, the influence of customary law structures is particularly strong, and often differs between the city and the country; in rural areas traditional customs are frequently more dominant than in cities in shaping people's lives. In particular, it is women living in villages or small towns who cannot read or write and do not know their legally established rights who become victims of traditional customs and patriarchal structures.

In Turkey and Afghanistan, for example, there is a custom of paying a price to the father of the bride rather than bride-money (which is paid to the bride). In Turkey, according to the provisions of the new civil law code (Turkish Civil Law Code, Article 151) women can fight back against such a marriage, and obtain a divorce on the ground that the marriage was forced on them. The classical Islamic bride-money no longer has any validity in Turkey. In Afghanistan, whose family law code dates from 1977, bride-money is legally regulated (Articles 99-101), but in practice a more important role is played by the so-called *walwar* (bride-price), which is paid to the bride's father and in some cases amounts to a considerable sum. The result is that women are not financially secure in the event of divorce or the husband's death.

Moreover, an investigation of legal practice in Egypt showed that the age of marriage was relatively high in urban areas; young men found it difficult to marry because of the bride-price and the cost of maintenance. In the countryside, on the other hand, the age of marriage was very low, often beneath the legal limit. The reason for this was, first, the lower bride-price in rural areas, and second, the idea that girls and boys should be married as soon as possible after reaching puberty to avoid sexual intercourse before marriage. The required birth certificate was applied for *post facto*, the parents claiming that the girl was not registered at birth. This shows the importance and significance of formal acts such as the registration of births, marriages, and deaths for legal protection and the modernization of societies. If the registrations frequently required by law are avoided and it is possible to receive such documents by whatever means, then traditional models of child marriage, divorce without legal proceedings, the refusal to provide maintenance, or the payment of bride-money will continue to exist.[43]

In Islamic law generally, conditions may be included in the marriage contract so long as they do not contradict sharia. This includes, for instance, the possibility of divorce if the man marries a second wife or is absent for a long time. In fact, the man thereby delegates to his wife his right to divorce in a specific case, for example when he enters into a second marriage. However, such a condition is also sometimes seen as unacceptable and therefore not practiced because it is considered restricting the husband's right to repudiate his wife. In Egypt, for example, as Nagla Nassar found out through empirical research, this kind of stipulation was, accordingly, not very common. In Iran, on the other hand, there have, for many years, existed standard marriage forms in which such conditions are already entered, so that the willing husband has only to sign them.

According to the same investigation by Nassar, for a divorce because of "injury," the possibility of which is established in Egyptian family law, the burden of proof fell wholly on the wife. She had to prove that she had in no way provoked her husband's violent behavior. The courts were most likely to grant a wife a divorce if her husband had been absent for more than a year.[44]

It is in Afghanistan where we can see most clearly the close connection between customary law, a traditional interpretation of Islamic law, and modern legislation. In the media, we find reports of girls fourteen years old or younger who have been married to sixty-year-old men, even though Afghan family law (Afghan family law code Article 70) sets the marriageable age for girls at sixteen, and for boys at eighteen. Here in particular we see the problem of the lack of registration of births, marriages, and deaths, which despite the legal requirement very seldom takes place. An investigation carried out in 2004-2005[45] showed that despite the establishment of human rights in the new Afghan constitution of 2004 and the family law code of 1997, various practices that violate both international conventions and Islamic law persist in certain regions of Afghanistan. One of these is levirate marriage, in which the brother of the deceased husband marries the latter's widow without her consent; another is the exchange of women without paying the bride-money. In general, honor (Persian *nāmūs*), in the sense of sexual honor, plays an important role, so that women and girls suspected of violations of honor frequently fall victim to violence on the part of their fathers or brothers. The handing over of women as compensation in the case of crimes of violence is particularly problematic and impossible to justify Islamically.

Polygyny is legally allowed by Afghan family law (Article 8) only if there are certain grounds, such as the wife's infertility. According to the results of the investigation cited above, polygyny is still or again relatively widespread in Afghanistan, despite the financial burden it imposes on the husband. In certain groups profiting from the war, and also in a new urban middle class, a second or third marriage is seen as prestigious and as attesting to the polygamous husband's financial and sexual power. Closely connected with this is the problem of divorce. According to Islamic law, divorce is generally possible, and the grounds for divorce open to women are established by Afghan law (Articles 176-191). In large areas of the country, however, divorce is not accepted; it is seen as injuring the honor of the wife's family. The result seems to be a greater pressure exerted on women to accept their husband's second marriage.[46]

In Afghanistan, as in other Muslim countries, women's and human rights organizations are battling these practices that violate not only human rights but also many Islamic legal precepts. They have to fight on numerous fronts: against the complaints of the scholarly establishments that the groups are trying to undermine Islamic law, against the patriarchal structures in families, and against the government and decision-makers who are still often thoroughly male-oriented. One of the women engaged in this struggle was Hamideh Barmaki (1970-2011), a professor of law at the University of Kabul. In 2009 she became the commissioner for children's rights in the Afghan Independent Human Rights Commission and from 2006 to 2011 had been active especially on behalf of children's rights. On January 28, 2011, she was killed in a Taliban suicide attack on a supermarket in Kabul, along with her husband, a physician, and her four children.

* * *

Whereas Afghanistan still has to fight hard against social structures based on customary law and patriarchy, and many female lawyers are working to put Afghani family law into effect, in Egypt and Morocco, and also in Iran, there have been public discussions regarding how existing legislation can be improved. In individual countries, the emphasis falls on different points in the debate and on different areas in which reforms are possible. The Pakistani jurist and professor of international law at Warwick University, Shaheen Sardar Ali, has described these differing versions of law and the various ways of viewing legal regulations as "Operative Islamic Law;" that is, as the specific blend of law which is in use in certain regions and states. This includes not only governmental legislation but also the arguments of civil organizations and Muslim feminists—male or female, traditional or modern.[47]

* * *

What should we retain from this overview?

- With respect to premodern law, legislation has made progress towards more gender equality. Codification itself led to certainty of law, and moreover in family law codes many regulations that contribute to greater gender equality have been established.
- This progress has been gradually achieved over the last century through difficult negotiations with representatives of the traditional clergy and the state. The importance of the women's movement and the encouragement of individual actors, both male and female, in the respective countries cannot be sufficiently emphasized. They have repeatedly brought the specific themes into public discourse, issued reprimands on the basis of international law, and at the same time elaborated and proposed justifications for more gender equality based on Islamic law.
- If the respective governments also act on behalf of more equality, the chances for an amendment of the law are good. In any case, in Iran many small and large reforms have been fought for, even against the government,

which provides further proof of the high level of commitment on the part of the women's movement.

- General discrepancies with human rights, the Convention on the Elimination of all Forms of Discrimination against Women (CEDAW), and the Convention on the Rights of the Child (CRC) exist, especially with regard to polygyny, divorce, and guardianship, but also with regard to Islamic inheritance law, which continues to be observed almost everywhere in the Muslim states.
- In the domain of criminal law, codification has not been advantageous for women; on the contrary, gendered regulations such as unequal blood money have been legally fixed.
- Law and society are closely related. This is clearly shown, for instance, by the different discourses in Morocco, where appeal to international law is possible, and in Iran, where it is not.
- Therefore the legislative process always has to be seen in its social affiliation and relevance. The education of women and girls, information regarding rights, the opportunity to pursue a profession, and public presence play a major role in this connection. This, along with steps taken against laws and traditions discriminating against women, is an indispensable supplement to revisions of legislation.

An important question in Muslim countries concerns the relation between legislation and international conventions, especially regarding questions of human rights. The conditions imposed on states in the various agreements, for instance the women's rights convention, compel national governments to submit regular reports to the international community, to change their legislation, and to make it possible for the international community to monitor their observance of human rights.

Sharia and Human Rights—Are They Incompatible?

The discrepancies between human rights as laid down in the international conventions and legislation in Muslim states consist chiefly of the following: the lack of religious freedom, Islamic criminal law, especially regarding cruel corporal punishments in those states where it is applied, and the question of gender equality, especially concerning polygyny, the husband's right to repudiate his wife, guardianship, and inheritance law. In addition, customary law often increases the discrimination against women. Is Islam compatible with human rights? The question is often asked but cannot be posed in this form, for as we have already seen, there is no such thing as "Islam" and thus "Islamic law." Instead, to use Shaheen Sardar Ali's categories, there are only various "operative Islamic laws" that differ depending on the nation, and perhaps also on the region, the level of the actors, and the perspective. This question therefore has to be discussed keeping in mind the legal domains involved, the country and its legal regulations, and also the legal and political discourse—that is, the respective operative Islamic law.[48]

In 1948, the United Nations approved the Universal Declaration of Human Rights (UDHR), which was signed by virtually all the states on earth. Among the Islamic states, the only one that did not sign was Saudi Arabia. Additional major international agreements include the Convention on the Elimination of All Forms of Discrimination against Women (CEDAW, 1979) and the Convention on the Rights of the Child (CRC, 1990). Both of the latter were signed by numerous Muslim states. However, almost 45 percent of all reservations regarding CEDAW, and almost a third of the reservations regarding CRC, proceeded from Muslim states. Particularly with respect to Article 2, paragraph (a) of CEDAW, there were a disproportionate number of objections by Muslim countries. This article reads:

> States Parties condemn discrimination against women in all its forms, agree to pursue by all appropriate means and without delay a policy of eliminating discrimination against women and, to this end, undertake:
> (a) To embody the principle of the equality of men and women in their national constitutions or other appropriate legislation if not yet incorporated therein and to ensure, through law and other appropriate means, the practical realization of this principle . . .

For example, Algeria's view was that the article contradicted the Algerian family law code. On the other hand, Bangladesh, Egypt, Libya, and Malaysia all specifically mentioned Islamic law and sharia as the basis for their reservations. For example, Egypt noted that:

> The Arab Republic of Egypt is willing to observe this article if its observance does not contradict Islamic sharia.[49]

Libya and the United Arab Emirates explicitly referred to Islamic inheritance law. Saudi Arabia and Oman attached a general "sharia reservation." But even with reservations, the international convention obligated the signatory states to submit reports concerning the adaptation of the national legislation and thus put in motion a process of debate with the United Nations regarding these norms.

Alongside the discussions on the level of the United Nations, tendencies to make independent Islamic declarations of human rights have emerged since the 1970s: for example, the Universal Islamic Declaration of Human Rights (UIDHR) of 1981, which was issued by Islamic councils in London and Paris; the Cairo Declaration On Human Rights in Islam (CDHRI) adopted by the Organization of the Islamic Conference in 1990; and the Arab Charter on Human Rights issued by the League of Arab States in 1993. The latter declaration shows a stronger commitment to equality and freedom of opinion and religion than the other two Islamic declarations, but it is less often appealed to in discussions. All these Islamic declarations include the so-called "sharia reservation;" that is, they refer to the regulations of Islamic law (which are as such unregulated). Thus they offer the option of a different—modern, but also traditional—interpretation. None of these declarations is internationally binding. Nonetheless, they document Islamic-influenced states' concern to demonstrate on the level of international politics as well the search for authentic formulations of cultural identity in the context of the "Islamic turn."

In connection with women's rights we should also mention the Declaration of Teheran issued by the Organization of Islamic Conference in 1995.[50] Here "only" women's rights are dealt with, and hence the declaration was elaborated by women. The first article refers not to the equality but to the complementary roles of the sexes; in the second article, the family is established as a fundamental concept of religion. In the third article, the mother's role as a natural task for women is described, and in the thirteenth article Islamic sharia is established as the fundamental framework for the interpretation of all articles in the declaration. On the other hand, in the preamble to the Islamabad Declaration on "The role of female members of Parliament in the process of peace, progress, and the development of Islamic societies," also issued in 1995, we find the following commitment to equality:

> Convinced that equality and elimination of discrimination in all spheres of life based on justice constitute the essence of democracy and guarantee the happiness and prosperity of the entire society, including men and women.[51]

Here there is also a reference to the role of women in politics and in the battle for freedom. Women's human rights are supposed to be realized at all levels "in the true spirit of Islam." In particular, an end to discrimination and violence against women is demanded, along with a place for women in the economy.

In general, we should note that the great majority of Muslim states have signed international pacts—even if with reservations—and have thus fundamentally committed themselves to the idea of universal human rights. However, the respective objections, especially those concerning sharia, still leave a significant room for maneuver for gaining access to modernity, but also for the contradictory conservative interpretations of personal law. Similarly contradictory ideas are found in the domain of sexuality and love.

3

Sexuality and Love

Premodern Ideas

Procreation and Contraception

Sexuality and the sex act are the most intimate human behaviors and, at the same time, the ones that have the greatest social importance; for that reason, they are regulated by all cultures. They are often subject to religious interpretive authorities and are closely connected with cultish-ritual prescriptions, such as those regarding purity. In the modern world as well, the definition of sex roles in connection with sexuality has become the central criterion of cultural self-understanding. Self-determined and free sexuality have gradually become the yardstick for measuring "modernity." The right to control one's own body was long withheld from women, even in European cultures. The close connection between sexuality, purity, and sacredness has already been discussed above; the sex act and especially ejaculation, but also menstrual blood, make a physical and metaphysical purification necessary before returning to the practice of religion.

The Islamic scientific tradition was influenced by the teachings of ancient authors. According to Hippocrates, men and women had equal parts in the conception of an embryo, whereas Aristotle assumed that the female was simply a receptacle in which the embryo, which grew from the male's semen alone, developed. In sura 76:2 we read that human beings sprang from a "mixed drop" (Arabic *nutfa amshāj*), which points to the participation of both sexes. According to the metaphor of light found in Ibn Ishāq's account of the procreation of the Prophet, the male semen is dominant. In sura 23:12-14, a drop, a clot of blood, and a clump of flesh are mentioned as stages in the development of human life. Scholars usually interpreted the text as meaning that there are three major phases of embryonic development, each forty days long. There are differing views as to the point at which the soul originates, sometimes on the forty-second day, sometimes on the one-hundred-and-twentieth day.

The physician Ibn Sīnā describes men's and women's sex organs as complementary. According to him, the man's penis and testicles, which are complete and are found outside the body, correspond to the woman's uterus, which is not complete and is found within the body, like a male organ that has been drawn inside. Ibn Sīnā's description reflects the tension in Islamic medical discourse between the idea of complementary sex organs and the notion that the woman's sex organs are smaller and less important than the man's. Male sexuality and female sexuality are both discussed, but the latter is usually described in relation to the former. However, the idea

that orgasm for both sexes plays a crucial role in the ejaculation of semen and conception has become an important part
of the Islamic concept of sexuality. According to Ibn Sīnā, mutual orgasm increases the chances of pregnancy. He therefore
recommends that men respect female sexuality if they want
to produce children.[1]

Contraception—and especially coitus interruptus, which the
Prophet is supposed to have practiced—was allowed, and
abortion was tolerated, at least according to some authorities,
up to the point at which the soul originates. Some schools of
jurisprudence insist on the wife's agreement in this case, since
she has a right to children and could suffer from the practice.[2]

Al-Ghazālī used the same metaphor as Ibn Sīnā to describe
the process of procreation. He argues against the rapid withdrawal of the man before the woman satisfies her craving and
reaches orgasm not just because this impedes conception, but
because it is harmful for the woman. This is why, according
to al-Ghazālī, the lawfulness of contraceptive measures, often
involving premature withdrawal or other techniques that
would compromise the woman's pleasure, is based exclusively
on the woman's agreement. This legal and ethical opinion is,
in turn, based on al-Ghazālī's understanding of the biology of
reproduction prevalent in Islamic scientific discourse.[3]

Dallal points with regard to the openness in the discussion
of sex, both in erotic treatises and in medical texts, to the
recognition that sexuality does not constitute a loss of control,
but sexuality is a deliberate and meaningful aspect of the natural and cultural make-up of men and women.[4] This might be
seen as opposite to the legal-religious discourse on *fitna* as
discussed below, which is clearly gendered and misogynistic.

Masturbation was tolerated, but regarded with disapproba-
tion. Other methods of contraception, especially the insertion
of tampons in order to stop the semen, have been discussed

only on the margins of the legal literature and especially in legal opinions that contain answers to believers' practical questions. However, there are clues suggesting that contraception was already practiced in the premodern period when "times were hard"—that is, in times of famine and natural catastrophes, people tried to reduce the number of pregnancies and births. Infanticide was morally abominated on the basis of the corresponding verse in the Quran.

Circumcision

Circumcision (Arabic *khitān*) is strongly connected to sexuality and purity. In the Muslim world it is a central ritual for boys, requiring the removal of the foreskin of the penis. It is closely related to the circumcision practiced by Jews. The point at which the operation takes place varies depending on the region and the time, but in general it is performed between the seventh day after birth and the age of fifteen. For boys, circumcision is accompanied by a major festive event.

The circumcision of girls is practiced chiefly in the Muslim states of North and East Africa. It involves the excision or reduction of the clitoris; in some cases, the inner labia are removed instead or in addition. Unlike circumcision for males, even so-called "light" female circumcision, in which part of the clitoris is removed, impairs the woman's sexuality. For that reason it is also, more aptly, called "genital mutilation."[5] In discussing so-called "lighter circumcision" legal scholars refer to a tradition according to which the Prophet told Umm 'Atīya al-Ansāriyya, a woman of Medina: "Don't cut it completely away, it's better for the woman that way and it gives the man more pleasure." Female circumcision is discussed in several works on law, sometimes as an honor for the woman.

Al-Jāhīz writes that an uncircumcised woman feels a joy in sexuality that a circumcised woman does not have, and that chastity is to be found among circumcised women.[6]

Other forms of female circumcision, such as the complete excision of the clitoris and sewing the labia together, frequently result in enormous damage to the woman's health.

Neither male nor female circumcision are mentioned in the Quran, but male circumcision is generally described by legal scholars as "necessary" (Arabic *wājib*) or at least "usual" (Arabic *sunna*), and is customary throughout the Islamic world. Indeed, it has become a fundamental characteristic of the Muslim male.

The circumcision ritual is obviously connected with marriageability and seems moreover to be considered an act of initiation that symbolizes inclusion within the religious community.

The Fear of Excesses

In general, religious and legal literature assumes that the wife's duty is to satisfy the man, and hence that a man's sexual needs are greater than those of a woman. Thus in sura 2:223,[7] men are addressed:

> Your wives are your fields, so go into your fields whichever way you like, and send (something good) ahead for yourselves.

Whereas in this verse the point of view is male and women appear as objects to be disposed of at will, in sura 2:183 a form of the couple relationship and sexuality more oriented toward gender equality is conveyed:

Permitted to you, upon the night of the Fast, is to go in to your wives; they are a vestment for you, and you are a vestment for them.

Here the basic conception of sexuality is positive, but bound by rules. In his work *Revival of Religious Sciences*, the theologian al-Ghazālī (d. 1111) argued for the unconditional recommendation of marriage, because it is a regulator for the sexual desire. As the advantages of marriage he mentioned, after the "calming of sensuality," "procreation, satisfying sexual desire, ordering the household, providing companionship, and disciplining the self in striving to sustain them." Marriage is thus described:

[It is a] fortification against the devil, curbing lust, warding off the excesses of desire, averting the eye, and safeguarding relief. To this the Prophet referred when he declared, "He who marries fortifies half of his religion, so let him fear God for the second half."[8]

As a "fortification against the devil," marriage is an important institution for everyone who is not penniless or impotent. For, if sensuality becomes too powerful and is not restrained by a strong fear of God, it leads to excesses. To this effect, the Prophet also cited God's assertion referring to the threatening turmoil and confusion in sura 8:74:

And those who disbelieve are the protectors of another. If ye do not so, there will be confusion [Arabic *fitna*] in the land, and great corruption.[9]

The Arabic word *fitna*—in the political history of early Islam this term was interpreted as meaning "civil war"—is transferred by al-Ghazālī to sensuality and sexuality, evoking "temptation" in the sense of confusion and chaos. The association of sexuality with *fitna*, with chaos, became a central theme in Muslim theological, but also public, discourse on gender. The female arts of seduction and the constant temptations to which men were allegedly exposed by women were seen to produce a chaos and revolt that had to be restrained by divine regulations.[10]

The fear of excesses, of transgressing divine boundaries, and ultimately of sexuality led to the segregation of the sexes on the basis of a categorizing dichotomy between "permitted" (Arabic *halāl*) and "forbidden" (Arabic *harām*, lit. "forbidden, sacred, taboo"). However, a *harām* is also a sacred place entrance to which is forbidden or at least restricted. The expression is used to refer to mosques and other sacred places, and especially to the most holy sites of Islam, such as the cities of Mecca and Medina. At the same time the term "harem" is also derived from this expression. The harem is the part of the home that is reserved for the family's women. The dichotomy *harām/halāl* is also applied to persons. For example, a woman is "permitted" if she is married to him and is not menstruating, and he can then have sexual intercourse with her. That is the formulation in the male-centered language of Islamic law. A woman is *harām* to her man during her menstrual period and puerperium. He is not "permitted" women who are closely related to him (e.g., mother or sister), as is stated in the Quran. Since "forbidden" things and persons are to be avoided, contact with such persons must be minimized, separate rooms for the two sexes are to be created, at least when they are not married or related to a degree excluding marriage. According to normative ideas, persons who are considered "forbidden" to each other are not allowed to share the same room. A tradition says:

> 4935: It is related from Ibn 'Abbas that the Prophet, may Allah bless him and grant him peace, said, "A man should not be alone with a woman unless he is a *mahram* of hers." A man stood up and said, "Messenger of Allah, my wife has set out to perform hajj and I am enrolled in such-and-such an expedition." He said, "Go back and perform hajj with your wife."[11]

The boundaries between the sexes have to be preserved. This is enforced not only by social and legal norms, but also by spatial separation and especially by clothing, in this case particularly the veil and a garment that covers the female body.

A married couple's life together does not escape legal scholars' propensity for regulation. Al-Ghazālī discusses, in addition to the wedding feast and good concord with the wife, the question of guidance and punishment, obviously addressing himself to male readers. Since tenderness is important before engaging in sexual intercourse, he advises men not only to call upon God at the beginning and to praise God before ejaculating, but also to start with "kisses and words." According to al-Ghazālī, a wife has a right to sexual intercourse:

> It is desirable that he should have intimate relations with her once every four nights; that is more just, for the (maximum) number of wives is four which justifies this span. It is true that intimate relations should be more or less frequent in accordance to her need to remain chaste, for to satisfy her is his duty.[12]

Al-Ghazālī assumes here that women have their own sexual needs, which have to be satisfied, so that "protection" can be read as referring to protection against temptation by the Devil (that is, uncontrolled sexuality) to which a sexually unsatisfied woman succumbs.

On the other hand, Al-Ghazālī also acknowledges the marital problems that many men would like to avoid. For instance, he attributes to the pious al-Hasan al-Basrī a statement according to which God, when he wants to do something good for a person, spares him concern with family and wealth.

Foreplay and kissing cannot conceal the fact that Al-Ghazālī sees the relationship between the sexes as male-dominated:

> However, if the discord is the woman's fault, it is the husband's right to chastise and induce her forcibly to obey, since men are guardians over women. Likewise, should she be remiss in performing her prayers, it is his right to force her to perform them. However, he should chastise her gradually: that is to say, first he should preach, then warn, then threaten; should he not succeed, he should turn his back to her in bed, sleep in another bed, or avoid her—while still remaining in the house—from one night up to three. Should all of this fail, then he should beat her but not excessively, that is, to the point that he would inflict only pain but without breaking a bone or causing her to bleed. He should not strike her face, for that is forbidden.[13]

The gender hierarchy and the included power relationship are reflected in the rules developed in classical law regarding the woman's "recalcitrance" (Arabic *nushūz*), as they are established in sura 4:38. Although the woman has a right to sexual satisfaction, al-Ghazālī's remarks make clear, she does not have the right to deny her body to her husband (or, in the case of slaves, to her master). That would amount to being "recalcitrant," and the resulting legal consequence is the withdrawal of maintenance. Al-Ghazālī also cites a few overtly misogynous statements, such as those of the second caliph, 'Umar (reigned 634-644), according to which a man should do the opposite of what women want.

The traditional Islamic understanding of gender roles is thus based on the separation of the two sexes (sura 4:1), to which different tasks and roles are assigned.

> Mankind, fear your Lord, who created you of a single soul, and from it created its mate, and from the pair of them scattered abroad many men and women.

Female virtues, which also include chastity and virginity and from which a Quranic conception of femininity can be derived, are listed in sura 66:5:

> It is possible that, if he divorces you, his Lord will give him in exchange wives better than you, women who have surrendered, believing, obedient, penitent, devout, given to fasting, who have been married and virgins too.

Homosexuality and Transsexuality

Although al-Ghazālī has in mind the heterosexual relation between husband and wife or master and slave, homosexual relations (Arabic *liwāt*), chiefly male, are also discussed in treatises on law. According to the legal scholars, those relations were to be rejected on basis of the Quran's verses concerning the people of Lot, which they interpreted as opposing it, and they even regarded it as punishable (suras 7:78-84; 11:77-83; 15:58-77; etc.), drawing parallels with illegitimate sexual intercourse. Female homosexuality was less often discussed and apparently not considered punishable to the same degree.

In a few medical treatises, such as that of Abū Bakr ar-Rāzī (d. 950), same-sex-relations are called an "illness" and attributed to a genetic defect. Rāzī saw the sex of the newborn child as being determined by the dominance of the male or female seed. If the dominant seed underwent an alteration during the process of procreation, in extreme cases the resulting child is neither male nor female. Thus a dominant but altered and thus defective male seed would result in an effeminate male child, and a dominant but altered female seed would result in a "masculinized" female child. According to this medical view, homosexuality was therefore always accompanied by physical signs. A homosexual man had a small penis and no testicles, while a homosexual woman menstruated little or not at all, and had a beard. In contrast, Ibn Sīnā rejected this explanation and suggested that a passive male homosexuality was psychologically and not physiologically determined. In an equally cursory discussion of hermaphrodites, Ibn Sīnā maintains that these may either lack male and female organs or have both; in the latter case, one of the organs is usually weaker and less visible, and only one of these two is usually used for urination.[14]

How much the legal reflections were theories is seen by the fact that the term *liwāt* has a different meaning in religious writings than in other contexts. In religious literature not all intercourse between persons of the male sex is *liwāt*; instead, a distinction is drawn between the person penetrating and the person being penetrated. Whereas penetration of the active part was socially acceptable, and was, for example, never used in invective verse as an argument against the object of the invective, the latter is one of the worst and most dishonoring accusations that can be made against a man, because it puts his social status in question. Conversely, women, as the "penetrated," were seen as passive and subordinate sexual partners.

It was thus generally acknowledged that the chief justice Yahyā b. Aktham (d. 857), otherwise a very strict judge of morals, had a special inclination toward *liwāt*. But this became embarrassing for him only when it was said that he was in fact one of the penetrated.[15] The classification of sexuality into hetero- and homosexuality that has been current in Europe since the nineteenth century can be applied in this context only in a limited way. A "man" was someone who both had the corresponding sex characteristics and played the dominant-active role in sexual relationships. Conversely, to be a "man" in one's own eyes and in those of others, a man had to limit his sexual activities to the active-penetrating role, while the role of passive sexual partner was assigned to women.

Other individuals who counted as passive sexual partners included "not-yet-men," who were young, "beardless" men (Arabic *amrad*), "no-longer-men," who were eunuchs, and *mukhannathūn* (the plural of *mukhannath*). In medical treatises like Rāzī's, the latter term was used to refer not only to children who were born with both a penis and a vagina, but also to transsexuals and homosexuals. Islamic legal scholars discussed at great length the status of such persons—for example, in relation to inheritance law—and raised the question of whether they should wear a veil. In premodern Islamic society, *mukhannathūn* had an established place, even if they were prohibited from exercising a masculine profession or occupying feminine roles. They were, for example, singers, jugglers, or comic actors.

Piety Does Not Disapprove of Love

In addition to treatises like those of al-Ghazālī, which related to sexuality and the conduct of marriage and here provide moral and concrete practical guidance, there is also the broad range of literature on love. As an example of the prose literature on this subject we may mention *The Ring of the Dove*, by the Spanish author Ibn Hazm (d. 1064). It combines subtle observational skill with psychological and formally perfected representation, describing the behavior of the beloved as well as her emotions. At the age of twenty, Ibn Hazm himself had become acquainted with a young slave and fallen in love with her, but she died very early, causing him great grief:

> Of Love—may God exalt you!—the first part is jesting, and the last part is right earnestness. So majestic are its diverse aspects, they are too subtle to be described; their reality can only be apprehended by personal experience. Love is neither disapproved by Religion, nor prohibited by the Law; for every heart is in God's hands.[16]

Ibn Hazm goes on to describe various ways in which humans can fall in love, such as love at first sight and love that develops only gradually, and also "falling in love with a quality and thereafter not approving any different." He sees subjection as positive, insofar as through love people with quarrelsome natures and difficult characters can become docile and devoted.

Ibn Hazm also has clear gender roles in mind when he writes:

> As for the reason why this instinct is so deeply rooted in women, I see no other explanation than that they have nothing else to fill their minds, except loving union and what brings it about. . . . Men on the other hand are divided in their interests; some seek to amass a fortune, some aspire to the company of kings, some pursue knowledge, some look after their families, some venture on arduous journeys, some hunt, some ply diverse crafts, some go forth to the wars, some confront armed rebellions, some brave fearful perils, some cultivate the soil.[17]

On the other hand, he reports that until puberty he grew up exclusively among women, who instructed him in the Quran and poetry and taught him how to write.

The ideas regarding procreation, sexuality, and love show that because of its importance for procreation, female sexuality was in some medical discourses given the same status as male sexuality, while on the other hand the female sex organ was considered subordinate because it was penetrated by the male. The various discourses in medical, legal, and literary texts reflect a multiplicity of perceptions and positions, but it can be argued that in legal and religious texts the danger of *fitna* emanating from women and threatening men played a dominant role and resulted in misogynist views.

Masculinity and Femininity in Modern Times

From al-Ghazālī to Fatima Mernissi

In the context of changing societies, globalization, and the international discussion regarding the status of women, a debate over the re-evaluation of sexuality has flared up in Muslim countries as well. However, the variety of the voices taking part in this debate requires us to proceed by studying a series of examples.

For years the voice of the Moroccan sociologist Fatima Mernissi has been heard; her book *Beyond the Veil* (1987) argued that unlike Christianity, Islam has developed a concept of active sexuality reminiscent of Freud. In this respect she is still operating entirely within the framework of the majority of scholars who see here a distinction between Christianity hostile to the body and an Islam that affirms sensuality and sexuality. However, she identifies female sexuality as active and even threatening, because it challenges the male sex. She bases herself on al-Ghazālī and Qāsim Amīn (d. 1908), a forerunner of the women's movement, and focuses above all on the importance of the fear of *fitna*, which we mentioned before and which she sees as fundamental for Islamic societies. As *fitna* is a chaos that breaks out when women's sexuality is unrestrained and against which the male part of society protects itself through the rules of the segregation, veiling, and the subordination of women in general, this clearly demonstrates women's power, albeit negatively connoted power.

Mernissi infers from Ghazālī's remarks that women do not have to play the passive role and men the active; on the contrary, she describes women as "hunters" and men as "prey." While the conception of *fitna*, in the sense of the chaos that erupts as a consequence of transgressing gender boundaries, appears in many texts, Mernissi has to acknowledge that what she calls the "explicit" theory of sexuality representing women as passive and men as active is still dominant in culture and society.[18]

Virginity and Chastity

In the twenty-first century Arab and Muslim world, the family is often still involved in the choice of a husband or a wife. Arranged marriages in the sense that the couple becomes acquainted in the family's living room are common. This acquaintance is normally followed by a long phase of contact in the form of excursions, meetings, and telephone conversations. In the conservative Gulf states the bridegroom relies on his female family network to handle the matchmaking and marriage arrangements. In North Africa and the Levant, however, professional matchmakers (Arabic *khātiba*) are also used. Around the Muslim world, young people increasingly meet in public spaces such as shopping centers and parks to flirt and date, using the Internet, Facebook, and blogs to transgress traditional gender boundaries. However, romances and affairs before marriage are generally kept secret. A man's reputation is not damaged by pre-marital encounters not guided by the family, but a woman's is. The cult of virginity still plays a role, but that does not mean that no pre-marital sexual relationships occur. However, the latter are kept more tightly secret than they are in Western countries. Sometimes the hymen is surgically restored before marriage, and in any case women fear malicious gossip.

After a betrothal, which usually takes place at a small ceremony in which the first, "opening" suras of the Quran are recited, the couple can date. The formal relationship begins with the marriage contract, but only with the marriage ceremony is the marriage completed (Arabic *laylat ad-dukhla*).[19]

Sexual restraint, chastity in marriage, and virginity before marriage, which constitute a restriction of female sexuality, are a consequence of the power relationship between the sexes. On the social level, however, they are closely connected with the conception of marriage according to which women's sexuality has to be controlled in order to preserve the family honor. This control of virginity and chastity is justified by the need to control the legal descent of children. For a long time, virginity was proven in a ritual that involved the newly married couple disappearing into the bedroom and, after a suitable time, displaying the bloody sheets. If the bride turned out not to be a virgin, the husband could, in accord with Islamic legal norms, return her to her family. Bloody sheets are now seldom displayed, but the husband continues to have the option of dissolving the marriage if the bride proves not to be a virgin. At the same time, however, the ritual also puts the male partner, who has to prove his virility in this situation, under considerable pressure. The underlying idea of virginity that characterizes Islamic "morality" and thus the Islamic form of femininity persists in many countries.

Let us take as our example Turkey, where a modern family law code exists but many traditional customs continue to be observed, and not solely in remote regions: for instance, until 2002 a decree issued by the ministry of education to the effect that "proof of unchastity" could lead to expulsion from school continued to be in force. The usual practice consisted of sub-jecting female students to a medical virginity test. In 1999, after strong protests by women's organizations, the ministry of justice issued a decree stipulating that the tests would be limited to circumstances such as rape, sexual relations with minors, or prostitution, and further that no woman could be subjected to such a test on disciplinary grounds, against her will, or in a way that might injure or torment her.

On the other hand, the demand for virginity has, in the meantime, led clinics in the Islamic world to offer restoration of the hymen. Whether this should be permitted is a matter of debate among scholars. At the meeting of the Islamic Or-ganization of Medical Sciences (IOMS) held in Kuwait in 1987, the Egyptian physician Kamal Fahmi presented a brief study concerning various medical situations in which doctors were requested or might be requested to restore the hymen, and what the possible responses to such requests were. The recommendation made at the end of the meeting was that any operation performed on the human body that results in de-ception should be prohibited.[20]

Sexual Taboo Subjects

Homosexuality is still a taboo subject in many Muslim coun-tries; in a few countries, such as Iran, it is even punishable.[21] However, the Iranian writer Ali Mahdjubi[22] has described a remarkably free and socially recognized practice of homo-sexuality when he was young, before the Islamic Revolution. He saw homosexual practices among young males as a matter

of course; they were later given up after marriage. According
to his account, in Iran homosexual couples had no difficulty
in renting an apartment together, though unmarried heterosexual couples did.

Studies on homosexuality among Muslims in European societies show that discussion of it is not always as open as
Mahdjubi suggests. Instead, it is mentioned as little as possible, and it is rather unusual and difficult for someone to acknowledge publicly that he or she is homosexual. When such
an acknowledgement is made, it commonly leads to extreme
conflicts in families. For example, a young Frenchman of Algerian descent reports regarding his mother's reaction to his
homosexuality:

> My mother said to me: "I'd rather you'd become a
> drug addict, a criminal, even a child molester or a
> rapist. . . . Anything but that. We'd rather you'd
> died. We'd have suffered, but the wound would
> have healed. This is a wound that will always re-
> main open, until the end of our days, because
> you're still here. You're alive, and you'll remain
> alive, so it will never heal."[23]

This reaction on the mother's part suggests, contrary to what
Mahdjubi says, that homosexuality is subject to a powerful
taboo and is seen as a deviant sexual practice. Gay people
have since begun to grapple with the Quran's regulations in
order to live as homosexuals and at the same time feel themselves to be faithful Muslims.[24] In many Muslim countries,
however, such an open discussion has not been possible up
to this point.

Masculinity and femininity, in the sense of the modes of
behavior and characteristics that are attributed to men and

women, vary according to culture, region, and social level, even if they are inherently connected with religious norms, they are certainly not reducible to Islam. Whereas the normative conception of gender, as it is also derived by Wadud from the Quran, consists of gender dualism or the centrality of the concept of the couple, the "third sex" was investigated by Unni Wikan in a field study she conducted in Oman in the 1970s.[25] She used the term "the third sex" to designate the *khanith*, a figure familiar from classical Arabian literature whose anatomy is described as being for the most part masculine, but effeminate and soft. In Oman, such men were frequently homosexual prostitutes during their youth, but later returned to the "normal" role of the man and husband. According to Wikan's research, the *khanith* wore special clothing that distinguished him from both men and women. Women spoke to him on the street, and he often appeared as a singer at marriages. He belonged to a group of men who acted in a feminine way and moved freely among women, and thus was able to cross gender boundaries that were normally respected in Islamic societies. Those people were not transvestites who wore the clothing of the opposite sex; instead, they could be described, because of their claim to be women, as transsexuals.

Whereas in the Western conception a sex change can be carried out only with the help of hormones or surgery, according to Wikan the Omanis saw this matter in an entirely different light. It is true that women always remained women, but men could cross the social boundary of their sex and come back again. Wikan notes the perspective of premodern literature according to which it is not the sex organ—i.e., the biological sex—that is of central importance; instead, sex is determined by the *act* of penetration. A man who acts sexually like a woman was seen as a woman. Since a *khanith* is anatomically a man, but acts socially in a way that no Omani woman would be allowed to act, namely as a prostitute, Wikan designates him as the "third" sex. A similar result had already been shown in premodern literature.[26] Moreover, her study makes it clear that Omani society tolerated these boundary-crossings, and also that it was possible to return to what was regarded, in accord with normative standards, as the "normal" condition of gender dualism.

Masculinity and Power

A feminine and thus passive sexuality was attributed to the *khanith.* The perception of the feminine role as passive and the masculine role as active has effects on the construction of a hierarchical gender relationship; the man's claim to power and strength is recognized.[27] An empirical study conducted in Morocco,[28] which investigated the masculine sense of a loss of power in connection with women's exercise of a profession, came to the conclusion that working women renegotiated traditional patriarchal power relationships, triggering ambivalent feelings among men. Since a man's financial situation determines his marriageability, men saw themselves put under pressure by women who work. Men related this socio-economic dimension to sexuality, and held it directly responsible for the fact that they took refuge in behaviors that they regarded as immoral, such as pre-marital sexual activity, masturbation, and homosexuality. On the other hand, conceptions of masculinity are connected with social level. According to this study, men from the upper classes clearly had fewer problems with social changes, not seeing their masculinity so much put in question by women's exercise of a profession.

Moreover, conceptions of masculinity shaped by Islam imply that the man, in the classical sense, is considered the provider for his family and the protector of its female members, whereby the dichotomy between the public and private spheres and thus the family's honor is to be preserved. Respondents in an empirical investigation described this conception as Islamic and considered it morally superior to the "Western" conception.[29]

According to the results of an investigation in Palestine, conceptions of masculinity (Arabic *rujūla*) take three forms: Islamic, liberal-secular, and situation-dependent.[30] The Islamic construction of masculinity is defined by an explicit rejection of Western culture and an appeal to Islamic values such as purity, morality, and a gender-based distribution of labor, while the liberal-secular conception accepts new ideas of motherliness and the role of women, and supports women's battle for equality. The third form adjusts pragmatically, referring to Arab traditions.[31] In addition, the previously discussed idea of honor, which men have to defend and whose bearers are women, plays an important role in Arab societies, for example in Yemen, but not only there. Ideas of family honor include the notion that men have authority over women and have a duty to control their sexual behavior. The result is an unambiguous power relationship.[32]

How I Killed Scheherazade

'Ali Shariati (d. 1977), an Iranian sociologist and intellectual forerunner of the 1979 Islamic revolution, outlined a modern Islamic conception of femininity. In his book *Fatima is Fatima*, which is dedicated to the Prophet's daughter, he criticized the subordinate role of women in religion and sexual segregation in Iran in the twentieth century. At the same time he opposed the uncritical adoption of Western gender conceptions by women belonging to the upper classes and the jet set in the Shah's time in Iran:

> Societies which only authenticate things in the economic terms of production, consumption, consumer goods and products only understand economics. Women are no longer creatures who excite the imagination nor speakers of true feelings. Neither are they the beloveds of the great lover nor do they have sacred roots. They are no longer spoken of in terms of mother, companion, center of inspiration and mirror of life nor are they faithful. Rather, as an economic product, women are bought and sold according to the positive-negative qualities of their sexual attractions.[33]

Instead of judging women on the basis of their "profitability," Shariati spoke out in support of their education and professional activity. Since neither the traditional nor the Western-oriented Iranian woman could be seen as a model, he modeled Fātima as the ideal-typical paradigm for young women in Iranian society of the last quarter of the twentieth century and projected onto her what in his opinion constituted the necessary quality of a Muslim woman in twentieth century Iran. He mentioned explicitly that Fātima had a close relationship to her father and played an important role in early Islamic society; she stands at the beginning of a new era introduced by Islam. The hard times she had to endure had shaped her, and her courage in the confrontation with the Prophet's companions and the later caliphs Abū Bakr and 'Umar had proven her righteousness, while her knowledge of the Quran and politics and her protest against materialistic tendencies were signs of her religiousness. 'Ali Shariati shows that Muhammad encouraged Fātima to complete her work on her own. Her personality was formed by religious strength, patience, social consciousness, and intellectuality.

With this creation of a role-model he vehemently attacked the Westernization of his society as well as the traditionally subordinate role of women in contemporary Iranian society. His book surely cannot be considered as an attempt to reconstruct the historical Fātima on the basis of a critical evaluation of the early sources, but rather as an inspired biography.

An entirely different concept of femininity is found in Joumana Haddad's *I Killed Scheherazade: Confessions of an Angry Arab Woman*, which appeared in 2010. In it, Haddad conceives the killing of Scheherazade as the killing of a historical myth in order to free the body and the soul, and deconstructs the characteristics of femininity generally connected with "Islam":

> Although I'm a so-called "Arab woman," I, and many other women like me, wear whatever we like to wear, go wherever we wish to go, and say whatever we want to say;

> Although I'm a so-called "Arab woman," I, and many other women like me, are not veiled, subdued, illiterate, oppressed, and certainly not submissive; . . .

> Although I'm a so-called "Arab woman," I, and many other women like me, do not live in a tent, do not ride camels, and do not know how to belly dance. . . .

And last, but not least, although I'm a so-called
"Arab woman," I, and many other women like me,
look a lot like . . . YOU![34]

In these lines she attacks the "Orientalist view," the stereo-
typed European perception of "the Orient" and "the oriental
woman." Haddad creates herself as independent, responsible
for herself, not corresponding to the cliché, and precisely not
veiled, obedient, uneducated, and oppressed. Her ancestry is
Christian, but she emphasizes that women from Christian
families are not automatically freer, since they too are under
the domination of a patriarchal society.

At the same time, as the editor of the magazine *Jasad* (Arabic *jasad*, "body"), in which erotic poetry, stories, and photographs are published, she opposes the numerous taboos in
her society, and this has led not only to criticism of her magazine but also to threats against her person. In her view, the
taboo subjects in Lebanese society and in Arab society in general are male and especially female circumcision, homosexuality, the question of sexual identity, and the critical
discussion of sex in contemporary novels. She defines her
femininity as "Fashion and culture: food for the body and
food for the mind. External beauty and internal beauty, completing, and enriching, each other."[35] In this way her concept
of femininity represents a self-assertive, body-oriented alter-
native to 'Ali Shariati's image of a humble, modest, educated
Islamic woman whose sexuality is not discussed. Haddad
sees herself as an intellectual, professional woman, and describes herself as a workaholic who enjoys both her femininity and the right to control her own body without making
herself a sex object.

As different as these ideas, practices, and concepts of masculinity and femininity may be, they show that in today's

Muslim world in general this subject is discussed and traditional role models are questioned, and that there is a multiplicity of possible ways of defining oneself as a woman. To women like Joumana Haddad, it seems natural that, at the beginning of the twenty-first century, a woman could realize herself in a working profession.

Marriage and Kinship Relations in anthropological Research

However, as we have seen, in the Islamic world marriage and kinship relations, gender roles, as well as hierarchical and egalitarian gender orders, were and are certainly influenced by religious ideas, and here again they are construed and experienced differently by various strata and groups. The following remarks, which are based on field research done by Andre Gingrich in Yemen, are well-suited to show how extremely diverse and complex these gender relations are and therefore how inappropriate it is to assume unified "Islamic" concepts, no matter how they are evaluated.

The tendency to understand everything in the Islamic world by reference to religion alone, which is rightly criticized, has long been contradicted by anthropological research that distinguishes between the so-called "great" and "small" traditions. The "great" tradition includes the standard written interpretations, inherited lore, and legal thinking that in the case of Yemen proceed from the Zaydiyyah, a Shiite school of thought that has been dominant in Yemen for centuries. The "small" tradition, in contrast, is shown in the multitude of local and regional manifestations that reflect local traditions.[36]

According to anthropological research, whereas cities and urban settlements are more heavily influenced by the "great" traditions, the "small" traditions, for instance those in the central and northern parts of the Yemeni highlands, are embodied primarily in the tribal cultures. Gingrich, who conducted intensive field research on gender roles, the idea of honor, and the use of space in the Yemen of the 1970s, argues that while basic Quranic principles cannot always be applied to all forms of gender relations in the Islamic domain, the patrilineal descent and filiation that are implicit in the Quran are nonetheless the most common forms of filiation in all tribal societies. He investigates gender relationships in three social groups in Yemen: the traditional upper class, the Sādāt (Arabic, "lords"), the tribes (Arabic *qabā'il*), which were, into the twentieth century, influenced to very different degrees by the "great" tradition of the Zaydiyyah, and the so-called Ahl al-Thulth (Arabic, lit. "people of the third"). Whereas the chief representatives of the "great" Zaydiyyah tradition can be seen as the Sādāt, who see themselves as the patrilineal descendents of the Prophet through his daughter Fātima, and who were and are closely connected with the ruling class and the house of the rulers of Yemen, and whereas the tribes derive their status from alleged eponymous ancestors in old south Arabian history, the Ahl al-Thulth are considered to be people of "unknown or baser" descent. They are forced to do jobs that other people leave to them, specializing in handicrafts and activities that others refuse to do, and the other two groups cover them with insults and abuse.

The gender image the Sādāt profess and propose as a model for the rest of the society is that of a wise, intellectually specialized, masculine actor and his wife, who manages his household in an upstanding way, but does not share his knowledge. An important component of this image is segregation by sex. Adult men are considered the representatives of their respective groups, and the hierarchical model of society based on colors, piety, purity, and honor is connected with men. For example, men's clothes are white, which symbolizes piety and purity, whereas women wear black. This image condemns women who do not conform to this ideal as "wandering women", impure and dishonorable.

However, there is more social mobility among female members of Ahl al-Thulth than among the Sādāt women. For example, they can accompany their husbands on business trips, a few of them can read and write, and they have developed methods of gaining access to local markets. In these markets Ahl al-Thulth women who belong mainly to the lower strata of this group sell their products and do their shopping. According to Gingrich's research, at the time of his investigation they were the only women who were allowed to be in the markets near the Sādāt areas. However, it was reported that, in order to be able to go to the market, women of all classes often "disguised" themselves by wearing the colorful veils and clothing worn by women of the lower classes. Gingrich's results indicate that despite their status as "impure"—from the Sādāts' point of view—and the sexual connotations associated with it, the majority of the Ahl al-Thulth women led a stable, prosaic, practice-oriented marital life. At the time Gingrich did his research, divorces were not as common in this group as they were in other parts of Yemeni society. The reason given for this was that the women were either important collaborators with their husbands (and fathers) or themselves involved in additional activities in the domain of textile or weaving work that provided indispensable sources of income for the family.

The third main traditional group is the tribal population, among which Gingrich studied the Munabbih group. In the tribal context there is a widespread code of honor that connects a man's honor (Arabic *sharaf*) with his ability to act on his own behalf and to support other members of the same rank in his tribe against third parties, as well as to act on behalf of his tribe and its chieftains, sometimes by bearing arms. He must protect "weak" parties, such as family, guests, traveling companions, handicapped people and the uncircumcised, that is, his "house" and his "country." In this context, women are used to moving about in public without concealing themselves, to greeting both men and women and speaking to them in similar ways. Their way of life is shaped by self-assurance and not by "hiding by covering up," as Gingrich puts it. The segregation of the sexes and the limitation of women to a household sphere are not consistently practiced and experienced in the corresponding regions, even if there is an obligation to emulate the ideal of the Sādāt precepts, which enjoys great prestige because it is legitimated religiously. The women of the tribe investigated played a prominent role in its most important rituals, such as marriage ceremonies, male circumcision celebrations, and sacrificial ceremonies meant to bring on rain. But they did not have a right to equal participation in ritual and legal life and to economic sources, though they could make their voices heard on all these matters, and were not limited to the private manipulation of preconceived, "public" opinions that were in fact male opinions. Gingrich concludes that, among the Munabbih, gender relations were less asymmetrical than among the Sādāt, and that women were not forced into segregation.

CHAPTER

4

Literary Reflections

Pious Women and Slavegirls

Storyteller or Cunning Character?

In Muslim countries, there were no female authors of books before the early twentieth century. For the premodern period we must therefore study female characters in literature. Among the most famous of these is Sheherazade, the story-teller in *One Thousand and One Nights* (this is the character who, in the title of her previously referenced book, Joumana Haddad says she has killed).[1] The story collection consists of a frame story—in which Sheherazade plays a central role—and collections of individual stories that do not, however, constitute a fixed canon. In the frame story, Shahryār, the king of an unnamed island between India and China, is shocked when he learns of his wife's infidelity. With his brother, who has suffered the same misfortune, he embarks upon a journey. First they meet a woman who orders both of them, on pain of death, to sleep with her. They cry out: "God, God, your cunning is great," and with this allusion to the story of Joseph in the Quran they yield to their fate.

Back in his kingdom, Shahryār commands his vizier to bring him a virgin every night, with whom he spends the night and has executed on the following morning. To put an end to the murders, Sheherazade, the vizier's daughter, offers herself. She begins the night by telling a story, and at dawn she has arrived at the most exciting part, so that the king must hear the rest. Spellbound by this tale and those told on the following thousand nights, he continually postpones Sheherazade's execution. In one variant of the story, during this time Sheherazade has borne the king three children, which is why the aspect of "saving time" or "storytelling to save one's life" frequently is pointed to. Her calculation with regard to the king is accurate; she is able to break the cycle of sex acts and killing. Her strategy diverts the king's attention from the sex act and leads from the bodily to an intellectual level: "from sex to text." This textual level is embodied in a woman. Three points thus come together: the woman's persuasive power, her "trick" or cunning, and the deliberate use of her sexuality.

Joumana Haddad explains her rejection of the character by arguing that in her culture Sheherazade is celebrated as a learned woman who escaped death by means of her inventiveness, but she feels Scheherazade's way of maneuvering with regard to the king to be a kind of bribery. In Haddad's interpretation, the storyteller seems to advise women to "persuade men, give them the things that you have and they want, and they'll spare you." She sees this as assuming the man's omnipotence and the subordinate position of the woman, which she consistently rejects.[2]

In addition to the story collections of *One Thousand and One Nights*, there also exists in premodern Islamic writing the wide-ranging *adab* literature (literally, *adab* means "good behavior," and in modern Arabic: "literature"), an unparalleled source of all kinds of norms and of stories that are both entertaining and serious. Many of these have didactic pretensions. The forms in which the *adab* literature has reached us range from monographs to encyclopedias focusing on different social groups. In the latter case, women usually find themselves on the bottom rung of a hierarchy conceived by men, along with marginal groups such as beggars and invalids.

On the basis of several exemplary passages of Ibn 'Abdrabbihi's *'Iqd al-Farīd* (10th century), which as an *adab*-encyclopedia evidences social and moral expectations, Isabel Toral-Niehoff shows that in medieval Arab society, a good mother was supposed to be honorable and chaste, in order to uphold her male offspring's respectability. Motherly love, in contrast, was a topic quite absent from medieval Arabic literature, a fact that has not been explained satisfactorily until now. She discusses various hypotheses: the general female social marginality, the incidence of wet nursing in urban classes, and the tendency to separate femininity into one sphere of sexuality and one of procreation.[3]

In the work of Ibn Qutayba (d. 889), *Book of Choice Narratives* (Arabic *'Uyun al-Akhbār*) we find a *Book of Women*, in which subjects such as sexual intercourse, bride-money, marriage, child-bearing, and divorce are discussed.

In *Tidings about the Intelligent* (Arabic *akhbar al-adhkiyā'*) by Ibn al-Jawzī (d. 1200), there is an exemplary chapter on women. Men are classified into professional groups such as rulers, judges, physicians, poets, and even thieves. Women, on the contrary, are put down simply as "cunning figures." Here we can discern three elements that also characterize Sheherazade's literary glitter: women's persuasiveness, their cunning, and their sexuality. Persuasiveness is described using examples taken from the most diverse social strata, ranging from the pious woman to the singing slave-girl. In general, the perspective is male-dominated.

One anecdote concerns a man who asks a slave-girl he wants to buy whether she can do anything with her hands. She replies: "No, but I can do things with my feet!" The text goes on to say that she was a dancer. A man's simple question and a woman's simple answer are commented upon, making clear the implicit sexual background of the man's question, which the woman seizes upon.

Al-Jāhiz (d. 869), a famous Arabian man of letters, relates: "I examined a slave and asked her: 'Can you play the lute (Arabic 'ūd) well?' She replied: 'No, but I can sit on it well,'" playing on the fact that in Arabic, the word 'ūd can also refer to a stick, which symbolizes the male sex organ.

These are typical, simply structured anecdotes with a man and a woman as protagonists engaging in a verbal duel. The man tries to define the woman, to pin her down, and she answers with a play on words that draws attention to her sexuality. Since the story ends there, the man is left speechless. Because the man's name is given but that of the woman is not, she stands for "woman" in general.

In another story al-Jāhiz was sitting and eating with a few people when he saw a very tall woman. Making fun of her, he said: "Come down here so you can eat with us!" To which she replied: "Come up here, so that you can see the world!" Whereas the man refers to what seems to him an abnormality of the woman's body, namely her height, she parries this disparagement with the implicit reproach that he lacks broad-

mindedness. The man relies on his power of sight when he
sees her as tall. She shows him that this is not sufficient, because he is not big enough to see the world. Here, for once,
the allusion is not to sexuality but to the woman's mental superiority.

Al-Jāhiz also relates that, one day, he met two women just
as his donkey broke wind. One of them said to the other, "It's
disgraceful that the scholar's donkey broke wind!" Annoyed,
al-Jāhiz stopped his donkey and angrily stating that no
woman had ever carried him without breaking wind. Thereupon the woman clapped her companion on the shoulder and
said: "This one's mother must have had a hard time for nine
long months for his sake!" Here al-Jāhiz's attempt to make
fun of the women and to bring his dominant sexuality into
play backfires. By being projected onto his mother, his sexual
bravado is made ridiculous; the woman has the last word and
thus the last laugh. The female body is used by both the man
and the woman, but it is the latter who proves victorious in
the end.

In medieval Arab literature there were also handbooks with
sexual and erotic content, written by authors such as
al-Tīfāshī (d. 1253) and Ibn Kamāl Bāshā (d. 1534). These
works were extremely popular. Al-Tīfāshī dedicated his work
almost entirely to the questions of forbidden love: how can
one practice illegitimate sexual intercourse (Arabic zinā')
undisturbed? How can one recognize a woman who is prepared to engage in such intercourse, despite her veil? The advantages of pederasty are described, hermaphrodites are
discussed, and a chapter is also reserved for lesbian love.

A distinction between intelligence and cunning (Arabic
kaid) is also drawn in the case of the women whom Ibn al-
Jawzī describes in his book on intelligent people. "Cunning"
includes the characteristics of deception and malice. At the

same time, the word *kaid* is also used to describe menstruation. A menstruating woman is, however, perceived negatively, since she is prevented from fulfilling religious duties or engaging in sexual intercourse.

The Model of Women's Cunning, a work by Ibn al-Batanūnī (d. 1494), can truly be seen as a perpetuation of the formula "Truly, you [women] are full of cunning." One story after another shows examples of women's deceit and trickery, and men are warned against them. Take, for example, the story of the Prophet's pious companion Fadlūn, with whom a woman falls in love. When he does not return her love, she accuses him of being a robber during the time he is supposed to be engaged in night-long religious exercises, and of stealing, raping, and killing her slave-girl. At his trial, 'Alī b. Abī Tālib, the Prophet's cousin and son-in-law miraculously shows up and announces that he will clear up the matter. He asks the woman whether she is prepared to accept the decision of her unborn child, and she says she is. 'Alī has a rod belonging to the Prophet, and lays it on her belly. The unborn child begins to speak and reveals the woman's whole web of deceit: his father is the woman's black slave, his mother is the murderer, and she is the one who staged the theft. 'Alī demands that the woman be punished after the birth of the child—which turns out to be black and dies on the spot. The woman is killed and the holy man spends the rest of his life in religious exercises. In this story, sex, violence, and magic come together. The crowning touch is the woman's sexual affair with her black slave. In these stories, women go to great lengths to avenge themselves and to satisfy their sexual appetites. Ibn al-Batanūnī apparently added a short chapter on pious women, but it has not been preserved; perhaps it might have provided a correction to his misogynist image of women.

"I Embraced Her, Then My Soul Wanted More"

Premodern poetry provides great scope for the representation
of gender relationships, including those with an erotic aspect.[4]
Here it is a matter not only of heterosexual but also of homo-
erotic relationships. This holds in particular for the so-called
ghazal or love lyric. However, there is no simple formula to
which the representation of women in the *ghazal* can be reduced. The representation of women repeatedly oscillates between allusions to God and love for God. In the early Arab
tradition of poetry (*qasīda*), the first part of the poem (Arabic
nasīb) refers to a lost love. The poet remembers the beauty
and tenderness of his beloved, and thus creates the gateway
to a male narrative of the female body and female behavior.
On the other hand, in his *Treatise on the Beloved* (Arabic
tashbīb) the poet describes a present love and his feelings.

In a love poem, Ibn ar-Rūmī (d. 896) writes:

> I embraced her, then my soul wanted more, but is
>   there any greater closeness than embrace?
> I kissed her lips to quench my thirst, but what I
>   tasted there made me all the thirstier.
> The fire of love is so great in me that no cooling
>   wind can extinguish it.
> The fire in my heart cannot be extinguished so long
>   as we have not become one with each other.[5]

Another love poem in which there is a similar allusion to
divine love was written by the mystic Abū Shaiba as-Sūfī
(tenth century):

> In love separation and union follow one another,
> until love has been fulfilled.

Whoever touches fire will be burned.
But what about someone who's already on fire?
How can he get burned?[6]

A general judgment regarding the representation of women in literary texts is not possible; the genre is too wide-ranging and the representations too varied. As it is everywhere in love poetry, the image of the beloved is influenced by the taste of the poet concerned, by the genre, and by the period. In some cases, feminine and feminized beauty become an expression of the intense mystical love for God, whereas in other cases they serve as the inspiration for purely sensual and physical narratives about erotic love. Nonetheless, there is a clear tendency to describe women in relation to their corporeality and their sexuality.

Female Ways of Seeing Things

From Correspondence to the Novel

The progress of education since the end of the nineteenth century made available to women in the Muslim world possibilities of communication that a considerable number of them knew how to use. At the beginning of the twenty-first century, writing novels, short stories, and poems has become an important form of expression for these women. Female voices in Muslim countries have become so numerous that they cannot all be mentioned here: thus in the following a small selection of them will be presented.[7]

We already know that by 1860 women were already

corresponding with one another. Around the turn of the twentieth century, Bāhithat al-Bādiya—who lived in Fayyum, an oasis west of Cairo—wrote letters to May Ziyāda (d. 1941), a poet and novelist. When their letters were published in newspapers they moved out of the private sphere. For her part, May Ziyāda also maintained a regular correspondence with Khalil Gibran (1883-1931), a Lebanese-American philosopher and poet. Around 1890, Eugénie Le Brun Rushdi, a Frenchwoman who had married an upper-class Egyptian and converted to Islam, held a salon in which upper-class women met and talked about their situations. In 1914, Hudā Sharāwī, the founder of the Egyptian Feminist Union (EFU), Bāhithat al-Bādiya, Nabawiyya Mūsā and May Ziyādah founded the Association for the Advancement of Women (Arabic *al-Ittihād al-nīsā'ī al-tahdhībī*), in which Egyptian and European women met for an informal exchange of ideas.

In this early stage people already knew each other and valued the revolutionary potential of writing: journalism and literary writing offered women an opportunity to escape their domestic world and converse with others. At the end of the nineteenth century, society found the idea of women writers provocative and morally threatening. When the Lebanese woman poet Warda al-Yāzijī (1838-1924) died, a group of Lebanese women wrote an obituary for her. That was the first time that women publicly honored another woman in their society.

Journalism, which in Egypt began in the nineteenth century, was closely connected with literary writing. In 1880 women were already writing for magazines edited by men. In 1892 Hind Nawfal (1860-1920), a Syrian woman living in Cairo, brought out the first Arab women's magazine, *al-Fatāt* (1892-1894), which avoided political and religious controversy and was devoted to women's achievements in literature

WOMEN IN THE ISLAMIC WORLD

and science. The first militant feminist periodical was *L'Égyptienne*, the EFU's journal. It appeared in French, with the subtitle "Monthly Review of Politics, Feminism, Sociology, Art" ("L'Égyptienne: Revue mensuelle politique, féminisme, sociologie, art") and ran from 1925 to 1940. The use of French indicates that the review's target audience was the upper class, but also that it sought to reach the international feminist community in order to correct Egyptian women's negative image.

At the end of the nineteenth century women had limited access to book publishers. Although a small number of liberal men supported female emancipation, the subject of patriarchy remained a thorn in women's side, because it was assumed that emancipation would lead to immorality and the spread of rebellious ideas. The Egyptian woman writer Alīfa Rif'at (1930-1996) reported that her husband could not bear to see her sentences published. In order to be able to write, she locked herself in the bathroom. In her short stories she wrote about the traditional life of women in her country. At the end of the nineteenth century, 'Ā'isha Taymūr (1840-1902) and Warda al-Yāzijī wrote and distributed poems and stories. They had grown up in liberal families and had fathers who resisted society's efforts to train girls in classic female skills such as knitting rather than in writing. Taymūr's lyric poetry was long considered traditional and "sexless," but an overt rage can be discerned in her 1909 poem "Knitted Ornaments":

> I defy my fate, my time
> I defy people's view
> I'm going to mock ridiculous rules and people
> That's how it will go; I'll fill my eyes with pure
> light

and swim in a sea of unbound feeling
I've defied tradition and my absurd situation
And gone beyond everything that time and place
allow.[8]

In 1958, a novel by a Lebanese woman writer caught the public's attention: Laylā Ba'lbakī's *I Live* (Arabic *anā ahyā*), which was described, like many other novels of this kind, as an "autobiographical report by a middle-class woman" regarding her revolt against social conventions. Her books show the influence of Simone de Beauvoir and are marked by a rebellious intellectualism. Her protagonists assume that they have the right and the freedom to participate in social life. Ghāda Sammān—who was born in Syria in 1942, later moved to Beirut, and then took a doctoral degree at the University of Cairo—is one of the most important authors of the women's movement in Arabic literature. Her works, which tell of the social sensibility and a perceptible turmoil in society, declare Arab women's breakthrough into literary production. In addition, she was the first woman author to address not only intellectuals but also the common reader.[9]

Autobiography as Processing

One of the earliest examples of a woman's autobiography is Taj al-Saltanā's *Memoirs* (Persian *Khātirāt*). Her account goes back to the encouragement of a friend and relative whom she was tutoring and who is repeatedly addressed directly in the work. Born in 1884 in the harem of her father, Nāsir al-Dīn Shāh Qājār (reigned 1848-1896), she was twelve years old when he died. In simple, clear language, she describes growing up in the harem, her upbringing and education, and her early marriage. Brief inserted dialogues with her friend serve to comment on her memories. Her report describes the life of a princess who saw her mother and father only once a day and was brought up chiefly by her black nursemaid. Thus she writes with pity about the humiliating living conditions of the black servants in the harem and describes, with a mixture of reproach and self-pity, her distant relationship to her mother. The description of her father is marked by awe and distance, but also by admiration; he was the only man she ever saw in the seclusion of the harem. Her book, which she wrote in 1914 at the age of thirty, is not only an autobiography in the sense of a self-reflexive realization and processing of her own life, but also a source of information regarding life in the isolated world of the harem. In this sober, partly self-pitying and depressive book, little remains of the eroticism and exoticism of the harem-perception as evoked in orientalism. Taj's education in the harem was not very substantial. Only later in her life did she appropriate knowledge concerning European, especially French, literature and culture. She was betrothed at a young age, and when the harem had to be broken up after her father's assassination, she moved into the home of her husband, the son of a high political dignitary who had been thirteen years old at the time of their marriage. From the outset, her married life was marked by frustration and disappointment. Only when she separated from her husband did she stop wearing traditional clothing, dressing in the European manner. She began to take an increasing interest in French literature and history—or at least, that is what she tells us in her book.[10]

Hudā Sha'rāwī, the founder of the Egyptian women's movement, also grew up in a harem and wrote about this experience in her memories. Value was placed on her education, even if, as she herself says, she did not make much progress in Arabic once the teacher no longer came.[11] She describes visits to the palace and reports on her engagement to her cousin, which was not discussed with her and thus came as a shock. She separated from him, but later returned. The marriage was not a happy one, as she says, but the Egyptian national movement brought her together with her husband at a time when she would actually have preferred to separate from him.[12]

A somewhat more recent counterpart of such a life history begun in a harem is presented by Fatima Mernissi. Born in 1940, she came from an upper middle-class family in the Moroccan city of Fez, which is known as conservative and religious. Her mother and grandmother were illiterate and led traditional lives marked by segregation and wearing the veil; her father encouraged her education but—and here we can see a parallel with Taj—was not very present in her life. After Quran school, she was able to attend a co-ed high school, and went on to study first law and then sociology in Rabat. Sojourns abroad followed. Her dissertation *Beyond the Veil—Male-Female Dynamics in Modern Muslim Society* appeared in the United States in 1975. After returning to Rabat, she taught sociology for a short time at Muhammad V University. Because her position did not provide suitable conditions for her critical research on society, however, she withdrew from teaching and worked as a writer and activist with several organizations, including UNESCO. She writes in both English and French, since for her Arabic is a language in which she cannot express herself freely. *Dreams of Trespass: Tales of a Harem Girlhood* (1995) describes her early youth in a Moroccan harem:

> I was born in a harem in 1940 in Fez, a ninth-century Moroccan city some five thousand kilometers

west of Mecca, and one thousand kilometers south of Madrid, one of the dangerous capitals of the Christians. The problems with the Christians start, said Father, as with women, when the *hudud*, or sacred frontier, is not respected. I was born in the midst of chaos, since neither Christians nor women accepted the frontiers. Right on our threshold you could see women of the harem fighting and contesting with Ahmed the doorkeeper as the foreign armies from the North kept arriving all over the city. In fact, foreigners were standing right at the end of our street, which lay just between the old city and the Ville Nouvelle, a new city that they were building for themselves. When Allah created the earth, said Father, he separated men from women and put a sea between Muslims and Christians for a reason. Harmony exists when each group respects the prescribed limits of the other: trespassing leads only to sorrow and unhappiness. But women dreamed of trespassing all the time. The world beyond the gate was their obsession. They fantasized all day long about parading in unfamiliar streets, while the Christians kept crossing the sea, bringing death and chaos.[13]

For her, this upper middle-class harem in Fez was her parents' home. Here she grew up with her mother, who actually did not want to live in a harem; her uncle's family; and a few unmarried female relatives. She describes a very sheltered world, since crossing the "boundaries" and getting around the doorkeeper, Ahmed, was not easy. In contrast, in her grandmother's harem in the country the door stood wide open, and there she missed the firm boundaries her father swore by. At the same time, this comparatively "open" space, which women could leave to go riding or to swim in the river, was also the space in which her grandmother, who suffered so much under her husband's second wife, had to endure repression and a lack of rights. These experiences marked Fatima Mernissi as a feminist and activist besides being a scholar in sociology who became an icon for the Islamic women's movement as a whole.

The Palestinian poet Fadwā Tūqān (1917-2003), known as the "Poetess of Palestine," wrote an autobiography entitled *A Mountainous Journey: A Poet's Autobiography* (Arabic *Rihla jabaliyya, rihla sa'ba*). In it she describes her life from birth to her return to Palestine after her education in England. The actual autobiography is framed by an introduction by the well-known Palestinian poet Samīh al-Qāsim and an epilogue in fragmentary form taken from the author's diary, which brings the reader up to the time of the Six-Day War of 1967, in which Israel took over the West Bank and the poet's homeland:

> I was unable to compose poetry; my inner voice weak in protest against everything that had caused my silence. I was expected to create political poetry while the corrupt laws and customs insisted that I remain secluded behind a wall, not able to attend assemblies of men, not hearing the recurrent debates, not participating in public life.[14]

As a poet, she is still operating in a literary genre that in the Islamic world has—in contrast to the novel—a long and prestigious history.

The Search for an Identity

Another widely read Palestinian woman author is Sahar Khalīfa (b. 1942). In her 1990 novel *The Saha Gate* (Arabic *Bab al-Sāha*), she describes how male and female representatives of various social groups meet in a bordello in the heart of the old quarter of Nablus. This "infamous building" is also the site of the unmasking of a duplicitous morality that holds women prisoner in ideal-typical value-images and thus denies them the status of agents with equal value and rights. Using the example of the protagonists' fate, Sahar Khalīfa demonstrates that, in contrast to its emancipatory rhetoric, the Palestinian liberation struggle is very far from being a struggle for "women's liberation". On the contrary: in agreement with the social forces arguing in conservative religious terms, the masculine heroes of the Intifada, the Palestinian resistance to Israel, seek to use covert and overt violence to preserve women's traditional roles and social barriers. Sahar Khalīfa's book is a critique of the patriarchal ideology and its constructions of femininity. Nonetheless, she sees herself as a convinced fellow warrior in the battle for liberation and the political renewal of her people.[15]

The Kuwaiti woman writer Laylā al-'Uthmān (b. 1945) frequently introduces into her stories women and girls who take lethal revenge against masculine violence and forced sexuality. This is no longer a mere intellectual safety valve in modern Arabic literature, but rather a new, striking form of the attempt to gain control of reality. Her latest title, *Diaries of Patience and Bitterness: A Slice of Real Life* (Arabic *Yaumiyyāt al-sabr wa-l-murr.*

Maqta'min sīrat al-wāqi' (2003), speaks for itself.[16] Assia Djebar (b. 1936), an Algerian writer and film director, is considered the most well-known woman author in North Africa, and her books have won many prizes, including the 2003 Peace Prize of the German Book Trade. Her works have been translated into many languages. In 1955 she was the first Algerian student to study at an elite French school. It is impressive, for instance, how in *A Sister to Scheherazade* (1987) two different female characters are opposed to each other: the intellectual and the simple woman who are both married to the same man:

> Two women: two wives: Hajila and Isma. The scenario of my story features a strange duet: two women who are not sisters, not even rivals, although—as one of them knows, while the other is unaware—they are both the wives of the same man—The Man—to echo the words that are murmured in Arabic dialect in the bedroom. . . . This man does not come between them, but nevertheless does not turn them into accomplices.[17]

Since 1978, Assia Djebar has also been making documentary films concerning the fate of women seen against the background of the colonial and post-colonial history of their countries.

A story of a quite different kind is found in the novels of the French-Moroccan writer Tahar Ben Jelloun (b. 1944), such as *The Sand Child* (1987) and *The Sacred Night* (1989). The latter presents variations on the same story of a Moroccan woman and her path to understanding herself. Her father feels humiliated because his wife has already born him seven daughters. For that reason he raises his eighth daughter as a son named Ahmed. Only after her father's death can Zahra begin to find herself as a woman.

In 2005, the novel *The Girls of Riyadh*, by Rajaa Alsanea

(Rajā' as-Sāni'), appeared. It was immediately translated into English and later into German as well, and became a bestseller. One of the reasons for the book's success was its unusual form as an e-mail correspondence, but it was also certainly due to the fact that it was written by a young Saudi-Arabian woman who describes her experiences in a sexually segregated world. Its themes are the classical taboo subjects in the Islamic world—homosexuality, virginity, and pre-marital sex—but it also deals with the ethnic tensions between Sunnis and Shiites in Saudi Arabia. The author was forbidden to publish in Saudi Arabia and was accused of discrediting "the" Saudi Arabian woman:[18]

> To: seerehwenfadha7et@yahoogroups.com
> From: seerehwenfadha7et
> Date: 2/13/2004
> Re: I Shall Write of My Friends
>
> Ladies and Gentlemen, you are invited to join me in one of the most explosive scandals and noisiest, wildest all-night parties around. Your personal tour guide—and that's *moi*—will reveal to you a new world, a world closer to you than you might imagine. We all live in this world but do not really experience it, seeing only what we can tolerate and ignoring the rest.
> To all of you out there
> Who are over the age of eighteen, and in some countries that'll mean twenty-one, though among us Saudis it means over six (no, I don't mean sixteen) for boys and after *ménarche* for girls.
> To everyone out there
> Who has got enough inner courage to read the

naked truth laid out on the World Wide Web and the resolve to accept that truth, with of course the essential patience to stay with me through this insane adventure.

To all who have

Grown weary of the "Me, Tarzan, you, Jane" brand of romance novels and have gotten beyond a black and white, good and evil view of the world.

To anyone who believes

That 1 + 1 may not necessarily be equal to two, as well as all of you out there who have lost hope that "Captain Majed" will score two goals to reach a draw in the last second of the episode. To the enraged and the outraged, the heated and the hostile, the rebellious and the bilious, and to all of you who just know that every weekend for the rest of your lives will be a total loss—not to mention the rest of the week. It's to you, it's for you that I write my e-mails. May they be the matches that set your thoughts on fire, the lighter that fuels a blaze of change.

The first Iranian woman novelist, Simin Daneshvar (b. 1921) tried, like many of her successors, to describe women engaged in positive social activities and with a political consciousness. Her novel *Savushun* is considered a masterpiece of twentieth-century prose. It takes place in Shiraz, in the first years of the Second World War and describes the occupation by Allied troops from the point of view of a wife and mother whose behavior is increasingly distant from the norms of her time.[19]

Forūgh Farrokhzād (1935-1967),[20] a woman poet and filmmaker, is one of the most important representatives of Iranian modernism. She married young but after a few years decided to get a divorce, which was not only frowned upon in the Iranian society of that time but also led to her losing custody of her child, which transferred to her ex-husband. In a personal crisis she attempted to commit suicide but survived. In 1958 she began to work at the Golestan Film Studio, whose director encouraged her to pursue her artistic activity. In 1963 she received a prize at the Oberhausen Film Festival in Germany for a film about a lepers' colony. She died in a car accident at the age of thirty-two, leaving behind her five collections of poems, a few short stories, and also films that display in an impressive way her critical encounter with gender categories, along with a merciless reflexivity and an intensive self-examination, but also the high price that she paid, as a creative women, for her self-realization. It is acknowledged that she had a high degree of emotional, psychological, and intellectual perceptiveness; she always transgressed and redrew for herself the boundaries that were set for her gender at that time.

Two novels by the woman writer Shamim Sarif (b. 1969) recount in delicate tones and with sensitive descriptions two love relationships between women. In *I Can't Think Straight* (2007), a Jordanian woman of Palestinian descent living in London falls in love with another woman, Leyla. In the novel *The World Unseen* (2007), Sarif depicts the love of Miriam and Amika in the racist, sexist, and homophobic atmosphere of South Africa in the 1950s. Sarif now lives in London with her wife and children.

Umm Kulthūm and Fairūz

In addition to literature, music is also, and perhaps even more, suited to transgressing boundaries and reflecting individual personality and identity. The history of music in the Muslim world, and especially song, cannot be described in a few words. Here a reference to a few outstanding figures will suffice.

In general, erotic power is attributed to the female voice, and all the more to female singing, which is why traditionalists regarded it as inappropriate and even partly prohibited it. Nonetheless, the Islamic world has produced singers such as Umm Kulthūm (1904-1975), who became a national symbol of Egypt. Her father was a prayer leader and Quran reciter in a village; he fostered his daughter's talents by teaching her religious songs. At first she sang at weddings, disguised as a boy, but after her family moved to Cairo in 1923 she was also invited to meetings of the EFU there and appeared at the "House of Women" founded in 1932. She had enormous successes, particularly during the Second World War and then during the period of independence in 1950s. Her repertoire ranged from religious to nationalist to love songs. When she died, Egyptian radio honored her—as it had only heads of state, up to that point—with recitations from the Quran, and millions of people attended her funeral procession. The Lebanese singer Fayrūz (real name Nuhād Haddād, b. 1934) was almost as famous; she was especially known for her songs about Palestine and the Palestinian Liberation Movement. Both drew from classical Arabic poetry for their lyrics.

Umm Kulthūm and Fayrūz are not the only examples of Arab singers; the Arab and Muslim world is, of course, full of female singers. Many popular female artists articulate their identity as Muslims through their music, often addressing issues that confront women in their own societies. The famous Algerian singer Cheikha Remitti, often described as the Edith Piaf of Rai, sang laments about the state of women and men in Algerian society in the first half of the twentieth century. Today there is a lively pop culture with many female Arab singers.

It is in the areas of family and celebration music that most Muslim women participate in the musical world of their communities. Women actively participate in music for weddings, lamentation, birth commemoration, healing, and harvest. Often referred to as women's music, these genres are considered legitimate and are often viewed as essential to the successful outcome of a celebration. In many communities where there is an importance placed on music, there are performance genres that are specifically associated with each gender.[21]

These necessarily isolated examples show that women in Muslim countries have increasingly won a place not only in literature but also in music. They are visible and frequently write from their viewpoint about subjects specific to women, sum up their experiences in a world that is still patriarchal, and thereby lend women a voice. The courage they have thereby displayed deserves great respect.

5

Women and Power

Domination on Stage and in the Wings

Men Have a Degree above Women

For the question of the power relationships between the sexes, sura 4:38 is the crucial verse. The interpretation offered by the modern exegete Amina Wadud has already been presented. In the premodern period, the interpretation of this verse given by al-Tabarī (d. 923) appears to base male dominance chiefly on finances, whereas in contrast Jalāl al-Dīn Maḥallī (d. 1459) and Jalāl al-Dīn al-Suyūṭī (d. 1505) base the divine dominance of men over women on "knowledge, understanding, and ruling force or guardianship [Arabic *wilāya*]."[1] The word *wilāya* should be understood here in both its legal and political senses. Jurists, theologians, and early

Quran interpreters, as well as the whole patriarchically-influenced society, considered it impossible that women could be rulers, and, according to the majority opinion of the legal scholars, it was also impossible for women to serve as judges or prayer leaders.

It is perhaps characteristic that in describing the presuppositions for holding the highest political office, the caliphate (also called, more generally, the imamate), it never occured to the constitutional scholar and theologian Abū l-Hasan 'Alī al-Māwardī (d. 1058), whose book *The Ordinances of Government* (Arabic *al-Ahkām al-Sultāniyya*) was the first fundamental work on public law, to explicitly exclude women. However, the exclusion of women is justified in another text where he discusses the office of judge. According to the Shafiite school of legal thought to which Māwardī belonged, women were in no case to have access to this office:

The second condition [for the assumption of the office of judge, IS] is masculinity, that he be a man. A woman cannot be appointed. However, Ibn Jarīr al-Tabarī allows women as well as men to be appointed judges, while Abū Hanīfa says that their activity as judges is permissible in areas in which they can also appear as witnesses, and he allows them to be witnesses in all areas other than criminal law [lit.: except for *hudūd*/Quranic penalties and *qisās*/retaliation, IS]. Ibn Jarīr connects permission to appoint women with the permission to issue legal opinions, whereas Abū Hanīfa links permission to be a judge with permission to make statements as a witness. The reference to the invalidity of the two opinions is found in the divine word: "Men . . . (4:38)," that is, in the understanding and in the meaning. Therefore they [women, IS] are not allowed to stand over men. And [furthermore the reference lies in, IS] the word of the Prophet: "Those who entrust their affairs to a woman will never know prosperity!"As it says in his word: "Prevent her in the way that God also prevents her."[2]

Māwardī's explanations show that in other schools of law, female judges were not excluded; especially in family law, women could theoretically act as judges. Thus, since Abū Hanīfa defined the permissibility of testimony by women as the presupposition, according to him, women could act as judges in family law, but not in criminal law. Here Tabarī, whose commentary on the Quran was cited earlier, apparently went a step further, seeing no reason why women could not serve as judges in all domains of law. However, his legal opinion, like that of the whole legal school he founded, did not succeed in establishing itself, in contrast to that of the Hanafite school based on Abū Hanīfa's teaching and the Shafiite school to which Māwardī belonged. Hardly any evidence for women serving as judges is to be found in the writings of historians.

Similar restrictions were put on eligibility for the office of prayer leader (Arabic *imām*). According to Ibn Rushd (1126-1198; also known as Averroës), there was no unanimity of opinion regarding the question as to whether a woman could act as a prayer leader before a congregation of men. Most theologians thought a woman should not be allowed to appear as a prayer leader before a group of men, and a few did not want to allow women to lead prayers even before a congregation of women. However, in the sources there is evidence that there were female prayer leaders and preachers, though they presumably appeared only before women. 'Ā'isha bt. Hasan (d. 1068) and Fātima bt. al-Baghdādī (d. 1144), both of whom came from Isfahan, Iran, were preachers, but in the case of 'Ā'isha it is explicitly stated that she preached only before women.[3]

If one had to be male to hold these two subordinate offices, this was even more true for political positions.[4] This view is also expressed in the *hadīth* cited by Māwardī: "Those who entrust their affairs to a woman will never know prosperity!" After the Prophet's death, the highest spiritual and political office was that of the caliph, which was occupied by the Prophet's follower Abū Bakr (reigned 622-624), 'Ā'isha's father. He called himself "caliph" (Arabic *khalīfa*), which means "representative," and conceived this office as that of the representative of God's messenger. Later on, the title was changed to "God's representative" (Arabic *khalīfat Allāh*). The historian, jurist, and sociologist Ibn Khaldūn (d. 1406) refers to the close connection between spiritual and worldly power, as well as between the office of prayer leader and the caliphate. Prayer was considered the central religious task, and as he lay dying, Muhammad transferred the leadership to Abū Bakr, who was then named the first caliph.[5] However, in the course of history a certain schism developed and caused the caliph's power to become steadily more restricted; in addition, from about the eleventh century on, the political office of the Sultanate gained importance. These factors made it possible, in individual cases, for women to occupy this position. We will discuss those cases in the following section.

Women in Power

In research on women since the 1980s, a trend has developed
that is concerned with Islamic history. This trend has helped
find in the sources female ruling figures who had always been
overlooked by earlier historiography, and to situate them with
relation to the political system and the society of their respective eras. In their research on women's studies in Islam Meriwether and Tucker point out that since the 1990s much has
been written on women and gender. They discern four fields,
the first of which is "Women Worthies," or the history of no-
table women who have played a visible role. Meriwether and
Tucker show that this kind of history writing has sought to
set the record straight by including women where before the
focus had been solely on males, and especially on rulers.
They also identify the problem of an elite bias and the dan-
gers of glorifying the past activities of an elite consisting of
only a few persons. In this approach women are "added" to
"normal" history.[6] In the following pages we will mention a
few outstanding examples.[7]

Sitt al-Mulk (d. 1023), an Egyptian princess from the Fatimid dynasty (reigned 909-1171) who had political ambi-
tions, planned to usurp power at the death of her father
al-'Azīz in 996, and to pass it on to her cousin. She was unsuccessful, however, and her half-brother al-Hākim (reigned
996-1021) was elevated to the throne. After a temporary improvement in her relationship with al-Hākim, who went down
in the history of Egypt as one of its most controversial rulers
because of his excesses, his cruelty, and his persecution of
Christians, the relationship ultimately deteriorated drastically.
However, historians have not been able to prove that she was
involved in the death of al-Hākim, who disappeared while
horseback riding in the mountains near Cairo.[8] Whether or

not it is true that she participated in any such plot, we know that Sitt al-Mulk assumed control of the government once it became clear that al-Hākim was gone for good. She ensured that her nephew received the oath of allegiance from the army and bureaucracy, rank upon rank, until all agreed. The historian al-Maqrīzī comments that the young caliph occupied himself with pleasure, leisure, and listening to music, whereas the affairs of the state were in the hands of his aunt, Al-Sayyida al-'Azīza, Sitt al-Mulk.[9]

One of the few women who actually ascended to the throne was Shajar al-Durr ("Tree of Pearls"), who lived more than two centuries later, also in Egypt. She was a favorite slave of al-Malik al-Sālih, the last ruler from the Ayyubid dynasty (1171-1250), who reigned over Egypt and Syria. After the birth of their son Khalīl, al-Sālih set Shajar al-Durr free and married her. When al-Sālih died after Louis IX's army of crusaders landed near the Egyptian port city of Damiette, and both his sons were murdered, the new dynasty faced a problem of legitimation. Shajar al-Durr therefore officially assumed the title of Sultāna on May 4, 1250; she derived her claim to the throne from her status as the widow of the deceased ruler and mother of the deceased son and heir, which was discernible in her name, Wālidat Khalīl, "mother of Khalīl." Her brief rule marked the dynastic transition from the Ayyubids to the Mamluks, who were recruited among Circassian and Kipchak bondslaves and ruled from 1260 to 1517, when the Ottoman Army conquered Egypt and parts of Syria.

Shajar bore the title of "Queen of the Muslims." Coins were minted in her name and she was mentioned in the Friday sermon, both of which were tokens of an Islamic ruler's power. She officially pledged fealty to the caliph in Baghdad, but was unable to win his recognition. Furthermore, the repressed Ayyubid dynasty opposed her, arguing that both her sex and her original status as a slave were grounds for denying the legitimacy of her rule. Since Syria thus seemed likely to be lost, on July 30, 1250 she abdicated in favor of her military commander, Aybak, whom she married, but until 1255 she continued to sign decrees with her throne name. In 1257 Aybak decided, presumably on the basis of a political calculation, to weaken her position and to take a second wife. This decision cost him his life, because Shajar had him murdered. However, her subsequent attempt to act as a king-maker failed, and on April 28, 1257, her dead body was found outside the citadel in Cairo.[10]

Tandū, a female member of the Jalayrid dynasty of Mongolian origin who ruled in Azerbaijan and Iraq, was first married to the Mamluk Sultan al-Zāhīr Barqūq (ruled 1382-1389) in Egypt. He had seen her while traveling and desired to take her as a wife. However, since the marriage did not succeed, after they divorced she returned to Baghdad and married Shāh Walad (reigned 1411-1421). The historian Sakhāwī reports that she ruled independently for a time. She was also mentioned in the Friday prayer, and coins were minted in her name. She died in 1419.[11]

In 1236, and thus somewhat earlier than Shajar al-Durr in Egypt, Radiyya (Persian Raziyya) al-Dunyā succeeded to the throne of her father, Sultan Iltutmish, in Delhi. Five years earlier, her father seems to have installed her already as ruler over Delhi during his absence, and soon afterward officially named her his heir. When he died, however, the army commanders and courtiers did not adhere to this nomination, and at first put a son of the deceased ruler, Firuz, on the throne. When the latter proved ineffectual and dissatisfaction with his extravagance grew, there was a popular uprising, in the wake of which Radiyya was elevated to the throne by the people and parts of the army, despite the scholars' religious and legal reservations. Toward the end of her reign, she is said to have appeared in public unveiled and in men's clothing. Her regency lasted three and one-half years before she was overthrown by the military and replaced by her half-brother. The Persian historian Menhāj is full of praise for her. He writes that "she was endowed with all the admirable attributes and qualifications necessary for kings; but, as she did not attain the destiny, in her creation, of being computed among men, of what advantage were all these excellent qualifications unto her?"[12]

Gabbay is especially concerned with Radiyya's use of male clothing, the "cross dressing." She argues that Radiyya's success in identifying as a man benefited from surprisingly flexible conceptions of gender in medieval Perso-Islamic culture. Although the categories of "male" and "female" were sharply delineated with the majority of positive attributes arrogated to men and negative ones to women, evidence also exists to show that, in certain cases, one's biological sex did not necessarily determine one's gender—that, in fact, by behaving as men, some women could become them, with all of the positive and powerful attributes associated with men at that time. By cross dressing, and by otherwise associating themselves with traditionally masculine symbols, titles, and imagery, Muslim women could raise their socio-political status and be considered worthy of achieving or maintaining sovereignty. Gabbay raises the question of whether Radiyya's relative success, based as it was upon a suppression of her femaleness, truly represents empowerment for women but concludes that Radiyya nevertheless symbolizes a "step forward for women."[13] However, even though Radiyya was able to divest herself of femininity during her reign, intervening centuries have served to re-feminize her. Medieval and even modern historians present heavily gendered and even erotically charged accounts of her reign and deposition.[14]

Zāhida Khātūn is supposed to have reigned over the southern Iranian city of Shiraz for twenty-one years, beginning in 1137, presumably during her husband's lifetime and after his death. She built a great educational institution (Arabic *madrasa*) and financed it through endowments. Money flowed to sixty scholars who taught at this institution.

Qutlugh Turkā, from the Qutlughanid dynasty, ruled the city of Kerman in southwestern Iran from 1257 to 1282. Qutlugh was named ruler after the death of her husband, because at that point her son was still not of age.

The historian Maria Szuppe argues that Turko-Mongol nomadic cultural tradition, as compared with the Irano-Islamic customs of settled people, imparted a much larger significance to women's social and political activities and to family blood ties on both paternal and maternal sides. Female members of ruling Mongol families were entitled to a share of booty and had the right to participate in the *quriltay*, the all-Mongol assembly. Not only did they become regents of their minor sons, but also under certain circumstances they could themselves lay claim to the throne. Even after Islamization progressed among the Turko-Mongol tribes, women retained much of their social position.[15]

Action on Behalf of Sons

However, power is not or not only connected with official offices that were difficult for women to obtain, since at least from a normative point of view women's room to maneuver was limited by the distinction between public and private spaces and the rule that men and women should not be in the same room, as well as by the conviction that women were not suitable for central positions in the government. We shall see later that in science and scholarship women left private spaces and taught and studied in spaces that were used by both sexes.[16] How women nonetheless managed to exercise power can be studied in the example of the Ottoman Empire during the period from the middle of the sixteenth century to the middle of the seventeenth century. From the end of the thirteenth century, the Ottoman Empire had been evolving out of small Turkish principalities in Asia Minor, and with the conquest of Constantinople and the end of the Byzantine Empire in 1453, a powerful state was established that brought under its control not only many parts of the Near East and North Africa, but also European territories, especially in the Balkans. Twice, in 1529 and 1683, the Ottomans besieged Vienna, but they never succeeded in overcoming this last obstacle separating them from Central Europe.

The highpoint of the Ottoman Empire came in the sixteenth century. At this time, politics in the Empire were especially influenced by women from within the harem, which was a strongly hierarchically-ordered institution. The Sultans' mothers established themselves through great political skill and influenced politics outside the harem on behalf of their sons, establishing networks and political relations to the political system and the military. Until the middle of the sixteenth century, it was usual for a woman in the harem who had borne a son to the Sultan to move to the provinces with the prince as soon as he was old enough to assume a governorship. But when Suleymān I (1495-1566) married the Sultana Hurrem, her sons competed for power at the palace of Istanbul. When competition began between her sons and those from the Sultan's earlier relationships, Hurrem worked against her step-sons and promoted her own sons with the aim of placing them in powerful positions.

In the subsequent period, the princes were no longer sent to the provinces as governors, but instead remained in the palace under the watchful eye of the ruler and almost without connection to the outside world. An institutional succession to the throne was developed, according to which the oldest member of the House of Osman mounted the throne. Since they now stayed in Istanbul, the harem women were able to influence politics at the center of power itself. In addition to participating in networks and palace intrigues, they also made use of relationships with the Janissaries—the elite troops stationed in the capital—and had considerable economic influence as well, as shown by donation records. The buildings they financed did not, for the most part, bear the name of the donor, but only her title: Vālide sultan ("the Sultan's mother", Arabic wālidat al-sultān). From the second half of the sixteenth century onward, the Sultan resided in the harem. Since his mother presided over the harem, the ruler spent a great deal of his time in her domain. From the middle of the seventeenth century on, the Grand Vizier once again gained more power, but we can see that in the course of the eighteenth century a more and more important role was played by other female members of the Sultan's family. This time, the crucial figures were his daughters and sisters, who were given palaces on the Bosphorus after their marriages to high dignitaries. These princesses helped shape the self-image of the Sultan's family, and only the establishment of a "neo-absolutist" conception of the Sultanate reduced their power again.[17] Some researchers think that women from the elite strata of the Turkish tribes had a more independent and autonomous position than women in Arab societies.[18]

Kösem Māhpeykār Sultān (d. 1651), the mother of Murād IV (reigned 1623-1640) and Ibrāhīm I (reigned 1640-1648), provides an example of a powerful Vālide Sultan. After the death of her husband Ahmed I, she saw to it that his brother Mustafā became his successor, and because of his weaknesses, she was able to exercise her influence under his rule. When her son ascended to the throne in 1623 as Murād IV, she held the reins of government in her hands for the following five years, until her son was of age. But even after he had taken over the business of governing, she remained his advisor and his deputy whenever he was out of Istanbul. She kept the Ottoman dynasty from dying out by preventing Murād, who had already gotten rid of the other claimants to the throne, from killing his last brother, Ibrāhīm. After Murād's death, Ibrāhīm mounted the throne in 1640, but proved to be an incompetent ruler interested only in his slave-girls; Kösem handled much of the state business. In collaboration with the highest representative of the state, the Grand Vizier Shaikh al-Islām—the supreme religious scholar—and other high officials, she arranged for Ibrāhīm's removal and the appointment of the seven-year-old Mehmet IV as sultan. She was granted the title of "Grandmother of the Sultan," but with this act she had made powerful enemies and finally fell victim to a palace intrigue. She had decisively helped determine the politics of the Ottoman Empire for over thirty years.[19]

The facets of power and the exercise of power, the establishment of political networks and influence we have described, along with the small number of female rulers, show that women in ruling houses were involved in power or took part in it to differing degrees depending on the region and the period, and that an investigation of political power should not concentrate on the few women who actually rose to the throne and officially enjoyed the trappings of power.

After the beginning of the early modern period, sources in Muslim countries became more numerous, so that images of women in the various strata of society, and not only in ruling houses, can be more easily reconstructed. With the slowly growing influence of Europe since the seventeenth century and the subsequent period of colonialism and imperialism, Islamic civilization was confronted with immense problems, at first military, and then especially economic, political, and cultural in nature. One of the most exciting developments is the controversy over the question of gender roles under the influence of European ways of seeing things and ideas about the Orient.

The Age of Colonialism and the Search for a New Identity

Not Only Arrogance and Exoticism

In his two-volume work *Modern Egypt*, Evelyn Baring, later Lord Cromer (1841-1917), who was the first British Consul General in Egypt (1883-1907) and thus a high representative of English colonial power, found forthright words to describe the oppressed status of the Egyptian woman in his time:

> The effects of polygamy are more baneful and far-reaching than those of seclusion. The whole fabric of European society rests upon the preservation of family life. Monogamy fosters family life, polygamy destroys it. The monogamous Christian respects women; the teaching of his religion and the incidents of his religious worship tend to elevate them. . . . Save in exceptional cases, the Christian

fulfils the vow which he has made at the altar to cleave to his wedded wife for life. The Moslem, when his passion is sated, can if he likes throw off his wife like an old glove.[20]

Colonialism, which had reached its highpoint at the end of the nineteenth century and the beginning of the twentieth, changed the political and social landscape of the Middle East and North Africa in an unprecedented way. Economic influence, military intervention, and also superior European technology not only led to reforms—first in the military, then in the area of politics and government—but in addition triggered a cultural crisis and an intellectual debate between native scholars that posed the question as to how Islamic civilization could meet this challenge.

Both on the side of the colonialists, as becomes evident in the quotation just given, and in Islamic culture's response, the debate focused particularly on gender roles. The colonial attitude assumed an exceptional status of women in Western civilization and in Christianity that was contrasted with a Muslim woman living in an inferior civilization, deprived of her rights by polygyny, segregation, and veiling. Negotiations concerning cultural identities, and even more often concerning cultural hierarchies, were and are carried out to a large degree through debates on gender roles.

In 1716, the English traveler Lady Mary Montagu (d. 1762) accompanied her husband Edward Wortley Montagu, a member of the House of Commons, on a diplomatic mission to Constantinople that lasted several months. In her letters from the Orient, she tried to prove that the widespread view just outlined was wrong:

'Tis also very pleasant to observe how tenderly he and all his brethren voyage-writers lament on the miserable confinement of the Turkish ladies, who are (perhaps) freer than any ladies in the universe, and are the only women in the world that lead a life of uninterrupted pleasure, exempt from cares, their whole time being spent in visiting, bathing, or the agreeable amusement of spending money and inventing new fashions.[21]

The harem, the veil, and gender segregation were the subjects that had always fascinated European travelers, and after Lady Mary's time fascinated them increasingly, since the spaces not accessible to male travelers stimulated extravagant fantasies. Lady Mary deliberately opposed this image of "appalling incarceration" to her provocative opinion that these women were "perhaps freer than all others on Earth." From her observation that these women lived in "uninterrupted, careless pleasure" it can be inferred that when she wrote this, she was thinking chiefly of the Ottoman upper class, to whose harems she had access and with whose women she carried on various conversations reproduced in her letters. In her description she sees veiling and the separation of the sexes not as a restriction of freedom of movement or a sign of oppression, but, on the contrary, as an opportunity for women to move about unhindered and unrecognized and to keep numerous "love affairs" secret. She thus sets against Lord Cromer's critical and pejorative description of the gender roles in Egyptian society a positive and even erotically influenced picture of the women in the Muslim world.

Unlike Lady Montagu, Edward William Lane (1801–1876) stayed in Egypt for a longer time, and used his sojourn in Egypt from 1833 to 1835 to write *An Account of the Manners and Customs of the Modern Egyptians*, an ethnographic study that is still engaging today because it is so detailed and insightful. He spoke excellent Arabic and dressed in the Ottoman manner, but without concealing his European identity; he sought contact with Egyptians and lived in a native quarter in Cairo. Lane went there as a scientist who showed interest in the civilization around him and tried to understand it. He describes meticulously his observations on customs and behaviors, drawing on his knowledge of classical Arabic literature and theology. He describes rituals performed in connection with birth and death, upbringing and education, superstition and magical ideas, and depicts domestic life as well as governmental and administrative authorities and their functioning. Thus he provides valuable insight into people's social and political life, their doings and dealings in everyday business, and their festivities. For example, he explains that Egyptian girls arrived at puberty much earlier than girls in other countries and generally married their cousins, which in his opinion made these marriages as a rule more enduring. He describes the negotiations between families that preceded betrothal, and notes that in general two-thirds of the bride-money was paid before the marriage contract was signed, whereas the last third was held back in case of a divorce or the husband's death, and describes the personal and annual religious festivities and rituals. In addition, he points out, like Lady Mary, that:

> Though the women have a particular portion of the house allotted to them, the *wives,* in general, are not to be regarded as prisoners (sic) for they are usually at liberty to go out and pay visits, as well as to receive female visiters (sic), almost as often as they please.[22]

The image of the oppressed Muslim woman, victim of the Islamic religion as well as the patriarchal society on the one hand, and the erotically fascinating description of the alleged freedoms under the veil became clichés that still commonly influence present-day representations of the Islamic gender order. The Western perception of women "in the Orient" oscillated between these poles of erotic fascination and pitiful contempt—between the erotic seductress in the harem, on the one hand, and the oppressed and incarcerated Muslim woman on the other. In the nineteenth century the "oriental" woman thus advanced to become a projection screen for various ideas of European origin.

In the depiction produced by the so-called orientalist painting that developed in Europe in the nineteenth century and was practiced by artists such as Jean-Auguste Ingres and Jean-Léon Gérôme, the harem was ultimately stylized as a space of pure and unlimited eroticism, for which an uninhibited acting out of male sexuality was imagined. Precisely in the representation of the bath, a common theme in Orientalist harem-painting, the lasciviousness of the naked female body served as a hint at its sexual availability for male-dominant sexuality. In Western painting, the idea of the eroticism of the harem was all the more electrifying because it was conceived against the background of the alleged knowledge of a complete gender separation (women in the private space, cut off from the public), and as controlled by men, but also by Islamic law. There is hardly need to add that those nineteenth-century European painters saw the Orient from a very masculine point of view.

The differing perceptions of the harem make one thing clear: harems differed. We have to distinguish them according to region and period, and, for instance, according to the social stratum to which they belonged—whether we are speaking of the Ottoman ruler's harem of the sixteenth and seventeenth centuries or about an upper middle-class harem in the middle of the twentieth century. It can be proven, as we have seen, that the sixteenth- and seventeenth- century Ottoman harem was the seat of the Sultan's mother and thus a center of political female power, and contrary to Europeans' erotic fantasies, it was largely inhabited by the ruler's female relatives, sisters, daughters, and aunts, who were subjected to a strict social hierarchy.[23]

To escape these clichés, we have to turn to concrete individual spaces and, if not abandon the concept of the "harem," which is uploaded with various cultural and symbolic notions, at least problematize it. Women in Muslim countries demanded this early on. Thus the English traveler Grace Ellison (d. 1935), who was well acquainted with the Ottoman Empire of her time and considered herself a feminist, once asked a woman from the Ottoman upper class how she, as an Englishwoman, could help Turkish women make progress. The lapidary answer was: "Ask them to delete for ever (sic) that misunderstood word 'harem,' and speak of us in our Turkish 'homes.'"[24]

A Look toward Europe

Whereas travel reports intially dominated knowledge of the Orient, this changed toward the end of the eighteenth century, and especially in the nineteenth century. Egypt was the first Arab land in modern times that had to endure a Western military intervention by a European power, even if it was a brief one. In 1798 Napoleon's troops landed in Alexandria in order to buttress their position against England, but by 1801 they had already left the country. This short campaign has often been considered a decisive turning point, the "beginning of the modern period" for Muslim countries. After Napoleon's withdrawal, the Egyptians were in fact able to throw off direct Ottoman control, and under the Viceroy Muhammad Alī the country, which was by then only nominally subject to the Ottoman Sultan, experienced a wave of modernization. Numerous reforms in the military, government, education, and economics were carried out. At the same time, Egypt moved to the center of the intellectual debate with Europe. Men like Muhammad 'Abdūh (d. 1905), Rashīd Ridā (d. 1935), and Qāsim Amīn (d. 1909), along with women like Malk Hifnī (d. 1918), worked out various answers to the question of whether Islam was capable of modernization at all, and if so, what such a modernization should look like. Since in these discourses, as in the area of the women's movement, Egypt played a pioneering role, the political development and the associated intellectual debate about the status of the sexes will be represented using this country as our example.

At the end of the nineteenth century, Egypt was under de facto British administration, even though it became a British protectorate only in 1914 and officially remained one until 1922. However, British influence continued to mark the country far into the 1950s. The harsh criticism of segregation and polygyny shown by the quotation from Lord Cromer given above is connected with a stereotypical opposition between superior Western and inferior Islamic culture. The civilizing mission seems clearly to proceed from this: "The whole structure of European society is based on the preservation of family life." According to Cromer, "the Christian," monogamous, respects women, whereas "the Muslim" despises them, "arbitrarily" throwing them away like an old glove. In this view, Christianity is connected with respect for women, monogamy, and a social order that preserves and maintains family life, all positive evaluations. Muslim civilization, in contrast, represents the corresponding negative foil, and is moreover based on the satisfaction of "passions." It is hardly surprising that this attitude aroused in the Islamic world a debate about cultural identity, the values of the society, and the role of Islam that was to shape the following period. Before we present this debate, however, it will be instructive to take a comparative look back toward the West, toward England.

Was the image of women in England actually so modern and emancipated? What did the role of women in Victorian and Edwardian England look like?[25] In any case, the "high esteem" for women mentioned by Cromer was not reflected in efforts to grant them equal rights. Precisely at this time, centuries-old prejudices, according to which the emotional and even irrational woman was inherently subordinate to the man, were taken up once again and justified with newly discovered evidence that was then considered scientific. Thus Charles Darwin (d. 1882) took it for granted that women's lighter brains were less developed than the heavy brains of men. Moreover, in accord with the *zeitgeist* of colonialism, he equated woman's constitution, characterized by an excess of emotion, intuition, and easier irritability, with the constitution of the "lower races." John Ruskin (d. 1900), an English social thinker, put it this way: "Man to command, and woman to obey; all else confusion." The "confusion" that results when the man does not command and the woman does not obey, makes us think of the "chaos" (Arabic *fitna*) that Islamic scholars feared when the barrier between the gender was crossed: the parallel with al-Ghazālī's urgent warnings about the chaos that would break out if men and women were to interact on the same level and without the restraining institution of marriage is evident. Similarly, in Victorian England the "woman question," which at the same time touched upon the politically controversial issue of voting rights for women, was discussed with reference to the separate spheres in which the sexes were supposed to operate: private for the woman, public for the man. Ibn al-Ḥājj (d. 1326), who came from Fez but lived in Cairo, and about whom we shall have more to say later on, would have seen this as confirming his views.

In his homeland, Lord Cromer himself was a founding member and for a time president of the "Men's League for Opposing Women's Suffrage," and thus a vehement opponent of a central demand of the women's movement at that time. Nonetheless, England was then ruled by a woman: Queen Victoria (reigned 1837-1901).

One might have expected Lord Cromer's criticism of the Egyptian gender order, along with the colonizer's alleged duty to civilize the colonized peoples, to have been accompanied by a women-friendly policy, for example in the domain of education. But this was not the case. In 1881, before the British seized power in Egypt, 70 percent of the pupils in state schools received government support for clothing, books, and fees. In 1892, ten years later, 73 percent already paid these costs themselves. Britain followed the same policy in relation to girls' schools. Thus we can hardly say that Lord Cromer acted on behalf of women and women's rights. As Leila Ahmed pointedly notes, feminism on the "home front"- and feminism directed against the white man—must be opposed, but when it occurs abroad and is directed against the culture of the colonized peoples it can be given at least rhetorical support.[26]

The Beginnings of Reform

One of the first and most vehement critics of polygyny in Egyptian society was Qāsim Amīn (d. 1908). Of Kurdish descent but born in Egypt, he was a pupil of the well-known reformer Muhammad 'Abdūh (d. 1905) and a friend of high political officials of his time. He had benefited from a French education and worked as a judge in Egypt. In a new interpretation of Quran verses 4:3 and 4:129 he developed an argument that is still often used in the Islamic world, and according to which one can at most say that polygyny is allowed, but not recommended. Consequently, the state has the right to prohibit it in the public interest.

Qāsim Amīn's teacher, Muhammad 'Abdūh, a scholar and influential predecessor of the Muslim reform movement in the late nineteenth century, argued for the schooling and education of women and criticized polygyny, though he did not go so far as to prohibit it. He traced the Prophet's permission to engage in polygyny back to the social and economic situation in seventh-century Arabia and argued that suras 4:3 and 4:129 make equal treatment for wives a condition. If this condition is not fulfilled, the permission is invalid. Another of 'Abdūh's students, Rashīd Ridā, published with his teacher a Quran commentary, *al-Manār*, in which he argued that the verse on polygyny (4:3) implies that a second marriage is invalid only if the husband is not able to fulfill his duty to treat his wives equitably. But, he says, polygyny became a strain on families because wives were not able to cope with their jealousy.[27] On the other hand, Ridā bases the permissibility of polygyny on the, in his opinion, well-founded fact that men throughout the world are naturally polygynous.[28] Whereas in the West men are forced to act hypocritically by taking only one legal wife while at the same time secretly having one or several mistresses, Islamic precepts are more natural and beneficent for both partners: the man can follow his natural inclinations, and all his wives are assured equal security for their living expenses, their children, and their heritage. Furthermore, Ridā sees polygyny as the solution in the event that the first wife is infertile or falls ill. A second marriage allows a man to ensure his posterity without having to repudiate his first wife.

Along with Qāsim Amīn, Malak Hifnī Nāsif (1886-1918), an Egyptian woman journalist also known as the "Seeker in the Desert" (Arabic *Bāhithat al-Bādiya*), is considered one of the founders of the women's movement. In her book *On Women's Questions* (Arabic *Nisā'iyyāt*), she writes under the title "Polygyny":

> This is a terrible word, so terrible that my fingers almost refuse to hold the pen as I write. It [polygyny, IS] is the bitter enemy of women and their only devil. How often has it broken a heart, unsettled a mind, destroyed a family, and caused misery![29]

In these lines, it becomes evident that the author's consternation results from her own life experiences. Before marrying in 1907, Malak Hifnī had attended one of the two Egyptian teacher-training schools that then existed. Only after she married did she learn that her husband was already married and had a daughter, whom she was supposed to take care of and educate. Nonetheless, she held on to this marriage, but worked for women's rights, and in 1911 wrote a ten-point program that she presented to the Egyptian Parliament, in which she called above all for the improvement of women's education and professional life. However, her demands for the abolition of polygyny and a reform of divorce law were unsuccessful. Even today, polygyny is entrenched in Egyptian personal law, which was reformed in 2000. However, the husband is now required to inform a wife when he takes another. Malak Hifnī's fate, entering into such a marriage without knowing that her husband already had a wife, has been legally excluded since 2000.

The need to educate girls and women was recognized by Egyptians long before the British protectorate. The scholar al-Tahtāwī (b. 1873), who traveled to Paris on Muhammad 'Alī's behalf with a delegation of students, wrote in his travel diary *An Imam in Paris*:

> As everybody is often asked about the condition of women among the Franks, we have lifted the veil that hangs over their situation. In summary, we can again say that the confusion with regard to the chastity of women does not arise from whether they wear the veil or not. Rather, it is linked to whether a woman has a good or bad education, whether she is accustomed to loving only one man rather than sharing her love among others and whether there is peace and harmony within the couple.[30]

After his return to Egypt, al-Tahtāwī worked to establish the educational system and in particular endorsed the demand for the education of girls and women.

In addition to education and polygyny, the third theme that was taken up by Egyptian intellectuals was the segregation of the sexes, and especially the veil. In his book *The Liberation of Women* (1899), Qāsim Amīn demanded the abolition of the veil, but by that he meant not the headscarf, but rather

the facial veil (modern Arabic *niqāb*), which was at that time
still commonly worn. Thus he writes:

> Had the Shari'a included specific passages to
> advocate the use of the veil as it is known among
> Muslims, I would not have researched the topic
> . . . because heavenly orders should be obeyed
> without question, research, or discussion. How-
> ever, the Shari'a does not stipulate the use of the
> veil in this manner. This custom is a product of the
> interactions among nations. . . . Muslims were at-
> tracted to the use of the veil, approved it, exagger-
> ated its use, and dressed it up in religious raiment,
> just as other harmful customs have become firmly
> established in the name of religion, but of which
> religion is innocent.[31]

Since veiling is not religiously determined and puts enormous
limits on women's freedom of movement, Amīn argued not
only for its abolition but also for the necessity of a general
cultural and social reformation in Egypt. For him, abolishing
the veil was the key to social progress, and he advocated the
visibility of women's faces and hands, if only to make them
recognizable as persons in legal matters, but also so they
would not be hindered in their everyday activities.

On the other hand, Malak Hifnī opposed an immediate
abolition of the veil, not on religious grounds, as she said,
since religion does not restrict people, but solely on social
grounds. She had grave reservations about the mixing of the
sexes that she saw as being promoted by the abolition of the
veil, and thought the result would be immorality. Her criticism of the Egyptian society of her time is unsparing. In her
view the middle class came off best, but because of the un-

avoidable mixing of the sexes in the necessary work done in factories and agriculture, the lower class, in Egypt as well as in Europe, had the worst morals. They were kept from falling into complete immorality by neither the veil nor customs, but only by their heavy workload. The corruption of village women was surpassed only by that of the urban underclass. On the other hand, upper-class women were marked by idleness and the freedom to do whatever they wanted. Supported by servants, these women devoted themselves to a life of inactivity and took advantage of every opportunity to take off the veil in an inappropriate way. But if they wanted to appear unveiled because they were proud of their freedom or because they felt the veil prevented them from studying with scholars or engaging in any other worthy enterprise, they should be permitted to do so. However:

> The women of Egypt are entirely ignorant, and the men—with a few exceptions—so wholly depraved that in general there can be no permission to mix. On the other hand, among Europeans men and women are educated, but they suffer from the wickedness of their society and the faithlessness of their spouses.[32]

Thus for Malak Hifnī, a sudden abolition of the veil for Egyptian women was not defensible; she feared negative consequences for the country and the society. Men would shout obscenities at unveiled women and publicly humiliate them. In any case, the majority of Egyptian women were as innocent as new-born babes. For instance, they did not even know the meaning of the words "constitution" (Arabic *dustūr*) or "colonialism" (Arabic *isti'mār*). She did concede that the number of educated women in Egypt was increasing, and that among them there were a few to whom the guidance of their sisters could be entrusted. At the end of her chapter on the abolition of the veil, Malak Hifnī outlines her idea of an autochthonous development of Egypt, and calls for reflection on a specific modernity of the Orient, on a civilization that is adapted to the nature and character of the country, but that would not prevent Egyptian men and women from enjoying the fruits of Western modernity.

In this whole debate, the conservative scholarly establishment represented the view that the wearing of the veil and status of women should remain just as they were. However, Qāsim Amīn was attacked not only by the religious scholars, but also by nationalists, who accused him of using the emancipation of women to weaken the Egyptian nation and sow immorality in society. They rejected the criticism of the legal and social position of Muslim women as an attempt to exert imperialist influence.

As Qāsim Amīn's and Malak Hifnī's statements show, reactions to the confrontation with European culture varied immensely. In his demand for the abolition of the veil, Qāsim Amīn was more radical, and he went a step further than Malak Hifnī in his analysis, arguing that the reason for wearing the veil was to be sought in the backwardness of Egyptian society. Especially in his second book, *The New Woman* (1901), he put the religious justification less in the foreground and argued more intensively on the basis of a general progress of cultures. For both authors, education played an important role, and unlike Lord Cromer, neither of them saw Islamic religion as an impediment to abolishing the veil or to the evolution of society. On the contrary, their arguments were based on religion as part of the Egyptian identity. Unlike Amīn, Malak Hifnī argued for a slow, autochthonous development, within which was supposed to emerge an independent modern Egyptian culture that could benefit from the positive aspects of European culture and science without sacrificing its own identity.

Feminism in the Nation-States

The debate concerning feminist organizations and the nation-state is based on the question of the relationship between gender and citizenship. As Suad Joseph argues, the concept of citizenship has always been gendered. For example, nowhere in the Middle East were women given the vote as early as men. Joseph furthermore argues that Middle Eastern states tend not to construct citizenship exclusively or primarily as individualized—as in the liberal Western tradition. Citizens are formally recognized, in various ways, as members of family units, religious sects, or ethnic, tribal, or other subnational groups. Thus, the Middle Eastern concept of citizenship is heavily influenced by patriarchal social structures. It conflates gender and kinship, along with the patriarchal structuring of kinship that allows people to view women in terms of family and states to mediate their relationship to women through their roles as mothers and wives. Thus, women's organizations in the Middle East are often organized by the state, run by the ruling family or elite members, and dominated by family relations. At times, women's organizations are merely extensions of the ruling political parties.[33]

Three Ideal Types

The feminism that emerged in Western culture includes a broad range of social theories and political movements. Can it be transferred to another society at all? Is it universal, and does it reflect the worldwide oppression of women by men? Can certain cultural differences be found among feminist movements? For the Islamic world, it seems useful to adopt the definition of feminism given in Azza Karam's book *Women, Islamisms and the State* (1998):

> I understand and use feminism as an individual or collective awareness that women have been and continue to be oppressed in diverse ways and for diverse reasons, [as well as] attempts toward liberation from this oppression involving a more equitable society with improved relations between women and men.[34]

This broad definition applies to the female activists who shape the Middle Eastern political and social context, but who do not all advocate complete equality but seek only "greater" equality between men and women. Malak Hifnī would certainly not have described herself as a "feminist," for one thing because the concept was not current in the Egypt of her day, and for another because she would presumably have felt herself thereby too closely bound up with a Western discourse that she rejected as a self-confident Egyptian and Muslim woman. She was far removed from the position of female feminists at the beginning of the twenty-first century. However, she did write and speak on behalf of greater rights for women. The Arabic word *nisā'* means "concerning women," and *nisā'iyya* is the corresponding abstract noun. It can be translated as "feminism," but also simply as "women's question" or "women's issue." That is what Malak Hifnī is concerned with, as indicated by the title of her book, *Nisā'iyyat*; she can certainly be seen as a champion of the cause of feminism in the broad sense defined above.

Unlike Malak Hifnī, Hudā Sha'rāwī, who founded the Egyptian Feminist Union (Arabic *al-ittihād al-nisā'ī al-Misrī*) in 1923, was thoroughly familiar with European discourses and especially with French culture. Sha'rāwī, who, as she herself admitted, wrote better French than Arabic, chose this title with a deliberate allusion to the European meaning of the word "feminism."

On the basis of her broad conception of feminism, Azza Karam distinguishes three ideal types of "feminists" in Egypt that could serve as a starting point for an initial classification of activists in Muslim countries.[35]

1. Islamist feminists. Islamism, commonly called "fundamentalism," has been described as a "retrospective" utopia. It is a twentieth-century ideological movement whose central hallmark is the politicization of the Islamic religion. It began with the Muslim Brotherhood, which emerged in Egypt in the 1920s, but it is now divided into many different groups. The radical nature of Islamism consists in its criticism of established traditions and doctrines, for example the schools of legal thought and their differing interpretations, and it opposes them with the image of the "unity" of Islam. Muhammad's congregation in the seventh century is supposed to provide the guiding standard. A central demand is the reintroduction of sharia, which these movements do not see as achieved despite the fact that family law in most contemporary Muslim countries is based on sharia. This sharia is to be redeveloped through "independent textual interpretation"

(Arabic *ijtihād*) on the basis of the sources, i.e., Quran texts and also the tradition of the Prophet, while the interpretations arrived at in the course of more than a thousand years of legal history are to be cast off as invalid and contrary to unity. The vision of a return to the unity of Islam, the utopian conception of a state based on the early Islamic state of Medina, and the recourse to texts: these are the central elements, but also the weak points of the movement. They suggest that "the" modern Islamic state can be created anew, but in reality the various thinkers and movements differ in the way they define and describe this state.

Islamist gender images are conservative with regard to gender-equality-standards in the international human rights conventions. Both male and female Islamists see women's naturals rights as based on their roles as wives and mothers, since the biological difference between the sexes also determines the different tasks of men and women in the family. Equal rights for both genders in the Western sense is not a goal; it is considered "unnatural" and detrimental to women's dignity and integrity. When men and women are seen as different, the demand for equal rights becomes obsolete. What is primary is not a woman's right to individual self-determination but rather her duties to society, which she performs first of all through her role as wife and mother. These duties are socially and politically redefined and seen as service to society. Islamist Muslim women do not view themselves as "feminist", regarding the term as inappropriate and having too strong a Western connotation. Nonetheless, they actively support greater rights for women, and are aware of an at least partial oppression of women, which they want to eliminate by returning to Islamist principles.

According to these women, wearing the veil (Arabic *hijāb*) is necessary and an expression of deep piety, cultural authen-

175

ticity with regard to the West, and solidarity with other Muslim women. It is not perceived as oppressive but rather as liberating, and many arguments for it are advanced; for instance, that it protects women against being seen simply as sex objects and against men's importunateness, and that it should be seen as part of Muslim identity. Unlike educated Muslim women from the eleventh to the thirteenth centuries, these women see their role not simply as handing down texts, but rather claim for themselves the same right to "independent textual interpretation" as that held by men. On many points, the conclusions at which they arrive on this basis deviate from those of the traditional, thoroughly male-oriented scholarly establishments in major colleges and universities such as the traditional Azhar University in Cairo, Qarawiyyin University in Fez, Morocco, Zaytūna University in Tunis, or the Center for Shi'a Scholarship in Qom. An oppositional force arises from these institutions that work on the same scholarly basis, namely the exegesis of the holy scriptures.

2. Muslim feminists. Muslim feminists see themselves as believers in the traditional sense of the Islamic religion, but are—and here lies the great difference between them and Islamist feminists—at the same time convinced that a general gender equality is also possible in their society and within the framework of their religion. They endorse international agreements such as the 1979 Convention on the Elimination of all Forms of Discrimination against Women (CEDAW) and the 1990 Convention on the Rights of the Child (CRC), campaigned to get their respective countries to sign it, and consider an Islamic foundation for human rights both possible and important. Members of these groups are more likely than Islamist feminists to see themselves as fighters for women's rights. Whether in individual cases they call themselves "feminists" depends not only on their self-alignment with Western feminist movements, but also and especially on their social circumstances, which make such a self-alignment acceptable or instead make it seem "Western" and defamatory.

These women also frequently base themselves on new interpretations of the Quran and the tradition, and in particular they challenge the encrusted patriarchal structures in the religious establishment. Like the Islamists, they issue their challenge on the basis of their own Islamic scholarly qualifications. For them as well, *ijtihād* and their own interpretation of the sources is the method for achieving reform. Unlike the Islamists, they postulate that the equality of man and woman can be derived from the sources, and that men and women should also have equal access to leading positions in politics and society. However, a few of them are somewhat more reserved and approach the question in a practical manner, seeking to achieve gradual changes in concrete rights and regulations.

3. Secular feminists. In their tenets and principles, these women come closest to the radical idea of a feminist, and base themselves on international human rights and the various human rights conventions, especially CEDAW and CRC. They argue for a greater or even a complete separation of the state from religion, and for the creation of a democratic state, because the latter is the indispensable presupposition for equality of the sexes and the achievement of full rights for women. They do not seek to harmonize religious discourses with concepts of human rights, to interpret religious sources, or to appeal to religious law. For them, religion is a private matter, not the basis for the emancipation of women. In this way they circumvent the problem of the position of woman in Islam and thus avoid attacking the patriarchal establishment, according to which the scriptures may not be interpreted by women. At the same time they thereby vehemently contradict the Islamist concept of the inequality of the sexes. They agree with Muslim feminists that reforms in family legislation and in many other legal, social, and political domains are necessary, and tactical and strategic alliances are frequently formed. Whereas Islamist and Muslim feminists justify their efforts to achieve more participation in the public sphere and in the labor market by arguing that in this way women can better perform their duties in society, secular feminists base their demands for participation on individual personal rights.

This classification is necessarily founded on ideal types. On the level of real politics, representatives of the three categories may combine various ideas and concepts in their worldviews; moreover, strategic and tactical alliances among the groups are possible. Furthermore, activity on behalf of gender equality is not connected with biological sex, as the example of Qāsim Amīn shows. When in 2008 the Iranian government proposed a new family law code that revoked acquired rights for women, the high-ranking scholar Ayatollah Sāne'ī, a representative of the much-maligned Iranian clergy, took the side of women battling to retain their rights. His reward was a newspaper headline calling him "The Women's Mufti." At the same time, among the ranks of the Islamists there are many activists, both male and female, who defend Islamist conceptions of the complementarity of the sexes as opposed to equality of the sexes.

Women's movements in Egypt, Iran, and Morocco offer insight into the various developments in the Islamic world. Two of these countries, Egypt and Morocco, were protectorates, whereas Iran was never officially under European control, but since the Islamic Revolution it has been seen as backward, especially in the Western world, with respect to gender equality.

Egypt: From the Charitable Association to Islamism

Since the nineteenth century, Egypt has been seen as the most progressive Islamic state, credited with exercising a strong cultural influence on the Arab world. A women's movement emerged early on in Egypt, and its first leaders were women from the very same upper class so mercilessly criticized by Malak Hifnī. It began with the aid organizations and charitable associations that arose around the turn of the century. Through direct contact with women in need, new networks beyond the private sphere emerged. Upper-class women thereby acquired an idea of the effects of poverty, ignorance, and family law legislation on women in the urban and rural under-classes. Charity was seen not only as a religious duty, but also as a national and civic responsibility to be fulfilled by both Muslim and Christian women as Egyptians.

The women's movement—if it can already be called that—entered a new phase[36] in 1919, when the conflict between the Egyptian nationalist movement and the administration of the British protectorate heated up. At the highpoint of the country-wide unrest in March, 1919, 150 to 300 members of the upper class assembled in the first women's demonstration in Egyptian history and demanded freedom and independence for their country. For the first time, women became visible on the political stage as sympathizers and active supporters of prominent male politicians. They appeared—and this was typical of many other countries in the Middle East, and also of Morocco—not in their own interest, but rather to support men in the battle for national independence.

In 1922, the Wafd Party government accepted the conditions for independence offered by Britain, and Egypt became formally a kingdom (1922-1952). In 1923, Hudā Sha'rāwī (1879-1952), who was married to the vice-president of the Wafd Party and also a founder and activist of the EFU, publicly stopped wearing the veil. The EFU's agenda demanded education for women and changes in family law, especially limitations on the husband's right to repudiate his wife and on polygyny. The women of the EFU saw feminism in their society as a specific expression of a universal phenomenon and not as exclusively Western; they considered it compatible with their own culture.

A new constitution was adopted in Egypt in 1923, and its third article read as follows:

> All Egyptians are equal before the law. They enjoy the same civil and political rights . . . without distinction on the basis of race, language, or religion.

This claim to equality was not honored in legislation, however. The family law code, which was strongly influenced by Islamic law, continued to be applied, and women were not granted the right to vote by the "general right to vote" of 1923. With the exception of the wives of ministers and high officials, women were excluded from the celebrations held in connection with the opening of the new Parliament. "All Egyptians" obviously referred only to men. The political engagement of Egyptian women against the occupying power had ultimately not paid off. This too is a repeatedly seen characteristic of the history of women's movements in Muslim countries.

In 1948, Duria Shafīq founded a women's organization

called "Daughter of the Nile" (Arabic *Bint al-Nīl*). This had been preceded by her journalistic activity as the editor of the periodicals *The New Woman* (French *La femme nouvelle*) and *Daughter of the Nile*. In 1951, she waged a campaign for women's political rights and organized a sit-in in Parliament. She thereby aroused the public opposition of the Muslim Brotherhood, which demanded of the king that he put these women's organizations and their demands for political rights in their place. Once again people like Duria Shafīq were slandered as imperialist agents who wanted to undermine Egyptian society.

In the economically difficult post-war period, the ideology and tactics of Duria Shafīq's organization seemed too bourgeois and conservative. A person like Injī Aflātūn (1924-1989) felt that she was more connected with socialist ideology, saw women's liberation as part of the general battle for social justice, and considered her feminist activities to be part of the class struggle.

In contrast, in the first half of the 1950s, under President Nasser (governed 1952-1970), room was left for only a few organizations independent of the state, and the women's movement was also strictly regulated. On the other hand, during this time legal advances toward more gender equality began to appear under Nasser's socialist government. The constitutions of 1956 (Article 31) and 1964 (Article 24) contained a prohibition on discrimination on grounds of gender, and labor laws were changed. Furthermore, the state now guaranteed women active and passive voting rights and introduced a reform of the educational system in order to make it easier for working mothers by providing childcare. The expression "state feminism" was coined for this phase, since the state intervened dirigistically, from above, to carry out reforms. This occurred absolutely for the welfare of women and greater equality between the sexes, but without independent organizations being able to develop their own agendas. Thus, for example, women in Egypt were not able to represent their interests independently, to discuss them openly and pursue them politically. Furthermore, during this time, no progress was made in the "core" of the discourse on gender, personal law, in which polygyny and the husband's unrestricted right to repudiate his wife were firmly anchored.

It was Anwar el-Sadat (ruled 1970-1981) who tried to reform personal law, though he did so by means of a presidential decree. As a consequence of this the constitutional court struck down his new family law code. In connection with this legal reform, Jehan Sadat (b. 1933), the president's wife, played an important role, which is why the bill became generally known under her name: Lex Jehan. In her autobiography *A Woman of Egypt*, she writes:

> Women. All my energies and projects kept coming back to advancing women. Stemming the birthrate. Eradicating illiteracy. Educating the young and, by my example, the older. Providing health care, nutrition, and child care. Creating jobs. Raising the standard of living. Urging women to become more involved. Women. In them lay the future of the world, for it was women everywhere who were the ones to pass down their values and principles to their children, who raised their sons to manhood, who set the example for their daughters to follow. As it is said: "The hand that rocks the cradle rules the world." Women were capable of much, but in many Muslim societies, were allowed to do so little. What a waste. And all because of the way men had interpreted Shari'a, the set of laws set down in

the Quran and the Hadīth, or collected sayings of
the Prophet.[37]

Sadat's statements reflect the disappointment of an intellectual woman resulting from her conflicts with the Islamic
scholarly establishment. As a Muslim, she criticized men's
interpretation of the holy scriptures; although the *Lex Jehan*
operated strictly within the framework of Islamic law and did
not abolish rulings such as polygyny and the right to divorce
for men, it nonetheless made crucial improvements in certain
areas. The bill was later taken up again and passed by the Parliament in 1985. In the tripartite classification of ideal types
outlined above, Jehan Sadat should be assigned to the group
of Muslim feminists.

In contrast, Nawāl al-Sa'dāwī (b. 1931) represented and
continues to represent a form of secular feminism, combined
with an explicit critique of imperialism. In her opinion,
women's situations are inseparable from an analysis of their
general social context. As a feminist socialist, she sees patriarchal oppression as closely connected with imperialist oppression and the exploitation of the poor by industrialized
countries, and her goal is the creation of a more just, secular-
ized, and classless socialist society on the basis of gender
equality. She does not regard Islam as the primary cause for
the oppression of women, since patriarchal values and practices already existed in the pre-Islamic period.

She came from a peasant background, studied medicine
and psychiatry at the university, and began a medical career.
In 1966 she became head of the Department of Health Education at the Ministry of Health. As a writer, she was concerned with the problems of Egyptian women, with whom
she came into contact in the course of her work as a physician, facing many cases of sexual oppression, genital muti-

lation, and incest. Her book *Women and Sexuality* (Arabic *al-Mar'a wal-l-Jins*) appeared in 1972, and enraged not only conservative scholars but also the state, so that she had to resign her position.

Nawāl al-Sa'dāwī's achievement is to have broken a taboo in Egyptian society by opposing genital mutilation, which is practiced in Egypt and in African Muslim states, as a violation of human rights in its effect on female sexuality. From 1973 to 1979 she worked at Ain Shams University in Cairo, conducting research on neuroses in women. From 1979 to 1980 she served as an advisor to the United Nations women's program in Africa and the Near East, which shows her orientation toward the international human rights convention. In 1981 she was arrested because she had spoken out against the peace treaty with Israel negotiated by Anwar el-Sadat, but she was released after he was assassinated by radical Islamists.

In 1991, after Islamists threatened to kill her, she moved to the USA, but returned to Egypt in 1996. Sa'dāwī is on the religious extremists' hit list. The Arab Women's Solidarity Association (AFSA), which she founded in 1982, was dissolved in 1991 as a result of what was presumably a politically-based charge of corruption, and its assets were conveyed to other non-governmental organizations. It was claimed that the articles published by the AFSA on marriage, divorce, and polygyny contravened the country's social and religious order.

Whereas Nawāl as-Sa'dāwī can be described as a representative of secular feminism, Zaynab al-Ghazālī (1917-2005) is surely to be considered as a representative of the Islamist women. She never called herself a "feminist," but rather was named the "mother of the Muslim Brotherhood." At first, she was connected with Hudā Sha'rāwī's women's movement, but in 1949 she went over to the Muslim Brotherhood movement and was active in the Muslim Women's Association (MFA; Arabic *Jamā'at al-sayyidāt al-muslimāt*). In an interview she explained her separation from Hudā Sha'rāwī on the basis of the incompatibility of their ideas regarding the position of women in society. Al-Ghazālī demanded the integration of Islam into all aspects of the Egyptian public sphere. In 1954, after the Muslim Brotherhood was banned following its instigation of an attempt to assassinate President Nasser, and in the course of a new wave of arrests Al-Ghazālī was also detained. During the time she spent in detention, she wrote a book entitled *Return of the Pharaoh: Memoir in Nasir's Prison*. Subsequently, after the MFA was prohibited, she remained active as a teacher and propagandist. In her view, Islam offered men and women all they needed: freedom, economic, political, and social rights, as well as public and private rights. It gave women rights in the family that no other society had granted women. For her, it was necessary to speak of liberating women in the Christian or Jewish domain, but the Muslim woman had only to study Islam "correctly" in order to see that her rights were contained in her religion.

This idea of a "correct" Islam is the starting point and at the same time the problem of the whole Islamist and many modern discourses on Islam and Islamic identity. Which interpretation is "correct"? The answer depends, of course, on the exegete's point of view, and one could provocatively argue that there are as many "correct" interpretations as there are believers. Arguments based on the "right" interpretation are thus untenable. Not recognizing this leads proponents to defend all the more vehemently and intensely their claim to have the "right" interpretation and to accuse the other to be wrong. The consequence is a straightforward clash between the political and religious groups using this argument.

Al-Ghazālī emphasized the importance of studying the texts, which she considered central for all Muslim women. She proposes the image of the ideal, socially active Muslim woman that deviates from the traditional one: female members of the Islamist movement are urged to educate themselves, to study Islam, to put out newspapers and magazines, lead discussions, be politically active and write up calls for action. This is generally connected with intensive social welfare work on the level of society. For example, the MFA ran an orphanage, offered help to poor families, mediated conflicts, and tried to give young people work by getting them involved in religious activities.

According to Al-Ghazālī—and she herself is the best example of this—Islam allows women to participate in public life, and does not discourage them from working or engaging in political activities, or from making their opinions known and developing themselves, on one condition: all of this must not conflict with their first and primary obligation, their duty as mothers. Marriage is an established component of the tradition; men and women must marry, unless they have an express excuse such as an illness. Al-Ghazālī certainly recognizes the pressure put on women who have children and are obligated to provide childcare. She was married twice and once admitted in an interview that she has been fortunate not to have any children who might have prevented her from pursuing her political activities. When she came to the conclusion that her first marriage was interfering with her mission, she succeeded in getting a divorce. The basis for the divorce was a stipulation in her marriage contract that in the event of major differences regarding her political activities, a separation was to follow and her husband had accepted this stipulation. Her second husband stated from the outset that he did not want to stand between her and her mission, but rather to support her in it.

Another prominent figure in the Egyptian women's movement is Hiba Ra'ūf (b. 1965), a professor in the University of Cairo's Political Science Department. For her as for al-Ghazālī, Islam serves as her identity and the source for her activities. According to Ra'ūf, on the basis of Islamic values women can hold the highest offices if they have the necessary qualifications. She distances herself from feminism in the Western sense, which she considers superfluous because Islam is not only an attitude toward life but also has a political dimension. She writes:

> Feminism aims only at women, has one ever heard of "masculinism"? In order to address the whole issue of women's oppression, one must address the whole society. It is both men and women who have to be targeted, especially since we must aim to change the traditional way of thinking of the whole fabric of society.[38]

For Ra'ūf, the family, as the heart of Islamic society, is inseparable from values that she sees as threatened by secularization. She attacks and cannot countenance, from her Islamic perspective, the relativism of Western societies and the relativity of values; for instance, she mentions the acceptance of homosexuality. Like al-Ghazālī, she does not consider family and children to be obstacles to engaging in professional activity and appearing in the public sphere. Her conception of the family as the essential core in which women must be active approaches the Western feminist idea according to which everything private is at the same time political.

Jihān Abū Zayd, the spokesperson for the organization

"Daughter of the Earth" (Arabic *Bint al-ard*), can also be described as a Muslim feminist. She sees herself as a Muslim, an activist, and at the same time a supporter of human rights principles. Unlike al-Ghazālī and Ra'ūf, she is quite willing to be called a feminist. The main object of her criticism is legislation that continues to disadvantage women.

These examples show the broad range of activities carried on by women, ranging from those who overtly support human rights conventions, such as Nawāl as-Sa'dāwī and Jihān Abū Zayd, and who do not hesitate to call themselves feminists, to Islamist activists such as Zaynab al-Ghazālī and Hiba Ra'ūf, who reject this term for themselves and argue on the basis of Islamic concepts of gender. They reflect the multiplicity of social and political discourses in a country that has been in a politically exceptional situation since the time of Mubarak and in which civil organizations are systematically hindered in their work and oppressed. The political upheaval that began in January and February of 2011, sweeping away the old regime, can be seen as well as a revolt against this long oppression. It can now be hoped that, on the basis of this upheaval, open discussions about political ad social rights, laws, and gender questions will make their way into politics and legislation. Against the background of the Muslim Brotherhood and Islamist feminists, who are also very active, we will see how the new processes of negotiation in Egypt will be shaped and at what conclusions they will arrive.

Iran: Regression and Progress

In contrast to Egypt, Iran was never under direct foreign control, but from the end of the nineteenth to the middle of the twentieth centuries it was subject to considerable British and

Russian influence. Unlike Egypt, Iran has been seen in the West as "medieval" since the Islamic Revolution of 1979, as a country that has regressed from the already relatively advanced development of women's status under the Pahlavi Dynasty (1926-1979). And yet numerous women played an active role in the Islamic Revolution, and many of these were from the lower classes and had been unable to benefit from the Shah's policy of modernization and education. Moreover, it is clear that, thirty years later, women have won back many of the rights that were taken away from them shortly after the revolution.

Women from the middle and upper classes of society, intellectuals and leftists, supported the revolution in the hope that it would overthrow a dictatorship and establish a free, democratic state. Their hopes were dashed, and after the establishment of the Islamic Republic they were oppressed and persecuted. Nonetheless, in the last twenty years, civil organizations have collaborated in the gradual improvement of women's legal and political situation.[39] After the revolution, the Iranian government tried to implement an Islamic gender concept that came close to that advocated by Zaynab al-Ghazālī in Egypt. In many areas it could successfully establish new rules and regulations—often with force—but in other areas it met criticism from associations, individual activists, and the press. Here, as in Egypt, negotiating processes took place in which the government, the scholarly establishment, civic organizations, and modernist intellectuals—both male and female—participated.

The origins of the Iranian women's movement go back to Qurrat al-'Ayn ("Eyebright", d. 1852), an independent and self-confident Muslim woman who participated in the religious movements of her time and fought for women's rights and for the abolition of the gender segregation and the wear-

ing of the veil. Qurrat al-'Ayns's activities and her achievements in gender equality in the religious and social domain
led, in her private life, to a divorce from her husband. He was
her cousin on her father's side, to whom she had been married
at the age of fourteen and to whom she had borne two sons
and a daughter.

A female observer, though not an activist, was Tāj al-
Saltana (d. 1936), the daughter of a Qajar ruler, Nāsir al-Dīn
Shāh (ruled 1848-1896). In her autobiography (1914), she
criticized the established distribution of gender roles and
complained about the restrictions on her freedom:

> My readers! How much I wish I could travel
> through Europe and meet all these women seeking
> freedom! I would say to them: how fortunate you
> are, fighting honorably for your rights and being
> victorious, just look at the Asian continent! . . . The
> life of Persian women consists of two things: black
> and white. When they go outside to walk about,
> they are dreadful images of black mourning. When
> they die, they are wrapped in white. I am one of
> those unfortunate women and I prefer the white
> burial shroud to the pall that shrouds that figure. I
> have always baulked at wearing it.[40]

The dramatic nature of these words conveys an impression
of how oppressive and restricting she found her life in the
harem and her imprisonment in the woman's traditional role
when she looked back on it.

In the early twentieth century, between 1906 and 1911, the
first insurrections against the ruling Qajar dynasty (reigned
1796-1926) and its corrupt and exploitative officials occurred, and ultimately led to the proclamation of a constitu-

tional monarchy on the European model. In this battle for more participation, many women protested in the streets alongside men, just as they had in 1919 in Egypt. Under the Pahlavi Dynasty, which seized power in 1926 with Reza Shah, an authoritarian state was established that strove to introduce secularization and modernization, based on the Western model. The influence of the clerical authorities, especially in the domains of upbringing and education and in the legal system, was curtailed. Against the stubborn resistance of the Ayatollahs, schools for girls were established and progressive newspapers published articles by men and women demanding more rights for women.

Mohtaram Eskandarī (d. 1925),[41] a pioneer of the Iranian women's movement, founded the first organization of this kind under the name "National Women's Group" (Persian *Jam'iyyat-e neswān-e watankhwāh*). This organization set as its goal the expansion of women's rights on the basis of Islam, especially in the domain of education. After the untimely death of its founder, the organization lost influence. In 1932 the second congress on "Women from the East," which was attended by women from many countries, especially Muslim countries, was held in Teheran. In their resolution, they demanded voting rights for women and equal opportunities in the educational system, the reform of family law, and the abolition of polygyny. In 1935, the Women's Center (Persian *Kānūn-e Banūvān*) was founded, and its director, Hajar Tarbiyat, declared war on the black chador, which made an unexpected return on the streets of Teheran forty-five years later, during the Islamic Revolution.

In 1942 Mohammed Reza Shah (ruled 1942-1979) ascended to the throne and reigned until the Islamic Revolution. During his reign the first independent women's organizations were formed, among which the communist Tudeh party's

Democratic Women's Organization (Persian *Jāme'e-ye demokrāt-e zanān*) was one of the strongest and best organized. Many Iranian women from the middle and upper strata organized themselves under its banner and fought for improved education and a political mobilization of women, and protested against the exploitation of women working in factories. In 1959 the government created the High Council of Women's Organizations (Persian *Shūrā-ye 'alī-ye jam'iyyathā-ye zanān-e Īrān*), which included eighteen associations and was led by the Shah's twin sister, Princess Ashraf Pahlavi. In the 1960s state influence increased further with the foundation of the Women's Organization of Iran (*Sāzmān-e zanān-e Īrān*). As in Egypt under Nasser, the government took the reforms in hand and thus deprived women of the opportunity to develop their own initiatives.

This paternalism aroused a counter-movement. In 1951 Safīya Fīrūz and Mehrangīz Dawlatshāhī, who would become Iran's first woman ambassador in the 1970s, founded the organization "New Path" (Persian *jam'iyyat-e rāh-e now*). Both of them met with the Shah and demanded voting rights for women, but did not succeed in gaining them until 1963; even in the Islamic Republic, women did not have to give up their active and passive voting rights. Moreover, the "New Path" was involved in working out a new family law code. The family protection law of 1975 contained regulations that were progressive for an Islamic country. For example, a divorce had to take place before the family court, and polygyny was allowed only when the court agreed and the first wife also gave her permission. The marriageable age for girls was raised to eighteen, and women were granted the right to represent their children legally after the death of their husbands.

The first female government minister, Farrokhroo Pārsā (d. 1980), who had been a biology teacher at a girls' school before she was elected to Parliament in 1963, immediately used her position in Parliament to campaign for voting rights for women. She helped write the revision of the family law code and was made Education Minister in 1968. In 1980, she was the first woman to be executed by the Islamic regime for her work as a minister.

Mahnāz Afkhamī (b. 1941), who had become government minister in the country in 1975, was in the United States when the revolution broke out in 1979, and decided not to return. Since then she has worked as a journalist supporting women's rights and the women's movement in Iran.

In the wake of the Islamic Revolution the well-known model was followed once again: women got involved, fought, and put their lives on the line. And once again, it was precisely the women of the left-wing parties and the intellectuals who were disappointed; largely driven out of public life and confronted by Islamist clothing regulations, many of them had to give up their professions. Iranian women were no longer allowed to become judges, and those who worked in government offices and in the administration had to get used to a strict dress code. The family protection law was abrogated, even though it remained unofficially valid; the marriageable age for girls was initially reduced to nine, but later raised again to fifteen. Even though she herself was heavily veiled, A'zam Tāleqānī (b. 1944), the spokesperson for the Women's Association of the Islamic Revolution (Persian *Jāme'e-ye zanān-e enqelāb-e eslāmī*) warned against forced veiling and in 2003 criticized the treatment of political prisoners and solitary confinement in Teheran's notorious Evin prison. In 1980 she represented Iran at the United Nations Conference on Women held in Thailand.

In the first post-revolutionary Parliament, of the 217 members 3 were women, and after the elections of 2008 there were

8 women among 290 members. In the summer of 1980 the Parliament decided to impose the veil on all female citizens. As a result, in 2011, in contrast to other Muslim states, when appearing in public Iranian women are required to wear a headscarf, a cloak, closed-toe shoes, and stockings. As of 2013, in the wealthy northern part of Teheran, the cloak must only reach to the knee, sandals can be worn without stockings, and the fit of the headscarf reflects ongoing negotiation with the police.

In the meantime, however, the level of education for women in the Islamic Republic has risen compared to the Shah's time. In 1978, 33 percent of university students were female; in 2009, the figure is more than 50 percent. The first university for female theologians was opened in Qom in 1984, and since 2010 it has been headed by female professors alone. Women can now reach the rank of *mujtahida*, the lowest level of Iran's clerical hierarchy, and this allows them to offer their own interpretations of the texts (Arabic/Persian *ijtihād*), i.e., Quran and sayings of the Prophet and the Imams. However, they cannot reach a higher position in the Shiite hierarchy—for example, that of ayatollah—and in any case the position of President of the Republic is not open to them, not to mention that of supreme "religious leader." In May 2013, several women tried to get accepted by the Guardian's Council as candidates for the presidential elections in June 2013, but did not succeed.

In the first phase after the revolution, the previously mentioned Women's Association of the Islamic Revolution and the National Women's Union (Persian *Ettehād-e- mellī-ye zanān*) were particularly prominent in continuing, with Islamic and leftist ideological goals, the work of the women's organizations founded by Princess Ashraf. Iranian women of the most diverse political persuasions committed themselves to this work. Among the Muslim feminists were the jurist and human rights activist Mehrangīz Kār (b. 1944), Shahlā Lāhījī (b. 1942), a journalist and publisher of feminist literature, and Shahlā Sherkat (b. 1956). Shahlā Sherkat made a name for herself as editor of the extremely popular magazine *Zanān* (*Women*), a magazine that supported women's rights more than any other. As a platform for discussion by women of various political allegiances, it offered opportunities for exchange from a feminist point of view regarding different approaches to Islamic rules and contained articles on urgent legal questions, information on health and society, film criticism, and interviews with important public figures. Concrete help in legal matters was a particular focus. The disadvantaging of women before the law and in society was discussed, and the authors of the articles sought to use new interpretations of the Quran and theological discussions to work out possible solutions for legislation that would offer equal or at least nearly equal treatment of men and women. The articles in *Zanān* expressed a feminism that drew its justification from Islam but also made use of Western sources. The basic assumption was that patriarchy is not a genuine Islamic institution and that there is no contradiction between fighting for women's rights and playing the role of a good Muslim man or woman. The magazine was banned in early 2008.

In 2008, under the increasingly repressive conditions in the country during Ahmadinejad's presidency (since 2005), the organization "One Million Signatures" was founded. It is a coalition of various non-governmental organizations whose goal is to collect signatures for a revision of legislation with the aim to implement gender equality, especially in family and inheritance law. Numerous websites were established to report on the activities of women's organizations and new developments. These websites were regularly blocked by the government, but were then renamed and restarted.

On July 22, 2008, a bill on the "Protection of the Family" that had been drafted by the judiciary and approved by the cabinet was submitted to the Parliament.[42] When the text of the bill was published, a firestorm of protest broke out, and many organizations as well as individual activists, both men and women, spoke out against various articles in the bill. An intense and exciting debate was conducted on the websites of feminist organizations. The criticism focused on Article 23, according to which a man who wanted to enter into a second marriage required legal permission, but no longer required his first wife's agreement. The movement that then formed, which was composed of the "One Million Signatures" organization and many individual activists with various political and ideological backgrounds, initiated a nationwide campaign with pamphlets containing information about the precise content of the proposed law, stickers opposing the "Law against Family Protection," interviews, and websites. In summer 2008, nearly a hundred female representatives of this broad protest movement appeared in Parliament, debated the law on the spot with the members and representatives of the corresponding committees, and were able to get Article 23 struck out of the bill.[43]

These events brought to public attention the influence that non-governmental organizations and civil society could have on legislation in the Islamic Republic: public discourse regarding the specific question of second marriage could ultimately not be silenced. Right up to the point when it was prohibited, the magazine *Zanān*, whose position could be regarded as "Muslim feminist", played a central role. However, the government tried to stifle these activities and struck back with full force: male and female activists were subpoenaed, arrested, and even imprisoned. Many representatives of a conservative Islam—who had views similar to those of the Egyptian Zaynab al-Ghazālī—openly campaigned against the movement, advocating their conservative gender conception. Female members of Parliament and female representatives of the government supported the legislation and criticized the protesting women's groups. In an interview in the Fall of 2008, Fātima Āliyā, a member of Parliament, opposed the withdrawal of the proposed legislation and called the women who had come into the Parliament "a small number of secular mud-slingers." This shows how reference to secular legislation or international human rights conventions is vilified by the government in Iran.

In the case of Iran, the above-mentioned classification of feminists into "Islamist," "Muslim," and "secular," which can in any case offer only an ideal-typical frame of reference, is confronted by still another challenge: the government itself promotes an "Islamist" conception of women that does not prohibit female activities in the public sphere but strictly regulates them by requiring the wearing of the veil and the segregation of the sexes, politicizes the role of wife and mother, and at the same time rejects the Convention on the Elimination of all Forms of Discrimination against Women (CEDAW). For this reason, women in Iran can also be divided into conformist and non-conformist depending on whether they go along with state policy.

For example, Shirin Ebadi (b. 1947), a jurist and the first female judge in Iran—an office she had to give up in 1979, however, when women were no longer allowed to be judges —is a secular Muslim feminist who thinks and acts in a non-conformist way. She is an advocate for democracy and the rule of law, and never tires of pointing out the violation of human rights, especially the rights of women and children, in contemporary Iran. After she was dismissed as a judge, she was active for many years as an attorney in Teheran, working energetically and vigilantly to defend victims of violence and political persecution. In 2003 she was awarded the Nobel Peace Prize for her efforts on behalf of human rights and peace. She received death threats from violent groups and her Center for Human Rights in Teheran was closed down in 2008; in 2009, she finally left her country.

Another position is represented by Farībā 'Alāsvand, a researcher at the Centre for Studies and Research for Women (Persian: Jam'iyyat-e Zahrā) in Qom who spoke out against CEDAW, which was endorsed by the Iranian Parliament in 2003 but was rejected by the superior authority of the Council of Guardians, which examines all laws with regard to their "Islamicity." According to Alāsvand, this international convention contradicts the laws and the constitution of the Islamic Republic of Iran as it contradicts Islamic jurisprudence (Arabic/Persian *Feqh*) and Islamic law. She sees no problem in the fact that the highest religious office is open only to men; she accepts polygamy and the male prerogative of divorce on the basis of what she explains to be biological and psychological differences between men and women.[44] Behind this stands an "Islamist" concept of gender roles that is in conformity with that of the state, according to which men and women are not equal and thus equal rights for both sexes such as those laid down by the human rights convention are not valid for Islam.

In Iran, conformist and non-conformist men and women, representatives of Islamist gender conceptions, and others who campaign for equal rights oppose each other, and the discussion is carried on publicly with great vehemence. However, overtly secular voices are not heard in the discourse on gender, and reference to the international conventions is avoided in the public debate, even when it is produced abroad in publications and lectures by women such as Shirin Ebadi.

Morocco: Approaches to Emancipation

The situation is different in Morocco, whose government and King Muhammad VI take an open and positive attitude toward human rights conventions, and in particular toward CEDAW.

During the French protectorate, which lasted from 1912 to 1955, the women's movement in Morocco was connected with nationalist resistance. Women's organizations arranged events and meetings in which they promoted nationalist ideology and were active in the domains of social work and literacy. The National Union of Moroccan Women (Union Nationale des Femmes Marocaines) was founded only in 1969, the Moroccan Association for Family Planning (Association Marocaine de la planification familiale) in 1971. In the period between 1974 and 1989, various organizations were formed with the goal of improving the political, social, and legal situation of women. For them, the fight against illiteracy was a priority.

The movement further strengthened its position by establishing women's sections within the existing political parties. New women's associations were created, and informal groups also emerged.

However, it was not until the 1990s that the feminist character of these groups became clearer. Their chief demands included the revision of the constitution to establish the equality of the sexes, the correction of personal law, the guaranteeing of women's political rights, and the signature of international conventions, especially CEDAW, without reservation clauses.

In the 1980s the battle for human rights was already openly connected with the battle for women's rights. For example, in 1993 a royal decree stipulated that a woman could sign her marriage contract herself, and in March 1999 the government presented its plan to improve women's position in Moroccan society (*Projet plan d'action national pour l'intégration de la femme au développement*).[45] In this plan the government referred expressly to the United Nations declarations and adopted the resolutions that had been passed in 1995 at the Conference on Women held in Beijing.

Alaoui M'Daghri (b. 1942), at that time Minister for Religious Endowments and Islamic Affairs, criticized the plan, which in his opinion violated Islamic law; he assigned a committee of Muslim scholars to write up an opinion on the question. This committee described the plan as an effect of secularization and an imitation of the decadent West, and claimed that the reformers were infidels influenced by the West. The targets of their attack struck back: they argued that the scholars' claim to be the only ones who had the right to interpret the sources and to control the legislature was based on the model of the Islamic Republic of Iran, that the Islamists were financed by petrodollars from Saudi Arabia, and that Islam had no clergy and thus no group had the unique right to interpret the holy scriptures. Instead, every believer had the right to make an "independent textual interpretation." The scholars' declaration was said to constitute a challenge to Moroccan society that could lead to civil war (Arabic *fitna*—we can here encounter once again the classical Arabic legal expression, which on the one hand does in fact mean "civil war" and "political upheaval," but on the other hand also refers, with regard to gender roles, to a threatening scenario of the chaos unleashed by transgressing the boundaries between the sexes and a provocative danger inherent in female sexuality.)

Women's groups and human rights organizations were supported by two prominent modernist Muslim scholars, Abdelhadi Boutaleb und Ahmed Khamlichi. And in one of the first speeches delivered after the death of his father, the new king, Muhammad VI, emphasized his support for equal rights for men and women. At the beginning of the new millennium, more Islamist groups opposed the planned legal reform, including the important "Association for Justice and Charity" (Arabic *jamā'at al-'adl wa-l-ihsān*), which was not, however, organized as a party, led by the charismatic Abdessalam Yassine (b. 1928). Speaking for the movement, Yassine's daughter Nadia Yassine (b. 1958) criticized the government's proposals in numerous interviews, but did not argue for the continued validity of the family law code; instead, as is usual for Islamist movements, she argued for a rejection of traditional law books in law schools and a return to the sources, that is, to the Quran and the sayings of the Prophet. In contrast, in this phase of the discussion Leila Rhiwi, a professor of communications at the University of Rabat, argued strongly for changes in the family law code. In an interview she said: "I am Muslim in the cultural sense, but it does not bother me to be called a secular feminist." Khadija Rouissi, the general secretary of the human rights organization "Forum for Truth and Justice" (*Forum Vérité et Justice*) and president of the organization "House of Wisdom" (Arabic *Bayt al-Hikma*), an organization that supports individual rights and the establishment of democratic values in Moroccan society as well as the protection of children against violence, also described herself as a secular feminist.[46]

The new family law code was passed in 2004 and can be regarded as a decisive step toward equal gender rights in many domains; examples of it were given above with a comparison to the premodern law:[47] The husband is no longer the sole head of the family; instead, this role is assigned to the husband and the wife together. Divorce has to take place at court and it has been made easier for women to get a divorce. However, polygyny continues to exist.

Aisha Chenna, a trained nurse and social worker who has received several prizes and awards for her work, can be considered a Muslim feminist. She once said of herself, "I am Muslim in my heart and worldly in my head." In 1985, on the basis of her experience and her relevant work in the welfare ministry, she founded the self-help organization "Female Solidarity" (Solidarité Féminine) for single mothers, who still suffer from social discrimination in Muslim states. As a result of her work on behalf of these women, Chenna was reviled and denounced by clerics as supporting prostitution. Despite this criticism, the organization managed to set up two food stalls and several kiosks that were supposed to provide a livelihood for single mothers, and later on the project was expanded to include a hammam or bathhouse that offered additional services such as therapeutic massages, a beauty salon, and a fitness center for those who were able to pay. Through this project, single mothers were able to work and be trained, while their children were cared for in the project's daycare center.

It is typical of the Moroccan government's more open way of dealing with the subject of equal rights and also with subjects that are taboo in many Muslim societies, such as single mothers, that Aisha Chenna received significant support from its policy. The Moroccan king's wife, Princess Salma, attended the opening of Chenna's hammam in 2004.[48] A discourse guided by international conventions and based on gender equality is possible in Morocco, and is conducted openly.

6

Education and Professions

A Glance at History

Educated Women

Among the Prophet's companions and wives who reported many of his sayings, we have discussed first of all his favorite wife, 'Ā'isha. The sayings she handed down were accepted just as well as those handed down by men. How the educational situation and role of women in science and scholarship developed in the following centuries is now difficult to reconstruct because the sources are extremely scarce. Above all, biographical lexicons, which do not provide a great deal of information and are in addition described in Arabic by the term "men's books" (Arabic *kutub al-rijāl*), include only a few biographies of women. For the most part, the statements made in these works cannot be cross-checked against other kinds of sources. In only a few cases can information regarding individual women—chiefly from ruling houses—be found in the sources or in documents such as the records of endowments or donations that enable us to make statements about the lives of these women based on historical evidence.

In his biographical lexicon of the lives of noble personages (Arabic *siyar a'lām al-nubalā'*), the Syrian writer al-Dhahabī (d. 1347) offers the following account of a woman's life:[1]

> The learned and outstanding professor and connoisseur of the tradition, Umm al-Kirām, Karīma, daughter of Ahmad al-Marwaziyya, residing in Mekka, studied with al-Kuschmīhanī the "Sound Traditions" (of the Prophet) of al-Bukhārī, studied with Zāhir b. Ahmad as-Sarakhsī and 'Abdallāh b. Yūsuf al-Isfahānī. When she presented the tradition, she compared it with the original. In her, understanding and knowledge were combined with charity and piety. She handed down the "Sound Traditions" on several occasions, once after reading Abū Bakr al-Khatīb in the days of the pilgrimage. She died a virgin and never married. . . . Khatīb al-Baghdādī studied with her . . .
>
> Abū l-Ghanā'im al-Narsī wrote: Karīma gave me a copy of the "Sound Traditions" of al-Bukhārī. I sat opposite her and wrote seven pages. I presented them to her and wanted to compare them alone, but she said, "No, compare with me," and then she compared together with me.

Abū Bakr b. Mansūr al-Sam'ānī said: "I heard how my father mentioned Karīma and asked: "Has anyone like Karīma ever been seen?"

Abū Bakr said: "I heard the daughters of Karīma's brothers say: 'She never married.'"

Her father was from Kushmīhan, her mother from the al-Sayyāri family, her father went with her to Jerusalem and returned to Mecca with her. She lived to be almost a hundred years old.

This is one of the twenty biographies of educated women mentioned by the author. Interestingly, early biographical works include a large percentage of women, precisely with regard to the sayings of the Prophet. Up to fifteen percent of those transmitting sayings were women, whereas their share in al-Dhahabī's fourteenth-century work was only two percent, and over the following centuries and in works composed during the Ottoman period it decreased again.

How is this to be explained? Was the increasing institutionalization of education from the eleventh century on, along with the introduction of scholarly and scientific curricula and degrees in educational institutions as a precondition for entry into the civil service, responsible?[2]

The biographies usually provide only a few bits of information about the persons named: the date and place of birth and death, and in Karīma's case, a journey to Jerusalem with her father, perhaps for the purpose of study, and the names of the teachers and students along with an assessment of her character as charitable and pious. We learn nothing about the place where she taught; was it her private home or her father's home, since she apparently never married, or was it a building specially used for educational purposes?

In Islamic culture, upbringing and education generally enjoy great prestige and are considered worthwhile, especially when they involve acquiring knowledge of the Quran, the tradition, and the sayings of the Prophet. In the early period, people taught and learned in mosques and private houses. Starting in the eleventh century, madrasas (Arabic *madrasa*, pl. *madāris*) appeared, though they did not replace other places of learning. Fixed curricula were established in the madrasas, just as they were in European universities, and permanent teaching positions were created, especially for jurisprudence, which was considered a presupposition for access to state positions such as judge or prayer leader. Characteristically, they included no women, either as teachers or as students.

Karīma was described as a professor (Arabic *shaikha*), and the title *musnida* was given to her, which identified her as a transmitter of the sayings of the Prophet and referred to the fact that ideally she herself was part of the chain of tradition (Arabic *isnād*) going back to the Prophet. She studied with several teachers and educated many male students. Her understanding and knowledge were praised, and were supplemented by the religious and social qualities of charity and piety attributed to her. All this was common in biographies of both women and men. In Karīma's case, however, her scholarly excellence is explained in greater detail: she worked with exactitude, compared the manuscript with the student's copy, and was thus considered a careful teacher who did not let her pupils get away with any imprecisions. The fact that she trained male students in direct contact with them is proved by Abū l-Ghanā'im, according to whom he sat opposite her and wanted to compare his copy with the original by himself, but was not allowed to do so, because she wanted to control his reading.

Despite gender segregation, education together and study together were evidently possible. Whether it was usual we cannot say. Moreover, from the passage quoted we can conclude that in this educational space a woman, as teacher, could give instruction to male students and thus exercised authority. The instruction may have taken place in Karīma's home, and perhaps elsewhere as well, but presumably not in a madrasa, because that would have been mentioned. This private space was nevertheless transformed into a public space by the fact that it was entered by male students who were not related to her.

The biographies of women in Al-Dhahabī's work appear to be generally shorter than biographies of men and contain only the sober facts noted above. Biographies of men are for the most part more comprehensive and also sometimes include anecdotal material. For instance, in the description of the life of Ibn Mandah, the teacher of a certain 'Ā'isha bt. Hasan, the following story is reported: a guard at the Prophet's tomb in Medina saw a man dressed in white and carrying a quill, paper, and inkpot enter the holy precinct around noon. Then the wall of the tomb opened up, he went in, and remained inside for a while. When the man had come out again, the guardian asked him what had done in there. The man introduced himself as Ibn Mandah and said that he had had to discuss an unclear point in a tradition with the Prophet. There is no doubt that this story is supposed to emphasize Ibn Mandah's role as a transmitter of the tradition who had a direct "line" to the Prophet and whose interpretation is therefore particularly inspired and corresponds to the Prophet's conception. Such entertaining stories enhancing the importance of the person concerned were apparently reserved for men; in any case they are not found in any of the biographies of learned women mentioned by al-Dhahabī. It is not unlikely to conclude from this that al-Dhahabī differentiated on the basis of gender not only in his assessment of the person concerned but also in the choice of persons for his lexicon.

However, on several occasions al-Dhahabī's work offers proof that education did not take place in separate rooms. For example, 'Ā'isha bt. Hasan wrote down in her own handwriting the words Ibn Mandah dictated, which suggests that she was physically present. It is said that Shuhda (d. 1178) often frequented learned circles, and that many of the people she met there visited her at home. In this connection the expression "diploma" (Arabic *ijāza*) or the title *shaikha* repeatedly appear. Only one example is mentioned in which a woman completed an "indirect" program of study, a kind of "distance learning" in which the physical presence of the student was not necessary. This woman, whose name was Safīya, had been forbidden by her father to pursue an education, but nonetheless got her diploma through her uncle's mediation.

Al-Dhahabī's biographical lexicon shows that women were not excluded from formal training, at least in individual cases. On the other hand, they apparently wrote no books, but functioned chiefly as transmitters. Neither are there any examples of women as pupils or professors in madrasas, which were primarily concerned with the education of government officials such as judges and prayer leaders. This exclusion reminds us in many respects of the situation in European universities, where the immatriculation of women was not legalized until the end of the nineteenth century.

On the other hand, we have proof that women endowed madrasas during the Mamluk period in Egypt—that is, from the thirteenth to the sixteenth centuries—and during the Ottoman period from the sixteenth century on.

Fields of Activity

The fact that women could appear as donators is based on the women's right in Islamic law to own assets and to dispose of them as they wish. The separation of property is an inherent characteristic of the classical Islamic marriage contract and meant that upper-class women could invest their money as they wished without male interference. Furthermore, every married woman, regardless of her social background and class, had a right to living expenses paid by her husband, and a right to bride-money as well as to inheritance, although women received only half the share of a man with the same degree of kinship. This was the normative rule, which in reality was surely not always respected. Nonetheless, it can be assumed that a wife's freedom to act independently in the economic realm was proportional to the extent to which her family's power and prestige allowed her to demand this freedom and to prevent her husband from encroaching on it.

Women from the ruling class in the Mamluk Empire are reported to have sometimes had great wealth at their disposal, which they invested in religious endowments (Arabic *waqf*, pl. *awqāf*) of mosques, madrasas, and mausoleums, and they occasionally went to court to fight for the control of their assets. Since Mamluk rulers were inclined to confiscate the property of their officials in times of economic crisis, shortages, and drought, many of the latter made their wives the stewards of their resources in the hope of thereby protecting their assets. Thus women frequently played the role of guarantors for the continuity of the family's property.

However, even women could not completely escape the Sultan's grasp. Thus for example in 1470 the Egyptian Sultan Qaytbay demanded that Sāda, the daughter of the keeper of the royal strongbox, make the "usual" gift, in order to finance one of his campaigns. Sāda at first refused, arguing that she was not obligated to pay anything, at which point the ruler put her property under sequestration and forbade her to make any private transactions. Then he organized an auction that brought in the desired amount, honored Sāda with a court ceremony, and allowed her to continue her lifestyle as before. Thus she suffered the same fate as many of her male counterparts, who had already lost part or even all of their property to the Sultan's confiscations.[3]

Reports regarding the lower strata of society are scarcer. There is information about individual cases, but it is difficult to interpret them before the social background. The aforementioned Ibn al-Hājj (d. 1336), who came from Fez in Morocco but lived in Cairo, was deeply concerned with the role of women in the Egyptian society of his time.[4] The public domain, he noted, should be dominated by men, and the household by women, which is where they should stay. He quoted a saying by the Prophet according to which a woman should leave her home only on three occasions: when she married and moved into her husband's house, when her parents died, and when she herself died. To his chagrin, Egypt's women obviously did not adhere to this view. Therefore he severely criticized common practices that violated the rule of gender segregation, and complained that the advice of religious scholars was ignored. Women who frequented markets and jewelry stores, women who opened up when peddlers knocked at their doors, and began negotiations with these men—all this was a thorn in his side. He advised shopkeepers to be careful. Should a woman come in to buy something, they must keep an eye on her behavior. Al-Hājj's rather misogynist statements and complaints allow us to reconstruct with all the desirable clarity the discrepancy between the norm and real life, and gain an enlightening insight into the manners and customs of Egyptian women in his time. Without realizing it, he contradicts himself; for example, on the one hand he speaks out vehemently against women spending time in public, but on the other hand he recognizes that:

> It is the husband's duty to teach his wife the relevant religious rules, if she does not know them. If he himself does not know them, then he must find someone to teach her, or he should allow her to go out of the home and seek religious instruction.[5]

As a solution to the problem of male peddlers, he even suggests that there should be female peddlers. The consequence, which he does not discuss, would of course be that then they themselves would have to leave their homes and work in the streets. Even such a dyed-in-the-wool advocate of the gender segregation as Ibn al-Hājj thus gets into difficulties when he tries to apply it strictly.

Women's occupational activity in strict patriarchal family structures seems to be connected chiefly with the social strata and personal living situations of those concerned. Work was inevitable for peasant women who were obliged to help with harvesting and other agricultural tasks, of course, but it was also inevitable in the cities for women who lived alone—widows, for example. The example of "educated women" showed that female members of the upper class who did not have to work for reasons of sheer financial necessity engaged in activities, though it is not clear whether they were paid for their work. Various other social groups are mentioned in the sources, but because of the scarcity of information it remains impossible to reconstruct their exact living conditions, their percentage, etc. These groups include, for example, female preachers and transmitters of the prophet's sayings, saleswomen, hairdressers, woman who worked in public bathing establishments or in the houses of the Mamluk princes, governesses and nursemaids, midwives, and prostitutes who offered their services in bordellos. Women prepared brides for their weddings, made them up and adorned them, worked as corpse-washers and professional mourners.[6]

A female slave had to serve her master as a concubine if he wanted her to do so; but in this case the law provided that if a child was born of their union, the slave would be set free after her master's death, and her child would in any case be free. In premodern Islam, female slaves played an important role in the household domain. Male slaves were commonly used as soldiers.

The sources also mention entertainment artists: for instance, in the ruler's palace there was a whole orchestra composed of slave-girls, and popular female singers were invited to the Mamluk princes' festivities, appearing with the palace orchestra.

Many women from the lower classes had no choice but to work on the streets or to go into the homes of others. They could not stick to the strict rules of gender segregation that were vehemently demanded by an author like Ibn al-Ḥājj. In contrast, at that time and also later in the Ottoman Empire, it was generally considered a sign of a higher social status not to have to go out of the house to do things like shopping, since this was seen as the task of servants. Thus, members of the upper class—whether male or female—who appeared on the streets were constantly accompanied by their servants.

For the late nineteenth century, we can gain a small insight into the economic situation of women in Iran from the petitions that some of them sent to Shāh Nāsir al-Din (ruled 1848-1896). If we compare the petitions for the years from 1883 to 1886 with those submitted by men, gender-determined peculiarities emerge. Many women who were single, widowed, or for some other reason unattached to a family seem to have eked out a living with a small piece of land or through pensions and payments made by the state to their husbands, which apparently continued to be paid after the latter's deaths. In the petitions investigated there is no example of self-supporting, working women, though there is an example of a group of women living in a rural area. In a petition from a village in northern Iran the inhabitants appealed to the ruler for help because their husbands had left the village and gone to a far-off town, presumably to do agricultural work. They asked to be granted the status of "subjects," and complained that in paying their taxes they suffered from the greed and exploitation of the local tax collector.

A large proportion of the petitions—for the most part, over fifty percent—came from widows, whereas in the collection there is not a single male petitioner who refers explicitly to his status as a widower. The female petitioners frequently report that their living situation (that is, the fact that they live alone and without family protection) has aroused the greed of their relatives and neighbors, against whom they cannot defend themselves alone.

In one case, for instance, three women complain that the official responsible for distributing pensions has deprived them of the pensions of their deceased fathers and given the money to his own son instead.

Unlike the official chronicles or biographies of high civil servants, the petitions offer us a view of the life of the lower classes, of the poverty and complaints of ordinary people not only in the city, but also in the countryside. In this context it is interesting to state that only five percent of the petitions in the collection investigated were submitted by women. A few of the formulations in the women's petitions reflect knowledge of the legal process and a self-confident assertion of their own rights, but at the same time they also reflect the hopeless dependence on arbitrary power in which these women found themselves and the humble position:

> These slaves [i.e., devoted humble women, not legal slaves, IS] have a little bit of inherited property which is the means of their living and is vital for their survival. Hājjī Āqā Ridā, son of Hājjī Mullā Mīrzā Hasan, has without any right usurped our property. A certain amount is destroyed, he has placed us in hard circumstances and made us poor. We requested an order [issued by the ruler, IS] that if he has a case according to *shar'* and *'urf*-law against us, he should first have litigation with us and then, whatever the judgment, it should be implemented, and prior to litigation he should cease to molest us![7]

From this text we can infer that the inherited property, presumably a piece of land or a building, was the women's main source of income, that up to this point they had not been able to defend themselves against the predations of the official, and saw no option other than to appeal directly to the ruler. However, they are well informed about their rights and point correctly to the necessary court-decision which the Hājjī cannot produce.

Emancipation through Education?

The Battle against Illiteracy

In modern society, education and training are a fundamental presupposition for equal opportunities for men and women. That is why literacy and education for girls and women was one of the first and most important demands of the women's movement in Muslim countries.

According to the Arab Human Development Report issued in 2005, the rate of female illiteracy in the Arab region is higher than the world average and higher even than the average for developing nations; it is still about 50 percent. Women and girls continue to find it difficult to gain access to education, and many children do not attend school. This contradicts the general perception in these countries that girls ought to be educated.[8]

As in Egypt, in the Maghreb the colonial power—in this case, France—did not seek to set up an educational system, and certainly not for the female part of the population. On the eve of independence in the mid-twentieth century, 90 percent of women were illiterate. In Morocco, during the period from 2000 to 2004, 63 percent of men could read and write, compared to only 38 percent of women. In Algeria, the rates were 79 of men and 60 percent of women, in Libya 92 and 71 percent, and in Egypt 67 and 44 percent.

Although the countries of northwestern Africa are generally more shaped by secular influence from their colonial past, Islamic religious education is a significant part of the national curricula. Thus, as of the beginning of the twenty-first century, twelve percent of the time during the first six years of elementary school is devoted to religious subjects.

The proportion of women on the national committees on education and upbringing, which are responsible for the instructional materials and the organization of pedagogical activities, as well as in the ministries, especially in leading positions, was at first not high, but steadily increased. Investigations showed that the national syllabi still reproduced patriarchal values and stereotypes regarding the capacities and roles of men and women. Whereas men were frequently represented in occupational surroundings and as accomplished and competent, women were represented primarily in caring and teaching occupations. Women seldom appear as active participants in the economic, social, and political process.

Women's organizations—particularly in North Africa, but also in countries such as Lebanon and Syria—worked to correct outdated role depictions in schoolbooks and put pressure on ministries and committees. This led to repeated controversies with the conservative scholarly establishment. For instance, when it proposed to remove Islamic-religious subjects from the secondary school curriculum, the Moroccan Education Ministry was unable to prevail over the opposition of the Islamic scholars, who wanted, on the contrary, a greater "Islamization" of the teaching material. Toward the end of the twentieth century and at the beginning of the twenty-first, civic principles and democratic norms were included in the curriculum in Morocco. The Tunisian government announced that, after a reform of the educational system carried out in 1991, gender stereotypes had been eliminated from textbooks, for which it was praised in 1995 by the UN commission charged with monitoring and assessing the implementation of CEDAW guidelines. On the other hand, in 1999 the commission recommended that the Algerian government make further efforts.

In 1838 American Presbyterians founded a school in northwestern Iran. However, this school, like other similar schools in Teheran and other large cities, was attended only by children belonging to the Armenian minority. Bībī Khanūm was the daughter of a female tutor named Khadīja, who had worked in Nāsir al-Dīn Shah's harem. During the controversy over the constitution, which lasted from 1906 to 1911, she published articles in newspapers and magazines concerning women's rights and especially the education of women and girls. After vehement protests from the ranks of the clergy, her girls' school was quickly closed, but it was allowed to reopen a few years later on the condition that instruction be given only to girls between the ages of four and six. In 1907-1908, another girls' school with the significant name *Nāmūs* ("Honor") was founded in Teheran by Tūbā Āzmūdeh.

During the Pahlavi era (1926-1979), the educational system was developed on the French model, which was characterized by a high degree of centralization. In 1935 the first co-educational schools were opened in Teheran. The Shah strongly supported the education of women, reformed the dress code, and in 1934 ordered teachers and students to appear without veils. In 1940, there were 670 primary schools for boys, 117 for girls, and 1,524 co-educational schools. School attendance was made legally compulsory in 1943. The goal of the public educational system, which in the Pahlavi era was secularly oriented, was to prepare Iranians for professions in government, management, teaching, and the sciences. The first public secondary school for girls was established in 1939. The content of education and training for women changed. The emphasis was no longer on religious subjects alone; instead, women were now to be trained in household management, child raising, hygiene, cooking, and crafts-tasks that were at that time seen as typically female. In 1976, on the eve of the Islamic Revolution, 28 percent of all students in Iranian universities were women. In the same year, the literacy rate for women was 35 percent; in 2006 it was 88.7 percent for men, and 80.3 percent for women.

With the Islamic Revolution of 1979 there also began the "Islamic cultural revolution" proclaimed by Khomeini, which sought to Islamicize the educational system. Schools were temporarily closed, teachers who were considered un-Islamic were dismissed, and the teaching materials were searched for un-Islamic contents. Islamicization also affected school uniforms: henceforth, from primary school on girls were to wear a headscarf that covered their head and shoulders but not their faces, along with long-sleeved clothing and dark stockings. Investigations of Iranian teaching materials show that the gender roles in the illustrations and texts are traditional—that is, men are shown in the exercise of professions or in connection with technology, while women are shown performing household tasks. In religious instruction, the Quran and the Arabic language play an important role, and in secondary education about one third of the instructional content concerns religion. After the revolution, sports for girls were at first banned in schools, but were later reintroduced. Since the beginning of the twenty-first century, sports in girls' schools— Iranian schools are strictly separated by gender—have been considered important for physical development and health.

In Egypt, the first efforts to provide education for girls occurred even before the end of the British protectorate. In 1832, a training school for midwives was founded,[9] and in the same decade religious societies from England, France, and the United States began to set up girls' schools. According to the research of the historian Fahmy Khaled, the school for midwives had not been established to disseminate knowledge or even to make professional opportunities available to women, but rather to carry out medical examinations of prostitutes, because they were held responsible for the spread of venereal disease in the army, and to tighten the state's grip on the bodies of male and female citizens.[10] The first Egyptian school for girls was established by the Coptic Archbishop. Since the English administration under Lord Cromer paid little attention to education, Egyptian nationalists founded numerous schools. Nabawiyya Mūsā (d. 1951), the daughter of a military officer, attended the 'Abbās school in Cairo, which had been set up in 1895, and took her secondary school diploma there. Afterward she enrolled in the teacher-training program and upon graduating in 1906 became a teacher herself in the girl's section of the 'Abbās school. She was eventually appointed director of the state Seminary for Female Teachers in Alexandria, and published a book entitled *Women and Work* (1920) that called for a reform of the typical education for girls in Egypt. She argued for giving girls access to high schools and universities, so that they could become physicians, attorneys, and teachers; she sought sponsors for the foundation of additional schools, and opened two private schools.

Many female activists justified the necessity of education by appealing to Islamic ideas and rules, and therefore referred to the Quran. For instance, in 1925 Ihsān al-Qūsī gave a lecture at the American University in Beirut in which she emphasized that the Quran endorsed education for women. She mentioned earlier Muslim women and referred in particular to 'Ā'isha as a transmitter of the Prophet's sayings, and to Zaynab, the Prophet's granddaughter. In 1923, the EFU, led by Hudā Sha'rāwī, demanded that secondary schools for girls be created. And in fact such a school was opened in 1925 in the Zamalik district of Cairo. It was considered progressive and offered a course on psychology, among other subjects. Hudā Sha'rāwī showed her approval by sending her two young nieces to this school, which in 1929 had sixteen teachers and eighty pupils. According to a report, in 1930 girls did better than boys on the final examinations: 43.3 percent of the boys passed, while 52.9 percent of the girls passed. At the same time, however, there were demands for a specifically female training in housework and child-raising, which were accommodated by the opening of such schools in the following years.

After independence was won in the 1950s and universal compulsory education for both boys and girls was introduced, the rate of illiteracy steadily declined. In 2003, 68.3 percent of men and 46.9 percent of women could read and write.

The Conquest of the Universities

Efforts to improve education in premodern Islam were not limited to primary schools and courses on the Quran. The history of Islam includes, as we have seen, very important educated women and scholars. Typically, women taught in private groups, but they also founded madrasas, in which they themselves could not study, let alone teach. A striking example of this is Fātima bt. Muhammad al-Fihrī, who, in 859, founded the oldest university in the Islamic world, Qarawiyin University in Fez, still one of the leading universities in the Muslim world today. It was only in 1947—more than a thousand years later—that the first woman was allowed to graduate from this university.

As of the beginning of the twenty-first century, higher education and university degrees are open to women as the presupposition for professional activity, and as many women as men are studying at numerous universities in the Muslim world, at least in certain departments. Today, about 50 percent of the university students in Arab countries are women. Since at the same time fewer girls than boys go to primary and secondary school, this shows the exceptional success of females in the educational system, even given their disadvantaged position.[11] However, this development began only after the First World War. In Istanbul, there had been female students in medicine since 1899. However, the reason for establishing female higher education was still only to enforce the idea of a gender segregated society in which, so far as possible, women would be treated by female physicians, girls would only be taught by women, etc. Not until 1921 was co-education introduced at the University of Istanbul, while in Iran a few young women were given grants in 1928 for study abroad, and 193 female students were admitted when the University of Teheran was opened in 1935.

In Egypt, catching sight of female university students was still very unusual in the 1930s. In 1929 the rector of the University of Cairo allowed women to enroll for the first time. The university was not generally gender segregated, but nonetheless felt it necessary to provide women with their own lounges. Women were gradually admitted to the various departments. In 1936, the first woman graduated from the medical school. With the 1952 revolution and Nasser's socialist, pan-Arab politics, educational policy put more emphasis on encouraging young women to attend universities and to implement gender equality. At the traditional theological al-Azhar University, courses for women were introduced in the mid-1930s, and in 1962 an Islamic Women's Faculty was established. In the mid-1990s, 3.8 percent of women in Egyptian society held a university degree, in comparison to 7.2 percent of men. The percentage of female students rose considerably, and by 1997 40.4 percent of those entering the university were women. However, we find the typical distribution, with women primarily in the social sciences and humanities and men primarily in the physical sciences and technology. In the 1990s, 67.8 percent of male university graduates became government employees versus 85.7 percent of the women. These figures have been connected with the good working conditions, short hours, and access to social services.

In Iran as well, the proportion of female students is not as small as is often assumed. In 1991-1992, women represented more than 50 percent of students in economics and 35 percent of those in teacher training programs. In 1983 the High Council of the Cultural Revolution (Persian *shūrā-ye 'ālī-ye enqelāb-e farhangī*) decided not to admit women to programs in engineering, technology, and agronomy, but this ruling was relaxed in 1989 under pressure from women's organizations. In 2010, all departments were open to women.

In Saudi Arabia, another traditional Islamic country, women now outnumber men in higher education. In universities, female students constitute 58 percent of the total, and 55 percent of the graduates are women. One problem is the limited choice of professions open to women after completing a degree. For women who want to become doctors, nurses, physicians, or teachers, it is often difficult to find positions in gender-segregated places.[12]

There are eight universities and sixty-five colleges, seventeen of which are reserved for women; educational institutions are thus conceived as being only for men or only for women. Sometimes, women students follow lectures given by male teachers on a television monitor. 60 percent of the professors are now female, and 56 percent of the lecturers.

Men and women have been studying together at the recently founded King Abdullah University of Science and Technology since 2009.[13] The government made a thirty-six square kilometer island available for the construction of this international university, sure that it would also gain international renown and advance international scientific collaboration. The legal system based on sharia is not to be applied on the island, with the exception of the ban on alcohol, and, unlike in the rest of the kingdom, women are to be allowed to drive. It remains to be seen whether this large project can be integrated into the overall context of the Saudi Arabian educational landscape and especially what impact it will have on the situation of women throughout the country.

The Difficult Road to the World of Work

Generally it can be stated that, in contrast to education, women's professional activity in the sense of paid professions has thus far not achieved the same social recognition and the same practical and political implementation through legal measures. The idea of the male head of the family and household who is the sole breadwinner is still prevalent, but in practice many women in Muslim countries do contribute to the family income. One reason for this is the difficult economic situation in many Muslim states, which makes women's income indispensable. On the other hand, women have, of course, been doing agricultural work for centuries. Early on, the women's movement, especially in Egypt, had begun to make women's professional activity a subject of public debate. In the 1930s, after the institutionalization of girls' schools had been achieved, the campaign for paid work for women became a central temamt of the EFU's agenda. The first women had graduated from universities and were now looking for work. Women from the urban lower classes and from rural areas who had always worked on the field without ever getting paid could now hope to find paid work, such as in textile factories. However, because of the persisting patriarchal family structures, paid work for women of the middle classes was seen as a greater demand, since they could thereby break out of the private sphere of the family, transgress the boundaries of domesticity, and become less dependent on their husbands. In any case, by entering the job market in large numbers, they were competing with men for jobs. When an author writing in the magazine *The Egyptian Woman* (Arabic *al-mar'a al-misriyya*) in 1920 pointed this out, the editor felt it necessary to distance himself from this opinion.[14]

The modernization in the early twentieth century changed above all the situation of women from the lower class. The state tried especially to include them in new, productive roles in the domains of healthcare and education. Great Britain used its influence and the power of its protectorate to delay this development, and even countermanded it in part, for not only was women's education cut back, but Englishwomen also occupied many of the posts in precisely the areas of healthcare and education in which Egyptian women were beginning to establish themselves. Here the British were supported by conservative Egyptian groups that saw the Egyptian woman's place as being in the home and with the children. Nabawiyya Mūsā has aptly called this development the "second colonization." After independence was won in 1922, women were marginalized even further, because then Egyptian men flooded into vocational careers with a vengeance. In the 1930s, even liberal representatives at the University of Cairo such as Tāhā Husayn, who had fought for the admission of female students, thought that women's true workplace was in the family. However, should women be forced to work outside the home, these liberals were generously willing to allow them to do so.[15]

Women's situation improved considerably under Nasser's presidency. Article 32 of the 1956 constitution guaranteed women political rights, and Article 4 of law no. 73 passed in the same year gave them active voting rights if they were on the electoral rolls. The constitution of 1971 confirmed women's political rights, and Article 11 stipulated that the state guaranteed the compatibility of work and family in the society.

In 1978, labor laws were passed that were intended in particular to help men and women working for the government reconcile familial and social obligations. Both spouses were granted the right to unpaid leave, for example for the purpose of raising children. According to the statistical yearbook for 1991, only 15 percent of Egyptian women worked, but they represented 33 percent of university graduates. Thus in Egypt as well, women's participation in production decreased. Women have been able to become judges in Egypt only since 2007, whereas the first Moroccan female judge was appointed already in 1961, and in 2010 the proportion of female judges in Lebanon was between 50 and 60 percent.

Since the 1990s, and in the context of economic difficulties, an intense debate has raged in Egypt regarding the question of whether women should return to their own homes and households. The new labor law of 1994 provided for restrictions such as the following: without special permission from the Ministry of Labor, women are not allowed to work between 8 p.m. and 7 a.m. (Article 90), women should not be employed in areas detrimental to their health and morals, and in addition they should not undertake any "hard" labor (Article 91). These regulations served less to protect women than to advance a clear gender politics with the aim to drive women out of the world of work. In 2011 women are present in the area of small business, but they are fewer than the men engaged in this area. Businesswomen are generally older: 34.6 percent are between the ages of 55 and 60, 23 percent between 40 and 45.

Although there are no legal obstacles, women in Egypt cannot take it for granted that they will receive official permission to open a business. Here as well, businesswomen are admired and respected if they are single, which usually means that they are divorced or widowed. The kind of business found "suitable" for them is still largely determined by cultural norms. It is still regarded as inappropriate for women to run coffee shops or sell car accessories. They are more likely to work in the areas of clothing and fashion or hairdressing.

According to an Amnesty International report, in states belonging to the Gulf Cooperation Council[16] women are generally underrepresented in the workplace, or even almost completely excluded from it, chiefly in Saudi Arabia. However, their governments have appointed women as members of advisory councils. Laws regarding retirement encourage women to retire early. This apparent concern for their welfare prevents them from rising to hold important positions.

In Saudi Arabia, women, like men, can become business owners at the age of sixteen, and enjoy the same economic rights. In 2005, they owned between 20,000 and 40,000 businesses. As a result of the gender segregation, however, custom requires the employment of a male manager in order to represent a business in public. Although a Saudi-Arabian woman who owns a business is not forbidden to go to the Economics Ministry or to participate in business negotiations, this is not the usual practice. Whereas women are not allowed to vote in the political domain, in the economic domain they have the right to vote both actively and passively on the relevant committees. In 2005, two women were elected members of the Jeddah chamber of commerce for the first time.[17] In 1963 Soraya Obaid became the first woman from Saudi Arabia to receive a government grant to study in the United States; from 2001 to 2010 she served as the Under-Secretary General of the United Nations.[18]

On the whole, the number of indigenous working women in these countries is small (29 percent). Female workers from countries such as Pakistan and Indonesia represent a high percentage of working women in oil-rich countries, between 20 and 40 percent. They are employed in the healthcare sector and in education, but especially in private households.

According to Amnesty International, these women are not covered by national legislation, and are therefore exposed to greater risks of sexual violence and exploitation, and often have no access to legal aid. On February 15, 2005, the Saudi Arabian Ministry of Labor acknowledged that male and female immigrant workers were frequently exploited and abused by their employers, and steps to protect them were taken for the first time.

On the whole, according to the 2005 Arab Human Development Report, between 1990 and 2003 the number of women working increased more in the Arab region than in any other region in the world. Nonetheless, at 33.3 percent, women's participation in economic activity in Saudi Arabia is the lowest in the world; the global average is 55.6 percent. Women work in agriculture and primarily in the least remunerative jobs in the service sector. Reasons for this cited by the developmet report include not only a male-dominated society in which families do not want their women to work and employers are not eager to hire women, but also numerous labor laws that apparently seek to protect women but in fact limit women's career opportunities, as we have seen in the case of Egypt.[19]

In November 2012, the Dubai Women's Establishment

hosted the Third Arab Women's Leadership Forum. Muna al-Marri, chairperson of the DWE, remarked, "While there are several inspiring examples of women leaders in the Middle East, their prominence and success mask the reality that there is still a lot more to be done, and we hope forums such as these offer real and conclusive pathways for women to progress to positions of seniority in regional boardrooms— through skill development, mentoring, and networking opportunities."[20]

Women in Politics

In 1925, Lebanon became the first country in the region to give women the right to vote; in most other Arab countries it was granted to them in the 1960s. Quotas for the Parliament were instituted in some countries, but according to the 2005 development report the proportion of women members of Parliament in Arab countries is generally low, around 10 percent. In Egypt, law no. 41, passed in 1971, guaranteed women at least thirty seats in Parliament. This law enjoined all citizens to register to vote, registration now being made obligatory for women as well. However, in 1986 only 18 percent of potential female voters actually registered. In any case, that same year the law was declared unconstitutional by the constitutional court. In Egypt, an election took place in November 2010 on the basis of a law passed the preceding year that guaranteed women sixty-four seats in Parliament. The quota was, however, limited to the period preceding 2020.

Connected is the question of whether and how women could acquire leading positions in politics. Hikmat Abū Zayd (b. 1922), who later became Egypt's first female minister, was able to study at the University of Cairo with the support of her father and graduated in 1940. She completed her studies by earning a master's degree at the University of London, and after her return to Egypt in 1955 she taught at the 'Ain-Shams University in Cairo. Her political activities led Nasser to take notice of her, and he appointed her Minister of Social Affairs. In an interview, she described her tasks and successes as a minister in the area of the family and education concerning the compatibility of working and housekeeping, the establishment of daycare centers, and the creation of jobs for women.[21]

The first female government minister in Oman was Sharīfa bt. Khalfān, who took over the direction of the Ministry of Social Affairs in 2004. In Bahrain, Shaikha Mayy bt. Muhammad al-Khalīfa was appointed Minister of Culture; she also serves as chair of the UNESCO World Heritage Committee. In the same year, Ma'ālī Rīm al-Hāshīmī became Minister of State in the United Arab Emirates. In Jordan, Rīma Khalaf became Deputy Prime Minister in 1999.

In the Islamic Republic of Iran, where the constitution excludes women from the office of president, a woman was named a government minister for the first time under Ahmadinejad; Marzīyeh Vahīd Dastgerdī (b. 1959) was made Minister of Health in 2009, and was the third female minister in Iranian history after Farrokhroo Pārsā (d. 1980) and Mahnāz Afkhamī (b. 1941).[22] As a member of Parliament, Dastgerdī spoke out against the signature of the CEDAW convention.

While women in many Muslim states in the central region of the Middle East face enormous difficulties gaining access to the highest political offices, we can find some exceptions to this rule in the Muslim world: in Turkey, a secular state, Tansu Çiller was prime minister from 1993 to 1996, while in Pakistan Benazir Bhutto was prime minister from 1998 to 1990 and from 1993 to 1996, and in Bangladesh Khaleda Zia was prime minister from 1991 to 1996 and from 2001 to 2006.

In many countries of the Near East and North Africa, the movement toward democracy and the rule of law can no longer be ignored. Many women took part in the revolution that took place in Egypt starting on January 25, 2011. Margot Badran, a social scientist who has studied Egypt and its women's movements for decades from a feminist point of view, was present at the outbreak of the revolution in Cairo. Overwhelmed, she wrote:

> With the overthrow of the authoritarian state in Egypt and the dismantling of the buttresses of its power, and with legal reform already underway with the creation of the committee tasked with drafting a new constitution, equality and justice in law and practice now have a renewed chance at re-alization. The harsh inequties that authoritarianism enforces were there for all to see, in their starkest, most extreme form, in the practices of the regime that the youth eventually took down. Will the youth now be willing to accept patriarchal authoritarian-ism sustained by the old family law, a law so out of sync with contemporary social realities—with their own realities? It is very hard to see by what logic they could do so.[23]

Badran thus positions herself on the side of those who hope for broader secularization and democratization, or at least for a development toward greater gender equality in law and so-ciety. She draws a parallel between the fall of the authoritar-ian state and "authoritarian" family law that refuses to give women equal rights.

How does the situation look a year and a half later, in the spring of 2013?

Arab Spring or Arab Ice Age?
The Role of Women in and after
the Revolution of 2011

What Happened in Egypt

Since we cannot discuss every country here, the focus here will be on Egypt, as it has been in many of the preceding chapters.

After Mubarak's resignation on February 11, 2011, he was initially replaced by a military junta consisting of high-ranking officers. However, when the demonstrations and violent conflicts with the police did not stop, and the demonstrators felt that their demands for freedom and democracy were still not met, Taḥrīr Square in Cairo continued to be a center of sit-ins and demonstrations. On November 28, 2011, the Parliamentary elections began, giving the Islamic and Islamist parties the upper hand. On May 14, 2012, the Muslim Brother Muhammad Mursi was elected president of Egypt, and hence resigned his position in the Muslim Brotherhood. A new constitution was drawn up that immediately aroused strong protests from the liberal citizens because it was seen as too "Islamic."[24] In addition to the legal and constitutional discourses (which will be further discussed below), however, numerous other subjects in Egyptian society concerning gender roles were discussed. The "politics of the body" can serve as an example.

231

The Politics of the Body

Whereas during the first weeks of the so-called "Arab Spring" women and men went side by side into the streets and camped together in tents—a situation which, as the quotation above shows, deeply impressed Margot Badran—the atmosphere changed over the following months. Attacks on women and sexual harassment on the part of the demonstrators and of the state were reported with increasing frequency.

In an interview given on January 9, 2012, Professor Khaled Fahmy, a historian at the American University of Cairo, analyzed the situation as follows:

> The human body has been front and center of this revolution since the early days of its outbreak last January. Even though the leading slogan of the revolution, Bread, Freedom and Human Dignity is abstract and does not make explicit reference to the human body, it is the 30 dark years of torture, hunger and ill-health inflicted on the bodies of Egyptian men and women under Mubarak's rule that give this slogan meaning and resonance. In the last weeks of 2011, women's bodies have emerged as a nexus for many of the principles and noble objectives of this revolution. It is now apparent that women, and more specifically the female body, occupy center stage in the most recent, highly delicate stage of the revolution; namely, the struggle against the military institution with its patriarchal authority, repressive machinery and premeditated determination to thwart the revolution and intimidate the men and women who are carrying it out.[25]

The question arises whether violence against women and sexual harassment are to be seen in the context of a patriarchal society, explained as a deliberately produced phenomenon of the authoritarian regime, which considers the citizen's body as a thing, or represents a new dimension of the state's encroachments on sexuality. In an interview, Magda Adly, a female physician, pointed out that in 2005 the regime had already used the tactic of verbally insulting women demonstrators and also using hired henchmen, the so-called Baltajiyya, to harass them.[26] It seems clear that especially the female body and the politics of the body—that is, the state's way of dealing with the bodies of both male and female citizens—plays an important role in the Egyptian public sphere, in which much is still concealed.

For example, Alia Magda Elmahdi's[27] nude photographs prompted an uproar. An art student at the American University of Cairo, she provoked her country with nude photographs in which she posed wearing only red patent-leather shoes, nylon stockings, and a ribbon in her hair, with a rectangular yellow bar across her pubic area, her mouth, or her eyes. The yellow rectangles stood for the "censorship of our knowledge, expression, and sexuality." The photos, which would have attracted hardly any attention in Western societies, stirred up a storm of indignation in the still very conservative Egyptian society. Not only conservatives but also liberals and representatives of the April 6 movement who explicitly claimed to be revolutionaries distanced themselves from the photographs. Elmahdi was condemned and vilified, but she also received encouragement. She defended herself against a society characterized by violence, racism, sexism, sexual harassment, and hypocrisy. On her blog, she confronts the vehement criticism and condemnation of her nude photos. In a rather bold cartoon with the title "What society thinks I do," we see a woman having sex with two men; next to it is a very chaste photo of her in the arms of a man, under which we read "what I really do." She criticizes not only hypocrisy and bigotry, but with her photos she also raises questions about property and control over one's own body and about control by external guidelines. Her photos convey the demand for sexual self-determination, and they are artistic, not pornographic. They show an incipient revolt in favor of a different view of women's bodies, a de-sexualized and de-politicized view.

In the fall and winter of 2012, this attempt to claim the naked female body for women or for self-determination is not, however, the dominant discourse. In the course of 2011 and 2012, along with an increasing involvement of the Muslim Brotherhood and the Salafists in politics, the news was filled with reports of brutal attacks against women demonstrators, who were stripped naked, insulted, and called "prostitutes." On the internet, videos of brutal beatings and denudations circulated. A video from December 18, 2011, showed a woman demonstrator being brutally beaten by the police; her dress is pulled up so that her blue bra can be seen. A booted soldier kicks the chest of the helpless woman lying on the ground. This video created a furor throughout the world. Azza Helal Sulaiman, who tried to defend the woman "with the blue bra," as she was called in the Western press, and ran forward to cover her up, was also beaten up by the soldiers and suffered a concussion, a cut under her eye, bruises, and severe loss of blood. Interviews with her that can be seen on YouTube were conducted in the hospital.[28]

Denuding the body—in art, as in the case of Aliya Magda Elmahdi, and through brutal violence, as in the case of the "woman with the blue bra"—shows two different aspects of control over the body: in the first case, a woman chooses to present her own body naked, confronting the conservative society that excludes the female body by covering it up. She demonstrates her right to reveal her body—to control it and her own sexuality, refusing to tolerate men's control over her body. In the cartoon, she unmasks the fantasies of patriarchal society and puts them in their place. In the second case, the other's body is debased and humiliated: women are stripped naked against their will and thereby dishonored and degraded by the state. Fahmy comments:

> These events show that the female body is at the heart of this great revolution in which women have emerged as a driving and galvanizing force.[29]

Azza Helal would like to shift the focus from gender roles and positions toward the state's general policy of repression, and argues that this revolution has made everything equal: everyone can die.[30] Male demonstrators were also treated brutally, as we can see in the same video, but the dishonoring is nonetheless specifically inscribed on the female body.

There is no doubt that the politics of the body in post-revolutionary Egypt is sexually coded. It went a step further with the controversies over the so-called virginity test. On March 9, 2011, Samira Ibrahim was one of many people arrested at a demonstration and was forced to undergo a forced virginity test. If this test showed that a woman was no longer a virgin, then she was charged with being a prostitute. Samira Ibrahim and other women were forced to undress in front of the soldiers. According to their reports during the medical examination soldiers repeatedly came into the examination room to take photographs of them, and they were beaten and tortured with electrical shocks. Only Samira Ibrahim had the courage to report this violence, and the persistence to go before a court to fight for her right to bodily integrity.

In "What Made Her Go There? Samira Ibrahim and Egypt's Virginity Test Trial," a report published on Al-Jazeera, March 16, 2012, the journalist Habiba Mohsen calls Samira's denunciation of the physician responsible courageous. But she also points out that in the patriarchal society of Egypt many people spoke up only to ask: "What made her go there?" and thus to shift the blame from the state to a woman who in their view simply should not have been where she was.[31]

These virginity tests undertaken by the state have a long history in Egypt. Already in the school for midwives founded in 1832[32] in Azbakiyya in Cairo they played a role. The women who graduated from this school were employed in police stations to do forensic work. When a woman died, they had to determine the medical cause of her death, but they were also expected to carry out virginity tests on women whose male relatives accused them of having had sexual intercourse. The historian Fahmy Khaled reports that police documents in the Egyptian national archives contained hundreds of such test results that read: "No longer a virgin," "her hymen is completely gone," "she has been used." Khaled concludes, "In this sense, the modern state in Egypt was never there for the benefit of Egyptian men and women."[33]

Virginity tests were prohibited by a court judgment handed down in December 2011. However, the military physician responsible for performing the tests, Ahmed Adel (Arabic Ahmad 'Ādil), was later cleared by a military court.

Women's general fear of sexual harassment remains; in 2012 attacks on women became more frequent, and the view that women should not be on the streets or in the public sphere became more widespread. There is now a website called "harassmap,"[34] where women can make these harass-ments public. Here, as on many other blogs and websites, women are speaking up more strongly than ever before.

The Voices of Revolutionary Women

Are women the winners in the Arab revolution? Activists and observers of the situation were asked to answer that question by the German newspaper *Taz* for its issue of January 14/15, 2012.

In Egypt, an eighty-year-old woman, Nawal Al Sa'dāwī,[35] was one of those who replied, "Yes, of course." However, she wanted to emphasize that women and men had contributed to the revolution in equal shares. She mentioned the virginity tests and the violation of female bodies, which many people saw as a dishonoring of women, but which was in fact according to her a dishonoring of the system.

Nouri Bouzid, a film maker and screenwriter, lives in Tunis. For him, the freedom of speech that the revolution won for women and men is the most important result. He sees no chance that the Islamists will be able to challenge the Tunisian family law developed by Bourguiba; he thinks women's rights are firmly established in men's and women's heads, and that the people's mentality has changed.

Rasha Hefzi, a management consultant and activist from Jiddah, Saudi Arabia, acknowledges that the question is difficult. At first, she would have said "yes": for one thing, the Arab Spring came at a time when the political parties and religious groups agreed that women are an important social factor. Second, the new media provided women with fresh opportunities for activity. Third, women's movements were growing in all countries. Women had begun to assume leading positions. However, she also sees the danger that, in the conflicts among the parties women's concerns, could quickly be marginalized. She believes that it will still take years before a democracy based on gender equality is possible, and that it will have to be accompanied by a change in culture.

Those who answered in the negative included:

Baho Tāhā, an Egyptian woman journalist and human rights activist from Cairo, sees the role of women and men as being equally threatened by the role played by the military. She does not understand Western journalists who inquire only about "women," since people in Egypt went into the streets because of gross social injustices that affected both men and women. In her view, the concentration on sexual violence is a preoccupation of Western journalism. Naturally, she does not deny that violence against women exists, and the picture of the beaten "woman with the blue bra" shocked her. But during the same weeks, seventeen men died, and in her opinion this clearly shows the severity with which the military acts against men.

Fatima Jeghan has worked as an art teacher in a poor neighborhood in Tunis for twelve years. She describes what happened in her art class on November 18, 2011. As the pupils entered the classroom—it was the first day of school after the examinations—there were two students wearing beards and traditional clothing waiting for her. She began class, when one of these two students said, "Stop. Don't you know that images are forbidden in Islam? This subject must be forbidden." She explained that the class was an elective, and he was not required to take it. But God loves beauty, she went on, and with art people can change the world. Thereupon the young man became aggressive and attacked her. According to her this example shows the danger that Salafists represent for a liberal society and for women engaged in public schooles. The group called her, an artist and an art teacher, an atheist and a whore.

Mohammed Moulessehoul, an Algerian author who writes under the pseudonym Yasmina Khadra (Arabic Yāsmīna Khadrā'), believes, on the basis of his experience in Algeria, that women's battles are still far from won. He also sees the danger posed by the triumphant Islamist parties, which want to decree a physical imprisonment of women by requiring them to wear the veil and by limiting their freedom of move-ment, their contact with men, and their civil rights. "So long as women are excluded, no reform can prevent youth and the future, the foundations of a modern society, from being threatened."[36]

Constitution and Law: Family Law, the Example of Egypt

At the present time (May 2013), it is still too early to make a final judgment regarding these recent events; the information is too contradictory, the forces in the individual countries too antagonistic, and the developments too complex. In Egypt, a deep division is emerging between the religious groups in-fluenced by the Muslim Brotherhood and the Salafists, on the one hand, and the "liberal" opposition, as it is commonly called in the Western press, on the other. The draft constitu-tion that was drawn up under President Mursi was approved by only 64 percent of the voters, although it is true that par-ticipation in the election was very low and amounted to only 33 percent of eligible voters. In this constitution, religious references continue to be strongly marked, as they were in the 1971 constitution, and they concern, as they did earlier, not only Muslims, but also Christians and Jews.[37] Article 33 prohibits discrimination, but Article 10 stipulates duties with regard to her family and to work. Article 44 now prohibits blasphemy: "the insulting or defamation of any religious messenger is forbidden," thereby limiting the freedom of speech guaranteed in Article 45. In Egypt, blasphemy could always be treated as a criminal offense, but now there is a constitutional warrant for prosecuting it. Obviously, this means that action will be taken against atheism. Moreover, Article 2 contains, as it did earlier, a reference to the religion of Islam and to *shari'a* as the foundation of legislation. What is new is Article 4, according to which the scholars at Azhar University must be consulted. This provision seems to curtail the rights and prerogatives of the constitutional court and aroused a debate about the "Iranization" of the Egyptian constitution, because in Iran, too, there is an institution, the Council of Guardians, which examines the laws that were accepted by the Parliament according to "Islamic" standards.

Despite their participation in the revolution, women have seen very little fundamental change in Egypt. In the *Global Gender Gap Report* for 2011[38] published by the World Economic Forum in Geneva, Egypt is 125th out of the 134 countries investigated with regard to gender equality. Only 5 of the 508 members of the newly elected Parliament are women. Whereas in the passage cited at the outset Margot Badran expressed enthusiasm and hope, in the meantime a debate over a re-renovation of the family law has flared up. This is the key area of the law passed in 2000, the regulation of *khul'* according to which a woman can dissolve the marriage, even against her husband's will, by foregoing the bride money or making a payment to her husband. Hoda Elsadda therefore calls Margot Badran's statement "premature wishful thinking." What is the background?

It was perhaps not to be expected that right at the beginning of the revolution radical social changes would be made in a society with many areas still strongly marked by patriarchal conceptions. However, what Elsadda describes as a "shock" is the hostility and violence against female demonstrators. They were not only accused of being prostitutes, but also of supporting Western, anti-Egyptian agendas and turning against Egyptian values. These accusations are not new; they were first made during the colonial period, when feminist activities were described as associated with the Western policy of intervention and thus discredited. Now, in 2013, the advocates of women's rights are described as "the followers of Suzanne," Mubarak's wife, and thus connected with Mubarak's corrupt and decadent regime. The laws she initiated are labeled as "Suzanne's laws" or "the laws of the Hanim" (Arabic *qawanīn al-hanim, hanim*, which means "madam" or "mistress" in Turkish and was used to designate Mubarak's wife). In this way, the divorce law could easily be connected with the former regime and discredited by Islamist agitators.[39] Suzanne Mubarak (b. 1941), the daughter of a doctor and a Welsh nurse who had married the air force officer Hosni Mubarak at the age of sixteen, was not only the chair of the Women's Popular Council (Arabic *al-majlis al-qawmī li-l-mar'a*), but also participated in charitable activities and literacy campaigns, and her name appeared on many schools and libraries. Since the spring of 2011 it has been removed from them. She was considered the driving force behind the plan to make her son Gamāl (Jamāl) her husband's successor. She was accused of enriching herself, and only barely escaped being put into investigative custody by handing over three million dollars to the state.

In fact, a member of Parliament, Muhammad al-'Umda, had proposed in April, 2004 that a wife's right to get a divorce against her husband's will should be abolished. His argument was that the law violated sharia. Moreover, he claimed that the deceased Shaikh al-Azhar, Muhammad Sayyid Tantāwī

(d. 2010), and others had been subordinate to the "earlier order" (*al-nizām al-sābiq*)—that is, to the old political regime. In his view, *khul'* divorce against the husband's will in fact conflicted with Quran 2:229. The commentary on the law stated that a woman could buy her freedom from her husband if she feared she would not be able to adhere to God's commands, and thus appealed to the text of the Koran. But, it is now asked, what if she only wants to be free, for example, to travel? The Egyptian Women's Union (Arabic *al-ittihād al-nisā'ī al-misrī*) replied promptly and energetically that the law did not have its origin in the former first lady's wishes, but in the necessity of a solution to social problems and the impossibility for women to gain a divorce against the husband's will, the many pending divorce cases before the courts, etc. The women also argued that the possibility of a *khul'* divorce was in accord with the divine will in a case where it is impossible to continue the relationship and where the husband willfully clings to a relationship that his wife no longer wanted. An attempt at reconciliation must occur. The reference to human rights, which Egypt has endorsed, is also found among the responses, but it is secondary to the religious arguments—that is, those based on the text of the Koran. The Union's reply ends with a demand addressed to the Parliament and the ministry of justice urging them not to endorse such a proposal and claiming that it would throw Egypt back a century. In its reply, the National Council for Women[40] (Arabic *al-majlis al-qaumī li-l-mar'a*) points out that the percentage of *khul'* divorces in 2009 and 2010 was very low, only 1.8 percent, arguing that this can in no way be interpreted as an increase of the rate of divorce. Dr. Nasr Farīd Wāsil, who was Mufti of Egypt from 1996 to 2002,[41] rejected the accusations and described the existing *khul'* law as being in conformity with sharia. Dr. Malika Yūsuf, professor of sharia at the University of Cairo, said that the claim that the *khul'* law contradicts sharia shows an ignorance of Islamic regulations, and the former Dean of the Faculty of Islamic Studies, Dr. Āmina Nasīr, explained that *khul'* was the women's right to divorce just as *talāq* (Arabic for "repudiation") was the man's.[42] The debate thus became increasingly intense, and the law's future is uncertain. We will have to wait and see how the discussion of family law will develop.

NOTES

1. The Beginnings

1. Ibn Ishāq: *The Life of Muhammad,* pp. 68-69.
2. Ibid., p. 82.
3. Unless otherwise noted, quotations from the Quran cite Arthur Arberry's English translation, *The Koran*. Because translation is always already an interpretation, these quotations will be further elaborated upon using Amina Wadud's Quran exegesis.
4. Al-Bukhāri: *The Sahih Collection of Al-Bukhāri*, trans. A. Bewley, chap. 70, Nr. 4834, in "The Book of Marriage."
5. Ibid., Nr. 4895.
6. Abdullahi Ahmed An-Na'im: "Toward an Islamic Hermeneutics for Human Rights."
7. The sources provide contradictory answers to the question of whether women might have engaged in battle or were there only to care for the wounded. The historian Asma Afsaruddin arrives at the conclusion that before the fall of Mecca in 630, women may have fought in battle: Asma Afsaruddin: *Reconstituting Women's Lives*, p. 471.
8. The abbreviation "bt." stands for *bint*, "daughter," and "b." for *ibn*, "son."
9. Asma Afsaruddin: *Reconstituting Women's Lives*, p. 465.
10. Ruth Roded: *Women in Islamic Biographical Collections*, pp. 15-43.
11. Denise Spellberg: *Politics, Gender, and the Islamic Past*, pp. 153-156.
12. Al-Bukhāri:*The Sahih Collection of Al-Bukhāri*, trans. A. Bewley, chap. 70, Nr. 4931, in "The Book of Marriage."
13. Denise Spellberg: *Politics, Gender, and the Islamic Past*, pp. 156-161.
14. Laura Veccia Vaglieri: "Fatima," in EI2.
15. Verena Klemm: "Die frühe islamische Erzählung."
16. Ruth Roded: "Umm Salama Hind bt. Abī Umayya," in EI2. However, other sources report that the Prophet stayed her hand.
17. See infra, pp. 97-108, 164, 200.

18. Denise Spellberg: *Politics, Gender, and the Islamic Past*, pp. 137-140, 149.

19. Denise Spellberg: *Politics, Gender, and the Islamic Past*, p. 155.

20. Fatima Mernissi: *The Veil and the Male Elite,* pp. 119-140.

2. Theology and Law

1. Al-Bukhāri: *The Sahih Collection of Al-Bukhāri*, trans. A. Bewley, chap. 70, Nr. 4822, in "The Book of Marriage."

2. Ibid., Nr. 4777.

3. Leila Ahmed: *Women and Gender in Islam*, chaps. 3 and 4. Leila Ahmed assumes that the Quranic verses refer to an equality that is not based on legal but rather on ethical and moral considerations; however, this remains to be proven.

4. Ibid., p. 42.

5. Irene Schneider: "Freedom and Slavery," see pp. 370-373; see also Irene Schneider: *Kinderverkauf und Schuldknechtschaft*, pp. 188ff., 317-326.

6. Irene Schneider: "Ḥadīth-Literature as a Source," pp. 248ff.

7. Al-Bukhāri: *The Sahih Collection of Al-Bukhāri*, trans. A. Bewley, chap. 6, Nr. 298, "Book of Menstruation." In his article: "Some Isnād-Analytical Methods," Juynboll deals extensively with this and other demeaning sayings, and through his analysis of isnād—that is, the chain of transmitters—and the texts, he shows that these sayings cannot be traced back to the time of the Prophet but all emerged at the end of the first century.

8. Quoted in Jane I. Smith and Yvonne Haddad: *Women in the Afterlife: The Islamic View as Seen from Qur'ān and Tradition*, p. 44.

9. Ibid. The authors emphasize that man's sins against God can in a certain sense be seen as paralleling woman's sins against man.

10. On the concept that men and women can enter paradise, if they have been virtuous, see p. 39. For Toral-Niehoff on the role and the image of the mother in medieval Islam, see p. 125. And for Al-Ghazālī on being a mother as women's first obligation, see p. 186.

11. Abdelwahhab Bouhdiba: *Sexuality in Islam*, p. 72.

12. Angelika Neuwirth: "Myths and Legends in the Qur'ān," in EQ.

13. Ibid.

14. Thomas Breuer: "Das ist wieder einmal eine List von euch Weibern . . ." ("That's another of your women's tricks . . .").

15. Laura Veccia Vaglieri: Article "Fātima," in EI2. Scholarly study of Fatima also came to differing conclusions: Henri Lammens (d. 1937) reconstructed from the sources a dismal picture of Fatima. For him, she was unattractive and of mediocre intelligence, completely insignificant and not much loved by her father, whereas Louis Massignon (d. 1962) describes her as a privileged, hospitable woman who was especially well disposed toward non-Arab converts. See also Verena Klemm's subtle analysis of the development of the image of Fatima in her article "Die frühe islamische Erzählung."

16. Margaret Smith: *Rabia the Mystic*, pp. 35ff.

17. See supra, pp. 26-27. See also Raga' El-Nimr's interpretation of this Quran verse, p. 56f. The word *qawwamūna* is nowadays mostly rendered as "protectors" or "persons in charge of," etc., but it can also mean "standing above." Cf. Rudi Paret's German translation of this verse. These differences show how difficult the text is not only to translate but also to interpret.

18. Al-Tabarī: Tafsīr, vol. 5, p. 57; Al-Mahallī, Muhammad, Al-Suyūtī, 'Abdarrahmān: *Tafsīr al-Imāmayn al-Jalālayn*, p. 110.

19. Muhammad 'Abdūh, Rashīd Ridā: al-Manār, Tafsīr al-Qur'ān, vol. 5, p. 55.

20. Amina Wadud: *Qur'an and Woman: Rereading the Sacred Text from a Woman's Perspective*, p. 3.

21. Ibid., p. 3.

22. Ibid., p. 8.

23. Ibid., p. 21.

24. Ibid., p. 59.

25. Ibid., p. 71.

26. See ZIF (Zentrum für Islamische Frauenforschung und Frauenförderung) (ed.): *Ein einziges Wort und seine große Wirkung.*

27. Kecia Ali: *Sexual Ethics and Islam*, p. 131.

28. In 2011, Vasmaghi left Iran; she now lives in Sweden.

29. Raga' El-Nimr: *Women in Islamic Law*, pp. 93, 95.

30. See supra, p. 38.

31. Irene Schneider: *Islamisches Recht zwischen göttlicher Satzung und temporaler Ordnung?* p. 140; on Egypt, see pp. 152ff., on Iran, see pp. 156ff.

32. Kilian Bälz: *The Secular Reconstruction of Islamic Law. The Egyptian Supreme Constitutional Court and the "Battle over the Veil" in State-Run schools*, p. 229.
33. Ibid., p. 236.
34. For examples from other countries, cf. Dawoud El-Alami and Doreen Hinchcliffe: *Islamic Marriage and Divorce Laws of the Arab World*; Aifa Quraishi and Frank E. Vogel: *The Islamic Marriage Contract*; Jamal Nasir: *The Islamic Law of Personal Status*.
35. Dietrich Nelle: *Marokko*. The articles are not translated but summarized.
36. Rudolph Peters: *Crime and Punishment in Islamic Law*, pp. 148-153, 169-181.
37. Cf. Silvia Tellenbach: *Strafgesetze der Islamischen Republik Iran*. The penal code has been revised several times, and a new draft is before the parliament, but so far as I can tell, it has not eliminated these punishments.
38. See Michael J. Casimir and Susanne Jung: *Honor and Dishonor: Connotations of a Socio-Symbolic Category in Cross-Cultural Perspective*; Lynn Welchman and Sara Hossain: *Honour: Crimes, Paradigms, and Violence against Women*.
39. On this, and on the role of honor in detail, including in European law, see Silvia Tellenbach (ed.): *Die Rolle der Ehre im Strafrecht*; see also Lynn Welchman and Sara Hossain: *Honour: Crimes, Paradigms, and Violence against Women*.
40. Irene Schneider: "The Concept of Honor."
41. Irene Schneider: *Kindeswohl im islamischen Recht*, pp. 182-187.
42. Susan Gildon Miller: "Sleeping Fetus," in EWIC, vol. 3, pp. 421-424.
43. Nagla Nassar: *Legal Plurality: Reflection on the Status of Women in Egypt*.
44. Ibid.
45. Irene Schneider: *Registration, Court System and Procedure in Afghan Family Law*, pp. 209, 212-217, 224-229 ff.
46. Ibid.
47. Shaheen Sardar Ali: *Gender and Human Rights in Islam and International Law,* pp. 187-190.
48. Anna Würth discusses this topic on a political and practical level: *Dialog mit dem Islam als Konfliktprävention? Zur Menschenrechtspolitik gegenüber islamisch geprägten Staaten*.

49. The human rights conventions ratified by governments—and their respective reservations— can be found on this website: http://treaties.un.org/Pages/ViewDetails.aspx?src=TREATY&mtdsg_no=IV-8&chapter=4&lang=en , accessed on 06/14/2013.
50. Shaheen Sardar Ali: *Gender and Human Rights*, Appendix 3, pp. 311-313 (draft).
51. Ibid., Appendix 4, page 315.

3. Sexuality and Love

1. Ahmad Dallal: "Sexualities: Scientific Discourses, Premodern," in EWIC, vol 3, p. 401-407.
2. B. F. Musallam: *Sex and Society in Islam,* pp. 10-38.
3. Ibid., p. 18; Ahmad Dallal: "Sexualities: Scientific Discourses, Premodern," in EWIC, vol. 3, p. 407
4. Ibid., p. 405
5. See, e.g., Amira El Ahl: "A Small Revolution," in Spiegel Online International, http://www.spiegel.de/international/spiegel/a-small-revolution-in-cairo-theologians-battle-female-circumcision-a-452790.html; see also Noor Kassamali: "Genital Cutting," in EWIC, vol. 3, pp. 126-132.
6. Noor Kassamali: "Genital Cutting," in EWIC, vol. 3, pp. 126-132.
7. In this case the Quran translation is by Abdel Haleem.
8. Al-Ghazālī: "Marriage and Sexuality in Islam," p. 59.
9. Ibid., p. 61.
10. See also Denise Spellberg: *Politics, Gender and the Islamic Past*, p. 138.
11. Al-Bukhāri: *The Sahih Collection of Al-Bukhāri*, trans. A. Bewley, chap. 70, Nr. 4935, "The Book of Marriage."
12. Al-Ghazālī: "Marriage and Sexuality in Islam," p. 107; id., *Ihyā'*, vol. 2, p. 51.
13. Al-Ghazālī: "Marriage and Sexuality in Islam," p. 108.
14. Ahmad Dallal: "Sexualities: Scientific Discourses, Premodern," in EWIC, vol. 30, pp. 421 ff.
15. Thomas Bauer: *Liebe und Liebesdichtung*, p. 166; in general, pp. 165-174.
16. Ibn Hazm: *The Ring of the Dove,* pp. 21-22.

17. Ibid., pp. 100-101.
18. Fatima Mernissi: *Beyond the Veil*, pp. 30-45.
19. Lisa Wynn: "Courtship," in EWIC, vol. 3, pp. 90 f.
20. Björn Bentlage and Thomas Eich: "Hymen Repair on the Arabic Internet," *ISIM Review* 19 (Spring 2007), pp. 20-21.
21. Cf. supra, the table on p. 76, as well as p. 77.
22. Ali Mahdjoubi: *Homosexualität in islamischen Ländern am Beispiel Iran.*
23. Michael Bochow: *Sex unter Männern*, p. 113.
24. Andreas Ismail Mohr: *Das Volk Lots und die Jünglinge des Paradieses. Zur Homosexualität in der Religion des Islam.*
25. Unni Wikan: *Behind the Veil in Arabia: Women in Oman*, pp. 168-186.
26. Cf. supra, pp. 103-105.
27. Various empirical investigations are summarized in: Lahoucine Ouzgane (ed.): *Islamic Masculinities*.
28. Don Conway-Long: *Gender, Power and Social Change in Morocco*, pp. 147, 151 and passim.
29. Daniel Monterescu: *Stranger Masculinities: Gender and Politics in a Palestinian-Israeli "Third Space,"* pp. 128-134.
30. Ibid.
31. Ibid., pp. 129, 131, 135. For instance, one person questioned explained why his daughter could not study elsewhere: "Because we're Arabs." Thus, this form of masculinity contains many typical patriarchal elements.
32. Mohammed Baobaid: *Masculinity and Gender Violence in Yemen*, p. 176. For the concept of honor and the code of honor, see supra, pp. 20, 38, 78-80, 84-85, 109.
33. Ali Shariati: *Ali Shariati's Fatima Is Fatima*, pp. 100 ff.
34. Joumana Haddad: *I Killed Scheherazade*, pp. 17-18.
35. Ibid., p. 97.
36. On this, see Andre Gingrich: *Ehre, Raum und Körper*, p. 225. The following remarks are based on Gingrich's research. His subtle decoding of gender relations and representations of the body provides enlightening insight into the complexity of a Near Eastern society, and his presentation of the themes of honor, space, and the body, using the example of Yemen, is well worth reading. The anthropological literature on the Near and Middle East is so wide-ranging that here we

can mention only a few titles. Dale F. Eickelman, *The Middle East:
An Anthropological Approach*, especially chapter 8, may serve as a
general introduction. The publications of Lila Abu-Lughod, for instance, her book *Veiled Sentiments: Honor and Poetry in a Bedouin
Society* (1986), are still outstanding on gender roles.

4. Literary Reflections

1. The following remarks are based on Fadwa Malti-Douglas, who in
   her book *Woman's Body, Woman's Word* has analyzed women's roles
   and gender relationships as represented in a broad selection of literature.
2. Joumana Haddad: *I killed Scheherazade*, p. 142.
3. Isabel Toral-Niehoff: "Paradise Is at the Feet of the Mothers"; on premodern concepts of women's sexuality and procreation, see also pp.
   93-102.
4. On a few women poets of the classical period, see Wiebke Walther:
   Women in Islam, pp. 143-153.
5. Al-Qālī: *Al-Amālī*, vol. 1, p. 226. I am indebted to Mohsen Zakeri for
   the reference to this poem.
6. Al-Khatīb al-Baghdādī: *Tārīkh Baghdād*, vol. 4, pp. 15-16. I am
   indebted to Mohsen Zakeri for the reference to this poem.
7. Many of the novels are also available in English translation. See Margot Badran and Miriam Cooke (eds.): *Opening the Gates*; see also the
   general historical introduction.
8. Ibid., p. 20.
9. Wiebke Walther: *Die Situation von Frauen in islamischen Ländern*,
   p. 678.
10. Taj al-Saltana: *Crowning Anguish*; Irene Schneider: *"Der unglück-
    lichste König der Welt"— Person und Politik des Qādjārenherrschers
    Nāsir ad-Din Schah (reg. 1848–1896) im Urteil seiner Tochter Tadj
    as-Saltana*, pp. 258-261.
11. Huda Shaarawi: *Harem Years: The Memoirs of an Egyptian Feminist*,
    pp. 39 ff.
12. Ibid., pp. 50-52, 111.
13. Fatima Mernissi: *Dreams of Trespass,* pp. 1-2.
14. From Fada Tuqan: *Difficult Journey, Mountainous Journey*, Nablus

(Palestine) 1984, quoted in Margot Badran and Miriam Cooke (eds.): *Opening the Gates*, p. 27.

15. Verena Klemm: *Sahar Khalīfas Bāb as-Sāha—eine feministische Kritik der Intifada*.

16. Wiebke Walther: *Die Situation von Frauen in islamischen Ländern*, p. 677.

17. Assia Djebar: *A Sister to Scheherazade*, p. 1.

18. Rajaa Alsanea: *The Girls of Riyadh*, pp. 1-2.

19. See article in: http://www.iranica.com/articles/suvashun, accessed 06/14/2013.

20. See article in: http://www.iranica.com/articles/farrokzad-forug-zamas, accessed 06/14/2013.

21. Sarah Weiss: "World Music," in EWIC, vol. 5, pp. 188-195.

5. Women and Power

1. Al-Tabarī: *Tafsīr*, vol. 5, p. 57; Al-Mahallī and Al-Suyūtī: *Tafsīr al-Imāmayn al-Jalālayn*, p. 110.

2. Māwardī: *Adab al-qādī*, pp. 625-628; Irene Schneider: *The Position of Women in the Islamic and Afghan Judiciary*, pp. 88-90.

3. Ibn Rushd: *Bidāyat al-mujtahid*, vol. 1, p. 145; Irene Schneider: *Gelehrte Frauen des 5./11. bis 7./13. Jh.s nach dem biographischen Werk des al-Dhahabī (st. 748/1347)*, p. 115.

4. In her book *The Veil and the Male Elite*, which is more a literary fiction than a historical reconstruction of the early Islamic period, Fatima Mernissi, a Moroccan sociologist and committed feminist, recounts an anecdote bearing on the question of "women and power." She writes (p. 7): "I asked my grocer, 'Can a woman lead Muslims?' Like most of the grocers in Morocco, he is a true barometer of public opinion. 'May Allah help me,' he replied indignantly, despite the friendship that bound us. Paralyzed by horror at the thought, he almost dropped a dozen fresh eggs that I wanted to buy from him. . . . A second customer . . . spoke up: 'A people that entrusts its affairs to a woman will never prosper!' . . . There was a silence. I had lost the game. In the Muslim theocracy a hadith is no small matter."

5. Ibn Khaldūn: *Muqaddima*, pp. 160-172.

6. Margaret Meriwether and Judith Tucker: "Introduction," pp. 3ff.

Other approaches to feminist and gender research include political and institutional history, with a special focus on feminist movements, and social and economic history examining women's contributions to economic and legal history. The last, most important approach Meriwether and Tucker name is cultural history and gender discourse in which the definitions of maleness and femaleness in a particular place and time as points of opposition are taken into account, always with regard to gender hierarchy and power relations. See Meriwether and Tucker: "Introduction," pp. 3-10.

7. In her book *The Forgotten Queens of Islam*, Fatima Mernissi undertook a literary appraisal of women rulers.
8. Heinz Halm: *Sitt al-Mulk*, in EI2.
9. Paul Walker: "The Fatimid Caliph," pp. 38 ff.
10. Ludwig Ammann: *Shadjar al-Durr*, in EI2.
11. Muhammad al-Sakhāwī: *Al-Daw' al-lāmi'li-ahl al-qarn a-tāsi',* vol. 12, p. 16.
12. M. Athar Ali: *Radiyyat*, in EI2; Gabbay: "In Reality a Man," p. 57.
13. Gabbay: "In Reality a Man," pp. 52, 61.
14. Ibid., p. 58.
15. Maria Szuppe: "Knowledge and Politics," p. 141.
16. See infra, pp. 220ff.
17. See Suraiya Faroqhi: *The Ottoman Empire*, pp. 95-97. This period when the Sultan's mother exercised influence is described dismissively in older research as "rule by women" and is associated with the decline of the Ottoman Empire. It is clear that this perception arises from an explicitly misogynist position taken by the researchers. Women like Suraiya Faroqhi in *The Ottoman Empire* and Leslie Peirce in her book *The Imperial Harems* have collected the evidence in the sources on this point and re-evaluated it with a focus on gender roles in power politics.
18. Carl F. Petry: *Custodians of Property*, p. 123; see also Maria Szuppe: "Knowledge and Politics," p. 141.
19. M. Cavid Baysun: *Kösem Wālide*, in EI2.
20. Lord Cromer: *Modern Egyptian*, vol. 2, p. 157.
21. Mary W. Montagu: *The Turkish Embassy Letters*, pp. 171-172.
22. Edward Lane: *An Account of the Manners and Customs of the Modern Egyptians*, p. 15.
23. Indigenous authors have described in a vivid and striking way their

experiences of growing up in a harem, for instance, Taj al-Saltana, an Iranian princess who grew up in late-nineteenth-century Teheran; Fatima Mernissi, who was raised in an upper-middle-class harem in Morocco in the 1940s; and the Egyptian feminist Hudā Sha'rāwī, in her book *Harem Years.*

24. Quoted in Reina Lewis: *Rethinking Orientalism*, p. 45.
25. Angela Schwarz: "They Cannot Choose but to Be Women."
26. Leila Ahmed: *Women and Gender*, p. 153.
27. M. Rashīd Ridā: *Tafsīr al-Qur'ān*, vol. 4, p. 285.
28. Ibid., p. 288.
29. Malak Hifnī: *Nisā'iyyāt*, p. 76.
30. Rifā'a al-Tahtāwī: *An Imam in Paris*, p. 364.
31. Qasim Amin: *The Liberation of Women*, p. 37.
32. Malak Hifnī: *Nisā'iyyāt*, pp. 64-65.
33. Joseph: "Gender and Citizenship."
34. Azza Karam: *Women, Islamisms and the State*, p. 5.
35. Ibid., pp. 9-14.
36. Margot Badran: *Feminists, Islam, and Nation.*
37. Jehan Sadat: *A Woman of Egypt*, pp. 326 f.
38. Karam: *Women, Islamisms and the State*, p. 224.
39. For the development through the twentieth century, see Parvin Paidar: *Women and the Political Process in Twentieth-Century Iran*; Hamide Sedghi: "Feminist Movements in the Pahlavi Movements," in: http://www.iranica.com/articles/feminist-movements-iii, accessed on 06/14/2013. See also Ziba Mir-Hosseini: "Feminist Movements in the Islamic Republic," in: http://www.iranica.com/articles/feminist-movements-iv, accessed 06/14/2013.
40. Taj Al-Saltana: *Crowning Anguish*, p. 285.
41. See the article by Hamide Sedghi: "Feminist Movements in the Pahlavi Movements," in: http://www.iranica.com/articles/feminist-movements-iii, accessed 06/14/2013.
42. Irene Schneider: *Civil Society and Legislation: Development of the Human Rights Situation in Iran 2008*, pp. 395-411.
43. Ibid.; Noushin Ahmadi Khorasani: *Iranian Women's One Million Signatures.*
44. Farībā 'Alāsvand: *Naqd-e konvensyūn.*
45. Léon Buskens: *Recent Debates on Family Law Reform in Morocco: Islamic Law as Politics in an Emerging Public Sphere.*

46. Wendy Kristiansen: "Islam's Women Fight for their Rights," in: *Le monde diplomatique* 8/4/2004; see: http://mondediplo.com/2004/04/02islamicwomen, accessed 05/31/2013.
47. See supra, pp. 63-71.
48. Sabra, Martina: "Secular in My Head, Muslim in my Heart," in: Qantara.de, 23.11.2009: http://en.qantara.de/Secular-in-My-Head-Muslim-in-My-Heart/8263c163/index.html, accessed on 05/31/2013.

6. Education and Professions

1. Al-Dhahabī: *Siyar*, vol. 18, pp. 233 f. , Cf. Irene Schneider: *Gelehrte Frauen des 5./11. bis 7./13. Jh.s.*
2. Cf. Ruth Roded: *Women in Islamic Biographical Collections. From Ibn Sa'd to Who's Who.*
3. Carl F. Petry: *Class Solidarity versus Gender Gain: Women as Custodians of Property in Later Medieval Egypt*, pp. 122-142.
4. See an analysis from the point of view of women's studies: Huda Lutfi: *Manners and Customs of Fourteenth-Century Cairene Women.*
5. Ibid., p. 101.
6. Cf. 'Abd al-Rāziq, Ahmad: *La femme au temps des Mamlouks.*
7. Irene Schneider: *Gender and Gender Relations in Petitions to Nāsir al-Dīn Shāh (r. 1848–1896)*, p. 237.
8. The Arab Human Development Report for 2005: http://www.arab-hdr.org/publications/other/ahdr/ahdr2005e.pdf , accessed 9/15/2012.
9. Margot Badran: *Feminists, Islam, and Nation*, pp. 38 ff. and 142 ff.
10. Khaled Fahmy, 09/01/2012: "Women, Revolution, and Army," in: http://www.egyptindependent.com/opinion/women-revolution-and-army, accessed 09/15/2012.
11. Margot Badran: *Feminists, Islam, and Nation*, pp. 38 ff. and 142 ff.
12. Larissa Schmid: *Symbolische Geschlechterpolitik in Saudi-Arabien.*
13. See: http://www.kaust.edu.sa/, accessed 09/15/2012.
14. Margot Badran: *Feminists, Islam, and Nation*, p. 165.
15. Ibid., p. 171.
16. Members include the following countries: Bahrain, Qatar, Kuwait, Saudi Arabia, Oman, and United Arab Emirates; see also "Amnesty International Document, Gulf Cooperation Council," in: http://www.amnesty.org/en/library/asset/MDE04/004/2005/en/479f6a41-d507-

11dd-8a23-d58a49c0d652/mde040042005en.html, accessed 06/14/2013.

17. Larissa Schmid: *Symbolische Geschlechterpolitik in Saudi-Arabien*, p. 97.

18. See: http://en.wikipedia.org/wiki/Thoraya_Obaid, accessed 06/14/2013.

19. "The Arab Human Development Report for 2005": http://www.arab-hdr.org/publications/other/ahdr/ahdr2005e.pdf, accessed 9/15/2012.

20. See Arab Women Leadership Forum: http://www.dwe.gov.ae/awlf/press-details.aspx?id=1, accessed 06/14/2013.

21. See: http://en.wikipedia.org/wiki/Hikmat_Abu_Zayd, accessed 06/14/2013.

22. See: http://en.wikipedia.org/wiki/Farrokhroo_Parsa, accessed 06/14/2013, and http://en.wikipedia.org/wiki/Mahnaz_Afkhami, accessed 06/14/2013.

23. Margot Badran: "Egypt's Revolution and the New Feminism," see: http://blogs.ssrc.org/tif/2011/03/03/egypts-revolution-and-the-new-feminism/, accessed 06/14/2013.

24. The constitution can be found in English translation here: http://www.egyptindependent.com/news/egypt-s-draft-constitution-translated, accessed 12/28/2012.

25. Khaled Fahmy, 09.01.2012: "Women, Revolution, and Army," in: http://www.egyptindependent.com/opinion/women-revolution-and-army, accessed 09/15/2012.

26. Egypt, Dr.Magda Adly, 2005: http://www.frontlinedefenders.org/node/344, accessed 06/14/2013.

27. See, for example: http://www.nytimes.com/2011/11/18/world/middleeast/aliaa-magda-elmahdy-egypts-nude-blogger-stirs-partisan-waters.html, accessed 06/14/2013. For Magda al-Mahdi's blog, see: http://arebelsdiary.blogspot.de/?zx=b074fb534a06dc29, accessed 06/14/2013.

28. See, for example, "Egyptian Woman Beaten by Military Speaks Out," https://www.youtube.com/watch?v=-ZCog-bgXvU&feature=related, accessed 06/14/2013.

29. Khaled Fahmy, 09/01/2012: "Women, Revolution, and Army," in: http://www.egyptindependent.com/opinion/women-revolution-and-army, accessed 09/15/2012.

30. Reem Gamil: Azza Helal. "What Happened to Me Didn't Change Anything Related to the Revolution, but It Changed How I Think and

Feel about SCAF"; see: http://whatwomenwant-mag.com/sections/magazine/article.php?AID=1135, accessed 06/14/2013.

31. Habiba Mohsen: "What Made Her Go There?" in Al-Jazeera, March 16, 2012; see: http://www.aljazeera.com/indepth/opinion/2012/03/2012316133129201850.html, accessed 06/14/2013.

32. Cf. supra, p. 218.

33. Khaled Fahmy, 09/01/2012: "Women, Revolution, and Army," in: http://www.egyptindependent.com/opinion/women-revolution-and-army, accessed 09/15/2012.

34. http://harassmap.org/

35. Cf. supra, p. 183f.

36. *taz*, 01/14-15/2012, 14. See: http://www.taz.de/!85598/, accessed 12/30/2013

37. For the remarks on the new constitution, I thank my collaborator, the constitutional lawyer Dr. Naseef Naeem.

38. *The Global Gender Gap Report*, in: http://www3.weforum.org/docs/WEF_GenderGap_Report_2011.pdf, accessed on 09/15/2012.

39. Elsadda: "Women's Rights," pp. 85ff.

40. See: http://www.ncwegypt.com/index.php/en/, accessed 06/14/2013.

41. See: http://en.wikipedia.org/wiki/Dar_al-Ifta_al-Misriyyah, accessed 12/28/2012.

42. See an article by Ahmad Jamāl: "Qānūn al-khul' yuthīru jadalan mutadjadiddan," in: http://www.lahamag.com/pages.asp?nbPage=0&articleId=20555; for a similar set of arguments, see: http://www.shorouknews.com/columns/view.aspx?id=11df45c7-1787-4cce-8fa9-ea958f85fdd5, accessed 06/14/2013.

GLOSSARY

abū: father

adab: good behavior; modern: literature

'adam al-infāq: failure to provide maintenance support

Allāh: God

amrad: beardless young man

anṣār: helper, Muslim from Medina

asbāb al-nuzūl: occasions of revelation

āya, pl. *āyāt:* verse

'ayb: stigma, stain

čādor: chador, full-body veil

ḍaraba: lit., "he has struck"

ḍarar: disadvantage

dustūr: constitution

fiqh: jurisprudence

fitna: turmoil, chaos, civil war

fiṭra: basic characteristics

ḥabs: imprisonment

ḥaḍāna: childcare

ḥadd, pl. *ḥudūd:* lit., "boundary," a punishment established in the Quran

ḥadīth—, pl. *aḥādīth—:* tradition, heritage (of acts and sayings of the Prophet)

ḥalāl: permitted, allowed

ḥarām: forbidden, sacred, taboo

ḥijāb: curtain, veil, headscarf

hijra: Muhammad's emigration from Mecca to Medina in 622 *h.*

ḥūr: virgins of Paradise

ʿidda: waiting period

ijāza: diploma

ijtihād: independent textual interpretation

imām: prayer leader, also leader of a congregation

inkāh, tazwīj: marriage ceremony

isnād: chain of transmission

jāhiliyya: pre-Islamic age of ignorance

jasad: body

kalām: theology

kayd: trick, ruse, intrigue

khalīfa: caliph, ruler, lit., representative

khalīfat Allāh: God's representative

khāṭirāt: memories

khiṭān: circumcision

khiṭba: betrothal

khulʿ: redemption of the wife

kutub al-rijāl: men's books, biographical lexicons

liwāṭ: male-male sex

madrasa, pl. *madāris:* institutions of higher education, madrasas

mafqūd: a long-lost person

mahr: bride money

maḥram: forbidden for marriage

mubāraʾa: divorce by mutual agreement

mukhannath—, pl. *mukhannāthūn:* lit., "double-sexed," effeminate

mutʿa: temporary marriage

nafaqa: maintenance

nāmūs (originally Greek: *nomos):* Persian/Turkish honor

nāshiza: disobedient (female)

nasīb: first part of a poem

niqāb: facial veil

nisāʾiyyāt: women's questions

nushūz: recalcitrant, rebelliousness

qadhf: false accusation

qānitāt: obedient wives

qaṣīda: early Arabic poem

qawwāmūna ʿalā: standing over

qiṣāṣ: retaliation

rāqid: sleeping

rujūla: masculinity

shaikha: female professor

sharaf: honor

sharīf, pl. *shurafāʾ:* descendents of the Prophet

siyāsa: the ruler's guidance of the community in the interest of the welfare of society;

modern: politics

sunna: custom, usual

sunnat al-nabī: custom of the Prophet, his statements and acts elevated to the rank of legally binding precedents

taʿaddud al-zawjāt: polygyny

tafrīq: divorce by court decree

tafrīq qaḍāʾī: judicial divorce

tafsīr: Quran interpretation

ṭahāra: purity

takhayyur: choice, selection

ṭalāq: repudiation

ṭalāq amām al-qaḍāʾ: judicial divorce

tashbīb: treatise on the beloved

taṭlīq bi-ḥukm al-qaḍāʾ: judicial divorce

tawḥīd: unity

tazwīj: marriage ceremony

ʿūd: lute, stick

umm: mother

ʿunna: impotence

valide sultan: see *wālidat al-sulṭan*

wa-ḍribū hunna: strike them (female)!

wa-hjurū hunna: avoid them (female)!

wājib: necessary

walī: legal representative, guardian

wālidat al-sulṭān: mother of the sultan

waqf, pl. *awqāf:* religious foundation

wilāya: guardianship, ruling power

Zahrā, al-: the radiant

zan, pl. *zanān:* Persian, women

zawj: pair, couple

zināʾ: illicit sexual intercourse

BIBLIOGRAPHY

Abbreviations

EI2: *The Encyclopaedia of Islam*: 2nd ed., P. Bearman et al. (ed.), Leiden, Brill, 2006. Online edition: http://www.brillonline.nl/subscriber/uid =3262/title_home?title_id=islam_islam.

EI3: *The Encyclopaedia of Islam*: 3rd ed., Gudrun Krämer (ed.), Leiden, Brill, 2007. Online edition: http://www.brillonline.nl/subscriber/uid= 3262/title_home?title _id=ei3_ei3.

EIr: *Encyclopaedia Iranica*: Ehsan Yarshater (ed.), London, Routledge & Kegan Paul, 1982–. Online edition: http://www.iranica.com.

EQ: *Encyclopaedia of the Qur'ān*: Jane Dammen McAuliffe (ed.), Leiden, Brill, 2001–2006.

EWIC: *Encyclopedia of Women & Islamic Cultures*: Suad Joseph (ed.), 6 vols., Leiden, Brill, 2003–2007.

'Abd ar-Rāziq, Ahmad: *La femme au temps des Mamlouks en Égypte*, Cairo, L'Institut français d'archéologie orientale du Caire, 1973.

Abu-Lughod, Lila: *Veiled Sentiments. Honor and Poetry in a Bedouin Society*, Berkeley, University of California Press, 1986.

Afsaruddin, Asma: "Reconstituting Women's Lives: Gender and the Poetics of Narrative in Medieval Biographical Collections," in: *Muslim World* 92 (2002), pp. 461–480.

Ahmed, Leila: *Women and Gender in Islam*, New Haven, London, Yale University Press, 1992.

Ali, Kecia: *Sexual Ethics and Islam: Feminist Reflections on Qur'an, Hadith, and Jurisprudence*, Oxford, OneWorld Publications, 2006.

Ali, M. Athar: "Radīyat," in: EI2.

Ali, Shaheen Sardar: *Gender and Human Rights in Islam and International Law: Equal before Allah, Unequal before Man?* The Hague, Kluwer Law International, 2000.

Alsanea, Rajaa: *The Girls of Riyadh*, trans. M. Booth, New York, 2007.

Amin, Qasim: *The Liberation of Women and the New Woman: Two Documents in the History of Egyptian Feminism*, trans. S. S. Petersen, Cairo, 2001.

Ammann, Ludwig: *Shadjar al-Dur*, in: EI2.

Ateş, Seyran: *Große Reise ins Feuer: die Geschichte einer deutschen Türkin*, Berlin, 2005.

Badran, Margot, and Miriam Cooke (eds.): *Opening the Gates: An Anthology of Arab Feminist Writing*, Bloomington, IN, 2004.

Badran, Margot: *Feminists, Islam, and Nation: Gender and the Making of Modern Egypt*, Cairo, 1996.

Bälz, Kilian: "The Secular Reconstruction of Islamic Law—The Egyptian Supreme Constitutional Court and the 'Battle over the Veil' in State-Run Schools," in: Badouin Dupres, Maurits Berger, and Laila al-Zwaini (eds.): *Legal Pluralism in the Arab World*, The Hague, 1999, pp. 229–243.

Baobaid, Muhammed: "Masculinity and Gender Violence in Yemen," in: Lahoucine Ouzgane (ed.): *Islamic Masculinities*, London, 2006, pp. 161–183.

Bauer, Thomas: *Liebe und Liebesdichtung in der arabischen Welt des 9. und 10. Jahrhunderts: eine literatur- und mentalitätsgeschichtliche Studie des arabischen Ġazal*, Wiesbaden, 1998.

Belarbi, Aicha: "Die organisierte Frauenbewegung in Marokko. Entstehung, Entwicklung und Perspektiven," in: Claudia Schöning-Kalender et al. (ed.): *Feminismus, Islam, Nation. Frauenbewegung im Maghreb, in Zentralasien und in der Türkei*, Frankfurt am Main/New York, 1997, pp. 125–136.

Bentlage, Björn, and Thomas Eich: "Hymen Repair on the Arabic Internet," in: *ISIM Review* 19 (Spring 2007), pp. 20–21.

Bochow, Michael: "Sex unter Männern oder schwuler Sex—Zur sozialen Konstruktion von Männlichkeit unter türkisch-, kurdisch- und arabischstämmigen Migranten in Deutschland," in: Michael Bochow and Rainer Marbach (ed.): *Islam und Homosexualität—Koran. Islamische Länder. Situation in Deutschland*, Hamburg, 2004, pp. 99–115.

Bouhdiba, Abdelwahab: *Sexuality in Islam*, trans. Alan Sheridan, London, 2004.

Bukhārī, Abū 'Abdallāh Muhammad al-: Sahīh, Rpt. of the 1896 Istanbul edition in 8 vols., Beirut, 1981.

Buskens, Léon: "Recent Debates on Family Law Reform in Morocco:

Islamic Law as Politics in an Emerging Public Sphere," in: *Islamic Law and Society* 10, no. 1 (2003), pp. 70–131.

Casimir, Michael J., and Susanne Jung: "Honor and Dishonor: Connotations of a Socio-Symbolic Category in Cross-Cultural Perspective," in: Birgitt Röttger-Rössler and Hans Markowitsch (ed.): *Emotions as Bio-Cultural Processes*, New York, 2009, pp. 229–280.

Conway-Long, Don: "Gender, Power and Social Change in Morocco," in: Lahoucine Ouzgane (ed.): *Islamic Masculinities*, London, 2006, pp. 145–160.

Cromer, Evelyn Baring: *Modern Egypt,* 2 vols., New York, 1908.

Dallal, Ahmad: "Sexualities: Scientific Discourses, Premodern," in: EWIC, vol. 3, pp. 401–407.

Dhahabī, Muhammad b. Ahmad al-; -siyar a'lām an-nubalā', S. 'Arna'ūt et al. (ed.), 24 vols., Beirut, 1983–1988.

Djebar, Assia: *A Sister to Scheherazade,* trans. Dorothy S. Blair, London, 1981.

Eich, Thomas: *Islam und Bioethik: eine kritische Analyse der modernen Diskussion im islamischen Recht*, Wiesbaden, 2005.

Eickelman, Dale F.: *The Middle East and Central Asia: An Anthropological Approach*, 2nd ed., Prentice Hall, New Jersey, 1989.

El Alami, Dawoud, and Dorreen Hinchcliffe Sudqi: *Islamic Marriage and Divorce Laws of the Arab World*, The Hague, 1996.

Faroqhi, Suraiya: *The Ottoman Empire: A Short History*, trans. Shelley Frisch, Markus Wiener Publishers, Princeton, NJ, 2009.

Gabbay, Alyssa: "In Reality a Man: Sultan Iltutmish, His Daughter, Raziya, and Gender Ambiguity in Thirteenth-Century Northern India," in: *Journal of Persianate Studies* 4 (2011), pp. 45–63.

Ghazālī, Abū Hāmid al-: Ihyā' 'ulūm al-dīn, 4 vols., Cairo, c. 1960.

Gingrich, Andre: "Ehre, Raum und Körper. Zur sozialen Konstruktion der Geschlechter im Nordjemen," in: Ulrike Davis-Sulikowski, Hildegard Diemberger, Andre Gringrich, and Jürg Helbling (eds.): *Körper, Religion und Macht*, Frankfurt am Main/New York, 2001, pp. 221–293.

Haddad, Joumana: *I Killed Scheherazade: Confession of an Angry Arab Woman*, Chicago, 2010.

Haug, Sonja, Stephanie Müssig, and Anja Stichs: *Muslimisches Leben in Deutschland (Forschungsbericht im Auftrag der Deutschen Islam Konferenz)*, 1st ed., Nürnberg, Bundesamt für Migration und Flüchtlinge, 2009.

Hoda Elsadda: "Women's Rights Activism in Post-January 25 Egypt: Combatting the Shadow of the First Lady Syndrome in the Arab World," in: *Middle East Law and Governance* (2011), pp. 84–93.

Hoffmann, Valerie J.: "An Islamic Activist: Zaynab al-Ghazali," in: Elizabeth W. Fernea (ed.): *Women and the Family in the Middle East*, Austin, University of Texas Press, 1994, pp. 233–254.I

Ibn-Hazm: *The Ring of the Dove. A Treatise on the Art and Practice of Arab Love,* trans. by A. J. Arberry, London, 1953.

Ibn Isḥāq, Muḥammad: *The Life of Muhammad: A Translation of Ishāq's Sīrat Rasūl Allāh*, trans. A. Guillaume, Oxford, 1955.

Ibn Khaldūn: *An Introduction to History. The Muqaddimah*, trans. Franz Rosenthal, abridged by N. J. Dawood, London, 1978.

Ibn Rushd, Abū al-Walīd Muhammad: *Bidāyat al-mujtahid wa-nihāyat al-muqtasid*, 6th ed., Beirut, 1983.

Jonker, Gerdien: "Religiosität und Partizipation der zweiten Generation— Frauen in Berliner Moscheen," in: Ruth Klein-Hessling, Sigrid Nökel, and Karin Werner (eds.): *Der neue Islam der Frauen. Weibliche Lebenspraxisin der globalisierten Moderne. Fallstudien aus Afrika, Asien und Europa*, Bielefeld, 1999, pp. 106–123.

Joseph, Suad: "Gender and Citizenship in Middle Eastern States," in: Moghissi Haideh (ed.): *Women and Islam: Critical Concepts in Sociology, Vol. III*, London, New York, 2005, pp. 47–57.

Juynboll, Gautier H. A.: "Some Isnad-Analytical Methods Illustrated on the Basis of Several Woman-Demeaning Sayings from Hadith Literature," in: Harald Motzki (ed.): *Hadith*, Aldershot, 2004, pp. 175–216.

Kaddor, Lamya: *Muslimisch—weiblich—deutsch! Mein Weg zu einem zeitgemäßen Islam*, München, 2010.

Karam, Azza M.: *Women, Islamism and the State: Contemporary Feminisms in Egypt*, London, New York, 1998.

Khatīb al-Baghdādī, Ahmad b. 'Alī al-: Tārīkh Baghdād aw madīnat al-salām, 14 vols. Cairo, 1931–1986.

Khorasani, Noushin Ahmadi: *Iranian Women's One Million Signatures Campaign for Equality: The Inside Story*, Women's Learning Partnership, n.p., 2010.

Klemm, Verena: "Die frühe islamische Erzählung von Fāṭima bint Muḥammad: Vom ḫabar zur Legende," in: *Der Islam* 79 (2002), pp. 47–86.

_____: "Sah.ar Ḥalīfas Bāb as-Sāh. a: "Eine feministische Kritik der Intifada," in: *Die Welt des Islams* 33 (1993), pp. 1–22.

Koran: translated and with an Introduction by Arthur J. Arberry, Oxford, reissued 2008.

Koran: translated and with an Introduction by R. Paret, 11th ed., Stuttgart, 2010.

Lane, Edward William: *An Account of the Manners and Customs of the Modern Egyptians: Written in Egypt during the Years 1833–1835*, London and New York, 1890.

Lewis, Reina: *Rethinking Orientalism: Women, Travel and the Ottoman Harem,* London, 2004.

Lutfi, Huda: "Manners and Customs of Fourteenth-Century Cairene Women: Female Anarchy versus Male Sharī 'a Order in Muslim Pre-scriptive Treatises," in: Nikki R. Keddie and Beth Baron (eds.): *Women in Middle Eastern History—Shifting Boundaries in Sex and Gender*, New Haven, CT, Yale University Press, 1992, pp. 99–121.

Mahallī, Muhammad al-, and 'Abdarrahmān Al-Suyūtī: *Tafsīr al-Imā-mayn al-Jalālayn*, Beirut, s.d.

Mahdjoubi, Ali: "Homosexualität in islamischen Ländern am Beispiel Iran," in: Michael Bochow and Rainer Marbach (eds.): *Islam und Ho-mosexualität—Koran. Islamische Länder. Situation in Deutschland*, Hamburg, 2004, pp. 85–98.

Malti-Douglas, Fedwa: *Woman's Body, Woman's Word: Gender and Dis-course in Arabo-Islamic Writing*, Princeton, NJ, 1991.

Māwardī, 'Alī Ibn-Muhammad: *al-Adab al-qādī*, 2 vols., Muhyī Hilāl as-Sarhān (ed.), Baghdād, 1971.

Meriwether, Margaret, and Judith Tucker: "Introduction," in: Margaret Meriwether and Judith Tucker: *Women & Gender in the Modern Mid-dle East*, Boulder, CO, 1999, pp. 1–24.

Mernissi, Fatima: *Beyond the Veil: Male-Female Dynamics in Modern Muslim Society*, Bloomington, IN, Indiana University Press, 1987.

_____: *Dreams of Trespass: Tales of a Harem Girlhood*, Reading, MA, 1995.

_____: *The Forgotten Queens of Islam*, trans. Mary Jo Lakeland, Cam-bridge, 1993.

Miller, Susan Gilson: "Sleeping Fetus," in: EWIC, vol. 3, pp. 421–424.

Montagu, Mary Wortley: *The Turkish Embassy Letters*, ed. Teresa Hef-fernan and Daniel O'Quinn, Peterborough, 2013.

Monterescu, Daniel: "Stranger Masculinities: Gender and Politics in a Palestinian-Israeli 'Third Space,'" in: Lahoucine Ouzgane (ed.): *Islamic Masculinities*, London, 2006, pp. 123–142.

Musallam, Basim F.: *Sex and Society in Islam: Birth Control before the Nineteenth Century*, Cambridge, 1983.

Na'im, Abdullahi, al-: "Toward an Islamic Hermeneutics for Human Rights," in: Abdullahi an-Na'im (ed.): *Human Rights and Religious Values: An Uneasy Relationship?* Amsterdam, 1995, pp. 229–242.

Nāsif, Malak Hifnī Bāhithat al-Bādiya: *Al-nisā'iyyāt*, parts 1 and 2, Cairo, 1998.

Nasir, Jamal J.: *The Islamic Law of Personal Status*, 2nd ed., London, 1990.

Nassar, Nagla: "Legal Plurality: Reflection on the Status of Women in Egypt," in: Bauduoin Dupret, Maurits Berger, and Laila Al-Zwaini (eds.): *Legal Pluralism in the Arab World*, The Hague, 1999, pp. 191–204.

Nelle, Dietrich: "Marokko," in: Alexander Bergmann, Murad Ferid, and Dieter Henrich (eds.): *Internationales Ehe- und Kindschaftsrecht*, Frankfurt am Main, issue 186, 2010.

Neuwirth, Angelika: "Myths and Legends in the Qur'ān," in: EI3.

Nökel, Sigrid: "'Neo-Muslimas'—Alltags-und Geschlechterpolitiken junger muslimischer Frauen zwischen Religion, Tradition und Moderne," in: Hans-Jürgen von Wensierski and Claudia Lübcke (eds.): *Junge Muslime in Deutschland. Lebenslagen, Aufwachsprozesse und Jugendkulturen*, Leverkusen Opladen and Farmington Hills, 2007, pp. 135–154.

———: *Die Töchter der Gastarbeiter und der Islam: zur Soziologie alltagsweltlicher Anerkennungspolitiken—eine Fallstudie*, Bielefeld, 2002.

Noor, Kassamali: "Genital Cutting," in: EWIC, vol. 3, pp. 126–132.

Ouzgane, Lahoucine (ed.): *Islamic Masculinities*, London, 2006.

Paidar, Parvin: *Women and the Political process in Twentieth-Century Iran*, Cambridge, Cambridge University Press, 1997.

Peirce, Leslie P: *The Imperial Harem: Women and Sovereignty in the Ottoman Empire*, New York, 1993.

———: "Seniority, Sexuality, and Social Order: The Vocabulary of Gender in Early Modern Ottoman Society," in: Madeline C. Zilfi (ed.): *Women in the Ottoman Empire—Middle Eastern Women in the Early*

Modern Era, Leiden, Brill, 1997, pp. 169–196.

Peters, Rudolph: *Crime and Punishment in Islamic Law: Theory and Practice from the Sixteenth to the Twenty-first Century*, Cambridge, 2005.

Petry, Carl F.: "Class Solidarity versus Gender Gain: Women as Custodians of Property in Later Medieval Egypt," in: Nikki R. Keddie and Beth Baron (eds.): *Women in Middle Eastern History—Shifting Boundaries in Sex and Gender*, New Haven, CT, Yale University Press, 1992, pp. 122–142.

Qālī, Abū 'Alī Ismā'īl Ibn-al-Qāsim al-: *Kitāb al-Amālī*, 4 vols., Beirut, 1926.

Quraishi, Asifa, and Frank E. Vogel (eds.): *The Islamic Marriage Contract*, Cambridge, MA, 2008.

Quran: See Koran.

Qur'an: A New Translation by M.A.S. Abdel Haleem, Oxford, 2004.

Ridā, Muhammad Rashīd: *Tafsīr al-qur'ān al-hakīm*, 12 vols., Beirut, 1999.

Roded, Ruth: "Islamic Biographical Dictionaries—9th to 10th Century," in: EWIC, vol. 1, pp. 29–31.

_____: "Umm Salama Hind bt. Abī Umayya," in: EI2.

_____: *Women in Islamic Biographical Collections: From Ibn Sa'd to Who's Who*, Boulder, CO, 1994.

Rohe, Mathias: *Muslim Minorities and the Law in Europe: Chances and Challenges*, New Delhi, 2007.

Sadat, Jehan: *A Woman of Egypt*, New York, NY, 1987.

Sakhāwī, Muhammad Ibn 'Abd-ar-Rahmān al-: *Al -daw' al-lāmi'fī ahl al-qarn at-tāsi'*, vol. 12, Cairo, 1936.

Schmid, Larissa: "Symbolische Geschlechterpolitik in Saudi-Arabien," in: Ulrike Freitag (ed.): *Saudi-Arabien—ein Königreich im Wandel?* Paderborn, 2010, pp. 89–105.

Schneider, Irene: "Civil Society and Legislation: Development of the Human Rights Situation in Iran 2008," in: Hatem Elliesie (ed.): *Beiträge zum Islamischen Recht* 7, Islam und Menschenrechte, Frankfurt am Main, 2010, pp. 387–414.

_____: "The Concept of Honor and Its Reflection in the Iranian Penal Code," in: *Journal of Persianate Studies* 5 (2012), pp. 43–57.

_____: "Der unglücklichste König der Welt—Person und Politik des Qādschārenherrschers Nās.ir ad-Dīn Šāh (reg. 1848–1896) im Urteil seiner Tochter Taǧ as-Salt.ana," in: *Saeculum* 48 (1997), pp. 254–274.

_____: "Freedom and Slavery in Early Islamic Time (1st/7th and 2nd/8th centuries)," in: *al-Qantara* 28 (2007), pp. 353–382.

_____: "Gelehrte Frauen des 5./11. bis 7./13 Jh. nach dem biographischen Werk des Ḏahabī (st. 748/1347)," in: Urbain Vermeulen and Daniel de Smet (eds.): *Philosophy and Arts in the Islamic World, Proceedings of the Eighteenth Congress of the Union Européenne des Arabistants et Islamisants Held at the Katholieke Universiteit Leuven September 3– September 9, 1996*, Leuven, 1998, pp. 107–121.

_____: "Gender and Gender Relations in Petitions to Nās.ir al-Dīn Šāh (reg. 1848–1896)," in: Ulrich Marzolph (ed.): *Festschrift Werner Diem*, Köln, 2011, pp. 217–249.

_____: "Ḥadīth-Literature as a Source of Social History: The Enslavement of Women in Early Islamic Times," in: *Proceedings of the XVII Congress of the UEAI 1994 in St. Petersburg*. St. Petersburg, 1997, pp. 247–255.

_____: "Islamisches Recht zwischen göttlicher Satzung und temporaler Ordnung? Überlegungen zum Grenzbereich zwischen Recht und Religion," in: Christine Langenfeld and Irene Schneider (eds.): *Recht und Religion in Europa—zeitgenössische Konflikte und historische Perspektiven*, Göttingen, 2008, pp. 138–191.

_____: "Kindeswohl im islamischen Recht," in: *Recht der Jugend und des Bildungswesens* 54 (2006), pp. 181–196.

_____: *The Petitioning System in Iran: State, Society and Power Relations in the Late 19th Century*, Wiesbaden, 2006.

_____: "The Position of Women in the Islamic and Afghan Judiciary," in: Nadjma Yassari (ed.): *The Sharī'a in the Constitutions of Afghanistan, Iran and Egypt: Implications for Private Law*, Tübingen, 2005, pp. 83–101.

_____: "Registration, Court System and Procedure in Afghan Family Law," in: *Yearbook of Islamic and Middle Eastern Law* 12 (2005/2006), pp. 209–234.

Schwarz, Angela: "They Cannot Choose but to Be Women: Stereotypes for Femininity and Ideals of Womanliness in Late Victorian and Edwardian Britain," in: U. Jordan and W. Kaiser (eds.): *Political Reform in Britain, 1886–1996*, Bochum, 1997, pp. 131–150.

Shaarawi, Huda: *Harem Years: The Memoirs of an Egyptian Feminist (1879–1924)*, ed. Margot Badran, New York, 2001.

Shariati, Ali: *Ali Shariati's Fatima Is Fatima*, trans. Laleh Bakhtiar, Tehran, 1981.

Smith, Jane I., and Yvonne Y. Haddad: "Women in the Afterlife: The Islamic View as Seen from Qur'ān and Tradition," in: *Journal of the American Academy of Religion* 43 (1975), pp. 39–50.

Smith, Margaret: *Rābi'a the Mystic and Her Fellow-Saints in Islam*, Cambridge, 1928.

Spellberg, Denise: *Politics, Gender and the Islamic Past,* New York, 1994.

Stowasser, Barbara: *Women in the Qur'an, Traditions, and Interpretation*, New York, 1994.

Szuppe, Maria: "Knowledge and Politics: Women in Sixteenth-Century Safavid Iran," in: G. Nashat and I. Beck (eds.): *Women in Iran: From the Rise of Islam to 1800*, Urbana, 2003, pp. 140–169.

Tabarī, Abū Ja'far M. al-: Jāmi' al-bayān 'an ta'wīl āy al-Qur'ān, 15 vols., Beirut, 1984.

Ṭahṭāwī, Rifā Rāfi' al-, *An Imam in Paris: Account of a Stay in France by an Egyptian Cleric (1826-1831)*, trans. Daniel L. Newman, London, 2004.

Taj Al-Saltana: *Crowning Anguish—Memoirs of a Persian Princess from the Harem to Modernity 1884–1914*, ed. Abbas Amanat, Waldorf, 1996.

Talhami, Ghada Hashem: *Women, Education and Development in the Arab Gulf Countries, Occasional Papers of the United Arab Emirates*, Abu Dhabi, The Emirates Centre for Strategic Studies and Research, 2004.

Tellenbach, Silvia (ed.): *Die Rolle der Ehre im Strafrecht,* Schriftenreihe des Max-Planck-Instituts für Ausländisches und Internationales Strafrecht, Strafrechtliche Forschungsberichte 111, Berlin, 2007.

Toprak, Ahmet: *Das schwache Geschlecht—die türkischen Männer: Zwangsheirat, häusliche Gewalt, Doppelmoral der Ehre*, Freiburg i. Br., 2007.

Vasmaghi, Sedigheh: *Women, Jurisprudence, Islam* (the English translation is forthcoming in 2013).

Veccia Vaglieri, Laura: "Fātima," in: EI2.

Wadud, Amina: *Qur'an and Woman: Rereading the Sacred Text from a Woman's Perspective*, New York, 1999.

Walker, Paul: "The Fatimid Caliph al-'Aziz and His Daughter Sitt al-Mulk: A Case of Delayed but Eventual Succession to Rule by a Woman," in: *Journal of Persianate Studies* 4 (2011), pp. 30–44.

Walther, Wiebke: "Die Situation von Frauen in islamischen Ländern," in: Udo Steinbach and Werner Ende (ed.): *Der Islam in der Gegenwart*, 5th ed., Munich, 2005, pp. 635–680.

_____: *Women in Islam: From Medieval to Modern Times*, Princeton, NJ, 2006.

Watt, W. Montgomery: *Muhammad at Medina*, Karachi, 2000.

Weis, Sarah: "World Music," in: EWIC, vol. 5, pp. 188–195.

Welchman, Lynn, and Sara Hossain: *Honour Crimes, Paradigms, and Violence against Women*, London and New York, 2005.

Wikan, Unni: *Behind the Veil in Arabia—Women in Oman*, Chicago and London, University of Chicago Press, 1982.

Würth, Anna: *Dialog mit dem Islam als Konfliktprävention? Zur Menschenrechtspolitik gegenüber islamisch geprägten Staaten*, Berlin, Deutsches Institut für Menschenrechte, 2003.

Wynn, Lisa: "Courtship," in: EWIC, vol. 3, pp. 90 f.

Zentrum für Islamische Frauenforschung [ZIF] und Frauenförderung (ed.): *Ein einziges Wort und seine große Wirkung: eine hermeneutische Betrachtungsweise zu Qur'an Sūra 4, Vers 34, mit Blick auf das Geschlechterverhältnis im Islam*, Köln, ZIF—Zentrum für Islamische Frauenforschung und Frauenförderung, 2005.

Literature on the Internet

Amnesty International Document, Gulf Cooperation Council, in: http://www.amnesty.org/en/library/asset/MDE04/004/2005/en/479f6a 41-d507-11dd-8a23-d58a49c0d652/mde040042005en.html, accessed 06/14/2013.

Arab Human Development Report for 2005: http://www.arab-hdr.org/publications/other/ahdr/ahdr2005e.pdf, accessed 09/15/2012.

Arab Women Leadership Forum, see: http://www.dwe.gov.ae/awlf/press-details.aspx?id=1 accessed 05/31/2013.

Badran, Margot: "Egypt's Revolution and the New Feminism," in: The Immanante Frame, see: http://blogs.ssrc.org/tif/2011/03/03/egypts-revolution-and-the-new-feminism/ accessed 06/14/2013.

Breuer, Thomas (05/22/2003): "Das ist wieder einmal eine List von euch

Weibern . . ."—Josef und die Frau des Potifar in jüdisch-christlicher und islamischer Tradition, see: http://www.theophil-online.de/vielf%E4lt/mff%E4ltig2.htm, accessed 06/14/2013.

Bukhārī, *The Sahih Collection of Al-Bukhari*, trans. A. Bewley, see: http://www.sunnipath.com/library/Hadith/H0002P0000.aspx, accessed 06/14/2013.

Bundeskriminalamt: Pressemitteilung zur Ehre: http://www.bka.de/pressemitt eilungen/2006/060519_pi_ehrenmorde.pdf, accessed 06/14/2013.

Dār al-iftāh, see: http://en.wikipedia.org/wiki/Dar_al-Ifta_al-Misriyyah, accessed 12/28/2012.

"Egyptian Woman Beaten by Military Speaks Out," see: https://www.youtube.com/watch?v=-ZCog-bgXvU&feature=related, accessed 09/15/2012.

El Ahl, Amira: "A Small Revolution in Cairo: Theologians Battle Female Circumcision," in Siegel Online International, http://www.spiegel.de/international/spiegel/a-small-revolution-in-cairo-theologians-battle-female-circumcision-a-452790.html, accessed 06/14/2013.

Fahmy, Khaled (01/09/2012): "Women, Revolution, and Army," in: http://www.egyptindependent.com/opinion/women-revolution-and-army, accessed 09/15/2012.

Gamil, Reem: Azza Helal: "What Happened to Me Didn't Change Anything Related to the Revolution but It Changed How I Think and Feel about SCAF," see: http://whatwomenwant-mag.com/sections/magazine/article.php?AID=1135, accessed 06/14/2013.

German Federal Criminal Police Office, see: Bundeskriminalamt.

Ghazali, Abu Hamid al-: *Book on the Etiquette of Marriage, Being the Second Book of the Section on Customs in the Book The Revival of the Religious Sciences*, by Abu Hamid al-Ghazali, translated by Madelain Farah, see: http://www.ghazali.org/works/marriage.htm, accessed 05/13/2013.

Global Gender Gap Report, see: http://www3.weforum.org/docs/WEF_GenderGap_Report_2011.pdf, accessed 09/15/2012.

Hanno, Nahla: Arab Women Writers: http://www.arabwomenwriters.com, accessed 06/14/2013.

Harassmap, see: http://harassmap.org/ accessed 06/14/2013.

Hikmat Abu Zayd, see: http://en.wikipedia.org/wiki/Hikmat_Abu_Zayd, accessed 06/14/2013.

Jamāl, Ahmad: "Qānūn al-khul' yuthīru jadalan mutadjadiddan," see: http://www.lahamag.com/pages.asp?nbPage=0&articleId=20555; because the page does not exist anymore, see, for comparable arguments: http://www.shorouknews.com/columns/view.aspx?id=11df45c7-1787-4cce-8fa9-ea958f85fdd5, accessed 06/14/2013.

Khaled, Fahmy (0l/09/2012): "Women, Revolution, and Army," in: http://www.egyptindependent.com/opinion/women-revolution-and-army, accessed 06/14/2013.

Kristiansen, Wendy: "Islam's Women Fight for their Rights," in: *Le monde diplomatique* 08/04/2004, see: http://mondediplo.com/2004/04/02islamicwomen, accessed 06/14/2013.

Magda el-Mahdi: http://arebelsdiary.blogspot.de/?zx=b074fb534a06dc29, accessed 06/14/2013.

_____: http://www.nytimes.com/2011/11/18/world/middleeast/aliaa-magda-elmahdy-egypts-nude-blogger-stirs-partisan-waters.html, accessed 06/14/2013.

Medick, Veit, and Anna Reimann: "Justifying Marital Violence," in: spiegelonline, see: http://www.spiegel.de/international/germany/justifying-marital-violence-a-german-judge-cites-koran-in-divorce-case-a-473017.html, accessed 06/14/2013.

Mir-Hosseini, Ziba: Feminist Movements in the Islamic Republic, in: http://www.iranica.com/articles/feminist-movements-iv, accessed 06/14/2013.

Mohsen, Habiba: "What Made Her Go There?" in: *Al-Jazeera*, 03/16/2012, see: http://www.aljazeera.com/indepth/opinion/2012/03/2012316133129201850.html, accessed 06/14/2013.

National Council for Women, see: http://www.ncwegypt.com/index.php/en/, accessed 06/14/2013.

Sabra, Martina: "Secular in My Head, Muslim in My Heart," in: *Qantara*, 11/23/2009, see: http://en.qantara.de/Secular-in-My-Head-Muslim-in-My-Heart/8263c163/index.html, accessed 06/14/2013.

Schiffauer, Werner: "Eine Lust am Schaudern," in: http://www.taz.de/1/archiv/archiv/?dig=2005/10/17/a0186, accessed 03/07/2011.

Sedghi, Hamide: "Feminist Movements in the Pahlavi Movements," in: http://www.iranicaonline.org/articles/feminist-movements-iii, accessed 06/14/2013.

Toral-Niehoff, Isabel: "Paradise Is at the Feet of the Mothers," forthcoming in: http://www.medieval.udl.cat/en/imagotemporis, 2013.

Wulff, Christian: "Valuing Diversity—Fostering Cohesion," see: http://
www.bundespraesident.de/SharedDocs/Reden/EN/ChristianWulff/
Reden/2010/101003-Deutsche-Einheit-englisch.html, accessed 05/25/
2013.

Yassine, Nadia: Interview with Daniel Steinvorth; Interview with Moroccan Islamist Nadia Yassine, in: Spiegelonline: 07/03/2007, see: http://
www.spiegel.de/international/world/interview-with-moroccan-is-
lamist-nadia-yassine-our-religion-is-friendly-to-women-a-492040.
html, accessed 06/14/2013.

INDEX OF NAMES

ABOUT THE AUTHOR
AND TRANSLATOR

Irene Schneider is professor of Arabic and Islamic Studies at the University of Göttingen. After completing her graduate studies at the University of Tübingen, she joined the Oriental Studies Department at the University of Cologne. In 2007, she was appointed full professor at the University of Göttingen, where she also served as dean of the School of Philosophy for the academic year 2012–2013.

Irene Schneider is the author of numerous books, including *The Petitioning System in Iran: State, Society, and Power Relations in the Late 19th Century*, *Kinderverkauf und Schuldknechtschaft, Untersuchungen zur frühen Phase des islamischen Rechts*, and *Das Bild des Richters in der adab al-qādī-Literatur*. She is the co-editor of several scholarly anthologies, including *Perspectives et Dynamique du Développement de la Société Civile* and *Recht und Religion*.

Steven Rendall is the freelance translator of more than sixty books from French and German. He has won the National Jewish Book Council's Sandra Brand and Arik Weintraub Award and the Modern Language Association's Scaglione Prize for his translations, and he was a finalist for the 2012 French-American Foundation translation award. He is also Professor Emeritus of the University of Oregon and Editor Emeritus of the journal *Comparative Literature*. He lives on a farm in southwest France with his wife, two dogs, three cats, and five chickens.

www.ingramcontent.com/pod-product-compliance
Lightning Source LLC
Chambersburg PA
CBHW020657270326
41928CB00005B/165